We and the World Around

We and the World Around

Manmohan Vaidya

यात्रा
YATRA
BOOKS
An imprint of Vani Prakashan Group

vaniprakashan.com

Hardback First Edition : 2023

Yatra Books is an imprint of Vani Prakashan Group

Head Office

4695, 21-A, Daryaganj, New Delhi-110 002, India
Phone : +91 11 23273167, 11 23275710

Registered Bookstores and Offices

Ashok Rajpath, Patna-800 004, Bihar
Coffee House Campus, Mahatma Gandhi Marg, Allahabad-211 001, Uttar Pradesh
Mahatma Gandhi International Hindi University, Wardha-442 001, Maharashtra
36-A, Shakespeare Sarani, Near Rani Birla Girls College, Kolkata-700017, West Bengal

sales@vaniprakashan.in
vaniprakashan@gmail.com

We and the World Around
by Manmohan Vaidya

ISBN : 978-93-5775-279-4
History/Political Science

Price : ₹ 550

Printed and bound in India at IBH Print & Bind Pvt. Ltd.

Foreword

Rashtriya Swayamsevak Sangh, an organisation working in Bharat, is well known among people either by its full name or by the initials, RSS. However, when discussing its goal, activities, and modus operandi, let alone the general public, even scholars lack accurate information about RSS. Those whose selfish motives are impeded or exposed by the Sangh activities churn out false information against Sangh and try to put a spanner in its activities. Such propaganda is saturated with malicious lies, irrational claims and misleading misnomers because Rashtriya Swayamsevak Sangh does not work against anyone or as a reaction to any incident. In the past, misleading people with such disinformation was possible in the absence of information or direct contact with Sangh. But now, with the ever-expanding ambit of Sangh activities, more and more people have a first-hand experience of the reality, hence spreading misleading messages is no longer as easy. Another factor may be responsible for doubts or confusion arising in one's mind about Sangh. Languages that have emerged from Bharatiya traditions contain words that encompass complex and distinct emotions of Bharatiya life experiences. Many concepts of Bharatiya thought are special and unique. Exact synonyms or near approximates of those concepts are not to be found in other languages of the world, which makes it impossible to find corresponding words that convey the right meaning of these concepts. Unfortunately, while the people of Bharat are in the process of losing the tradition of getting to know Bharat through the medium of Bharatiya languages, viz. their mother tongues, and their ancient texts, they make attempts to understand Bharat through inaccurate translations of foreign languages which inadvertently convey the wrong meaning. This obviously leads to errors in comprehension. This book is an attempt to remove that veil of confusion and ignorance by taking cognizance of the mistakes in expressions about Sangh and Bharat made knowingly or unknowingly, intentionally or unintentionally, while offering the correct meaning in its stead.

Dr. Manmohan Vaidya is a *Sah Sarkaryawah* (Joint General Secretary) of RSS. Since childhood, he has been fulfilling various responsibilities of Sangh, travelling across Bharat and abroad. His work has occasioned contact with many enlightened people in the society. He has inherited the legacy of Sangh as well as proficiency in writing from the same source – his father. His articles have been published in the media of Bharat as well as other countries and read widely. He continues to study many subjects. In this book, comprehensive discussions on several topics of importance have been offered with logical reasoning as well as examples.

This book is not merely a refutation of misinformation related to Sangh or the errors in understanding Sangh. The responses that the Sangh perspective generates when the world of ideas of a Sangh *swayamsevak* meets with the ideas of the world are also to be found herein. It is the nature of a *swayamsevak* to proactively study any event or idea through the Sangh point-of-view and use the essence of the analysis to enrich his approach as a *swayamsevak*. The same process unfolds in the mind of a *swayamsevak* as he observes and examines people from all angles of life whom he comes in contact with, as well as friends and relatives. All these things are at the core of this piece of writing, which can be noted on reading.

You will find a discussion of complex concepts like *dharma* in this book alongside candid advice with regard to contemporary issues discussed in the media and the society, occasioned by some incidents related to Sangh. The article where Dr. Manmohan Vaidya has penned a heartfelt memoir of his father, not only expresses his feelings but is a succinct example of how one *swayamsevak* observes and takes inspiration from the life of another senior and experienced *swayamsevak*.

Dr. Mohan Bhagwat

Sarsanghachalak,
Rashtriya Swayamsevak Sangh

Preface

It is imperative for every nation to know who they are as people to decide about their priorities and tread the future path of progress. After the terrorist attack on the World Trade Centre on September 11, 2001, in the USA there was much churning about "who we are" as USA.

In the book "*Who Are We*" published in the aftermath of September 11, Samuel Huntington notes that-

"We Americans" face a substantive problem of national identity epitomised by the subject of this sentence. Are we a "we," one people or several? If we are a "we," what distinguishes us from the "thems" who are not us? Race, religion, ethnicity, values, culture, wealth, politics, or what? Is the United States, as some have argued, a "universal nation," based on values common to all humanity and in principle embracing all peoples? Or are we a Western nation with our identity defined by our European heritage and institutions? Or are we unique with a distinctive civilization of our own, as the proponents of "American exceptionalism" have argued throughout our history? Are we basically a political community whose identity exists only in a social contract embodied in the Declaration of Independence and other founding documents? Are we multicultural, bicultural, or unicultural, a mosaic or a melting pot? Do we have any meaningful identity as a nation that transcends our sub-national ethnic, religious, racial identities? These questions remain for Americans in their post-September 11 era. They are in part rhetorical questions, but they are also questions that have profound implications for American society and American policy at home and abroad.

In the 1990s Americans engaged in intense debates over immigration and assimilation, multiculturalism and diversity, race relations and affirmative action, religion in the public sphere, bilingual education, school and college curricula, school prayer and abortion, the meaning of citizenship and nationality, foreign involvement in American elections, the extraterritorial application of American law, and the increasing political role of diasporas here and abroad. Underlying all these issues is the question of national identity. Virtually any position on any one of these issues implies certain assumptions about that identity. So also with foreign policy. The 1990s saw intense, wide-ranging, and rather confused debates over American national interests after the Cold War. Much of this confusion stemmed from the complexity and novelty of that world. Yet that was not the only source of uncertainty about America's role. National interests derive from national identity. We have to know who we are before we can know what our interests are."

Since ages, Bharat has had a unique view of life that shaped the personality of Bharat, and consequently the people of Bharat possess some distinctive qualities. While addressing the Parliament of World Religions in Chicago in 1893, Swami Vivekananda said, "I am proud to belong to a religion which has taught the world both tolerance and universal acceptance. We believe not only in universal tolerance but we accept all religions to be true. I am proud to tell you that I belong to a religion in whose sacred language, the Sanskrit, the word 'exclusion' is untranslatable."

After reading this it dawned upon me that it's true because Bharat has a worldview that is all-inclusive and hence is not exclusive. This intrigued me to understand something unique Bharat or Hindutva is or sees.

Sister Nivedita, (Margaret Noble, an Irish by birth), the famous disciple of Swami Vivekananda has written insightful books on Bharatiya ethos and values and about how Bharat thinks and behaves differently, uniquely. In her book "*Religion and Dharma*" she emphatically states that, "In spite of its seemingly vast mythology, the actual content of Hinduism is infinitely less dependent on mythological ideas than any other religion whatsoever. He who is driven to abandon the historicity of Western beliefs has but sorry ground henceforth to stand upon. Not so the Hindu. There is no shade of the search after truth that is not looked upon here as religious heroism. We are in no danger of persecuting a man for no better reason than that he can see farther and deeper than we! Giordano Bruno would never have been burnt, Galileo would never have been put to torture if India had been their home and birthplace. The *Sanatana dharma* sanctions and endorses every form of honest striving after knowledge. It is jealous and suspicious of no form of truth. Perhaps in this lies the true crown of Hinduism."

Bharat believes in pursuing a continuous search for Truth and the Truth can have various interpretations. Take the case of the Bhagavad Gita. There have been innumerable interpretations of the same text of Bhagavad Gita and many more may come.

Gurudev Rabindranath Thakur in the seminal essay, *"Swadeshi Samaj"* echoed similar sentiments. He opined, "To experience unity in diversity and to establish unity amongst variety—this is the inherent *dharma* (the spirit) of Bharat. Bharatvarsh never interpreted diversities as hostility and neither considered the outsider as an enemy. Thus, without sacrificing our own, without destroying others, Bharat aspires to assign a distinct place to everyone in one vast ecosystem. Thus, it is willing to accept all ways of life and acknowledges the greatness of each in its own way. As Bharatvarsh possesses this trait, we would never get frightened by visualising any society as our opponent. With every new dissension, we inevitably will grow. The Hindu, Bauddha, Muslim and Christian would not fight with each other and die in Bharat. Rather they would find a balance, a meeting point here. This balance will not be non-Hindu, but very specifically Hindu. However foreign maybe its body parts, its life and spirit will be of Bharat."

Bharat has a history and tradition to welcome, accept and give space to new thoughts and religions for them to flourish and enriches them by adding Bharatiya content. Hence calling Bharat a *Ganga-Jamuni* culture is not correct. In Bharat when the two mighty rivers (Ganga and Yamuna) meet (*sangam*) at Prayagraj the river that flows beyond Prayagraj still continues to be referred to as "Ganga". This Ganga meets with river Saryu and it is Ganga only that flows further. Meeting, accepting many such small or large rivers like Gandaki, Kosi and others, it is Ganga that moves on and merges into the sea to form that which is called Ganga Sagar. This is exactly what Gurudev Rabindranath had to say about Hindutva.

Dr. S. Radhakrishnan in his seminal book, "*The Hindu View of Life*" has said, "Today the world has become a much smaller place, thanks to the adventures and miracles of science. Foreign nations have become our next-door neighbours. The mingling of populations is bringing about an interchange of thought. We are slowly realising that the world is a single cooperative group. Other religions have become forces with which we have to reckon, and we are seeking ways and means by which we can live together in peace and harmony. We cannot have religious unity and peace so long as we assert that we are in possession of the light and all others are groping in the darkness. That very assertion is a challenge to a fight. The political ideal of the world is not so much a single empire with a homogenous civilisation and a single communal will, but a brotherhood of free nations differing profoundly in life and mind, habits and institutions, existing side by side in peace and order, harmony and cooperation, and each contributing to the world its own unique and specific best, which is irreducible to the terms of the others.

"The cosmopolitanism of the eighteenth century and the nationalism of the nineteenth are combined in our ideal of a world commonwealth, which allows every branch of the human family to find freedom, security and self-realisation in the larger life of mankind. I see no hope for the religious future of the world if this ideal is not extended to the religious sphere also. When two or three different systems claim that they contain the revelation of the very core and centre of truth and the acceptance of it is the exclusive pathway to heaven, conflicts are inevitable. In such conflicts, one religion will not allow others to steal a march over it and no one can gain ascendancy until the world is reduced to dust and ashes. To obliterate every other religion than one's is a sort of bolshevism in religion which we must try to prevent. We can do so only if we accept something like the Hindu solution, which seeks the unity of religion not in a common creed but in a common quest. Let us believe in a unity of spirit and not of organisation, a unity which secures ample liberty not only for every individual but for every type of organised life which has proved itself effective for almost all historical forms of life and thought can claim the sanction of experience and so the authority of God. The world would be a much poorer thing if one creed absorbed the rest. God wills a rich harmony and not a colourless uniformity. The comprehensive and synthetic spirit of Hinduism had made it a mighty forest with a thousand waving arms each fulfilling its function and all directed by the spirit of God. Each thing in its place and all associated in the divine concert making with their various voices and even dissonances, as Heraclitus would say, the most exquisite harmony should be our ideal. That the Hindu solution to the problem of the conflict of religions is likely to be accepted in the future seems to me to be fairly certain."

Many modern thinkers and philosophers are echoing the same after seeing the conflict-ridden war-mongering tendencies to acquire (rather grab) political, economic and military power and control over resources at the cost of humans and humanity.

Fritjof Capra, the well-known Austrian-American physicist, seems to be hinting at this Hindu solution. In his book "*The Web of Life*", Mr. Capra notes very emphatically, "The paradigm that is now receding has dominated our culture for several hundred years, during which it has shaped our modern Western society and has significantly influenced the rest of the world. This paradigm consists of a number of entrenched ideas and values, among them the view of the Universe as a mechanical system composed of elementary blocks, the view of human body as a machine, the view of life in society as a competitive struggle for existence, the belief in unlimited material progress to be achieved through economic and technological growth, and last not the least–the belief that a society in which the female is everywhere subsumed under the male is one that follows a basic law of nature. All of these assumptions have been fatefully challenged by recent events. And, indeed a radical revision of them is occurring.

"The new paradigm may be called a holistic worldview, seeing the world as an integrated whole rather than a dissociated collection of parts. It may also be called an ecological view if the term "ecological" is used in a much broader and deeper sense than usual. Deep ecological awareness recognises the fundamental interdependence of all phenomena and the fact that as individuals and societies, we are all embedded in (and ultimately depend on) the cyclic process of nature.

"Ultimately, deep ecological awareness is spiritual or religious awareness. When the concept of the human spirit is understood as the mode of consciousness in which the individual feels a sense of belonging, of connectedness, to the cosmos as a whole, it becomes clear that ecological awareness is spiritual in its deepest essence. It is, therefore, not surprising that the emerging new vision of reality based on deep ecological awareness is consistent with the so-called perennial philosophy of spiritual traditions."

This perennial philosophy of spiritual traditions described by the enlightened souls above is precisely the Bharatiya or the Hindu view of life. Bharat has this knowledge, history, tradition, and legacy and hence the responsibility to show the world by example how a multi-cultural, multi-religious, multi-ethnic human society can live in prosperity, peace and harmony together with limited resources on our planet – Mother Earth.

Gurudev Rabindranath Thakur, in *Swadeshi Samaj* emphasises the importance of becoming what "we" are. He notes-

"We have fully understood today that just by lying low we cannot protect ourselves. The only way of self-protection is by evoking and directing our innate strength in every possible way. This is the rule of the divine. The English would continue to control our mind until we come out of our comfort zone and start toiling. Sitting on the fence and constantly ruing imminent ruination would yield no fruit. Aping the English in every sphere and disguising ourselves in an attempt to survive is analogous to disregarding ourselves. We can never be true English and even by mimicking the English we cannot bring them to a halt. Our intellect, our heart, and our taste are auctioned off at very low rates every day. The only way to prevent it from happening is by becoming what "we" are consciously, strongly, actively, and completely."

These observations riveted and inspired me to write about the unique way Bharat looks at the events taking place in Bharat and around. Unfortunately, some colonised minds, intellectuals and people with vested interests are seen trying to create misunderstandings about Bharat's integral and holistic view of the world.

This book is a compilation of articles written at different points in time [mainly in the last seven years (2017-2023)] that have featured in some of the premier national and international media. As a whole, these articles try to emphasise how the worldview of Bharat is different in its approach and understanding from the rest of the world (particularly Western). As these articles were published in the span of seven years in various media, the readers may find some repetitions. We have kept those as they are. Each article should be read in its entirety.

The readers may notice that in my writings, instead of 'India and Indian' I have chosen the words 'Bharat and Bharatiya' as they connote an ancient and rich meaning. While quoting the texts I have maintained the original words India and Indian. In the same way, Hindutva (Hinduness can be its apt translation in English) is chosen against Hinduism as this "ism" is alien to Bharatiya knowledge system and traditions.

I feel obliged to and express deep gratitude towards my father Late Shri M. G. Vaidya for inspiring and moulding me as a writer and also for suggesting an apt title— *"We and the World Around"* for this book. I am greatly indebted and extend my heartfelt gratitude to *Sarsanghachalak* Dr. Mohan ji Bhagwat for writing the foreword of this book. I am also grateful to Mrs. Namita Gokhale and Mrs. Pragya Tiwari for pursuing the idea of bringing out the compilation of these articles in a book form. Also, I thank Ms. Kaustubhi Shukla, Ms. Cherish Rajpurohit, Ms. Advaita Kala, Shri Prafulla Ketkar, Shri Hitesh Shankar, Shri Rajiv Tuli, Shri Bharat Bhushan, and all others who were instrumental in the publication of this book. I am thankful to the publisher Vaani Prakashan for undertaking this task and bringing out a book which I hope will guide many generations of Bharat to come.

Dr. Manmohan Vaidya

Sah-Sarkaryawah,
Rashtriya Swayamsevak Sangh

आषाढ़ शुक्ल एकादशी, गुरुवार, युगाब्द 5125
Ashadh Shukla Ekadashi, Guruvaar, Yugabd 5125

June 29, 2023
Bhopal, Bharat

सत्यमेव जयते

उपराष्ट्रपति
भारत गणराज्य

VICE-PRESIDENT
REPUBLIC OF INDIA

MESSAGE

We and the World Around, an incisive and analytical discourse by Shri Manmohan Vaidya of complex issues like dharma, is bound to enlighten and enrich the reader as also stir inquisitiveness. This fascinating book aptly focuses on essential elements of our civilizational ethos, rendering lucid elucidation of perennial idea of Bharat and *Bharatiyata.*

The book from eminently recognised ERUDITE ideologue would certainly help the reader understand and appreciate our cultural authenticity.

In ***We and the World Around*** Shri Manmohan Vaidya unfolds Bharat's view on various aspects. Chapters on ***'RSS and Freedom Movement'*** and ***'Gandhiji and Sangh'*** are informatively absorbing.

Shri Vaidya also raises several issues of contemporaneous relevance and brings forth rational perspectives, premising on the wisdom of celebrated thinkers to contextualise the idea of Bharat.

Congratulations to Shri Vaidya for his thoughtfulness in filling the much needed knowledge-gap on several aspects.

Jagdeep Dhankhar

12th October, 2023

New Delhi

Contents

Reflections

Inspiration Continues

Sangh and Samaj

1

Celebrating RSS Centenary

Rashtriya Swayamsevak Sangh was founded in Nagpur in 1925 and on the Vijayadashami of 2022, the organisation will celebrate its 97th anniversary. While Sangh is approaching its centenary, its reach and influence continue to grow manifold, despite opposition and obstacles. Consistent hard work, penance, the sacrificial spirit of Sangh workers, accrescent support of the society and blessings of the Almighty have made this possible. This achievement fascinates many, the world over. Lately, people are also curious to learn how RSS would celebrate its centenary.

RSS founder Dr. Hedgewar was very clear in his vision in which he saw Sangh not as an organisation operating within the society, but as the organisation of the entire society. One of Sangh's luminaries, Shri Dattopant Thengadi remarked, "conceptually RSS and Hindu society are co-terminus and psychologically they are one."

Therefore, the centenary of RSS cannot be confined to the organisational level. Since Sangh is synonymous with the society, and Dr. Hedgewar opined that our mission to unify the entire society under Sangh's vision should be fulfilled even before the celebration of the silver jubilee, accomplishing Sangh's mission before the centenary would be the ideal centenary celebration.

A Sangh song goes like "कार्यमग्नता जीवन हो और कार्यपूर्ति ही विश्रांति" (*Karyamagnata Jeevan ho aur Karyapurti hi Vishranti*) Meaning- "to live is to be absorbed in work and only its completion is to rest."

The journey of the monumental expansion of Sangh operations has seen four major phases. The period spanning the foundation of RSS up till the nation's independence should be considered the first phase, wherein the focus was on 'organisation' since it was necessary to make people believe that Hindu society can be united and speak about Bharat and *Hindutva* as a unified chorus. While *swayamsevaks* participated in the ongoing freedom movement and other social reform movements in their personal capacity, Sangh as an organisation completely absorbed itself in organising the collective.

The second phase of Sangh's expansion began in 1949 after Bharat's independence. A thousand-year-long struggle followed by the inspiration of the freedom movement called for a need to envision a social and national blueprint based on our real identity or self ("*Swa*"). Rooted in the traditions of Bharat, many initiatives were propelled by *swayamsevaks* in several segments like education, student welfare, politics, labour, tribals and farmers. While the organisation carried on with its core activities, many people's initiatives addressing the needs of the entire spectrum of human lifespan also shaped up alongside. Today, Sangh's *shakhas* are conducted in over 90% of the development blocks and more than 35 community-driven initiatives are addressing different needs of the society.

The third phase commenced following Dr. Hedgewar's birth centenary in the year 1989-90. The mission to weave the society as one with affection and affinity resulted in the outreach to the deprived, weak and the backward within our society. *Sewa Vibhag* (social service initiative) was established in 1991 to work towards their upliftment.

In the same spirit, every volunteer takes an oath, "I have become a constituent (volunteer) of Rashtriya Swayamsevak Sangh for the all-round progress of the nation." It is irrational to assume that the volunteers alone can bring about all-round progress. Many influential and well-intended people want to contribute toward society's betterment. In 1994, the *Sampark Vibhag* was set up for collating information about the activities and contributions of such social achievers, making them aware of Sangh's vision and cooperating in areas of mutual interest.

Take for example the matter of conversion that has been debated since the freedom movement. In 1967, under Congress governments, Madhya Pradesh and Odisha passed a bill to curb Christian conversion. Since then this issue has single-handedly been taken up by the Bharatiya Janata Party only and most of the bills to curb conversion were passed during the BJP government in various states with the exception of Himachal Pradesh. In 2006, the Congress government led by Shri Virbhadra Singh passed a bill against conversion there. Just a few years ago, some officials of the Sangh *Sampark Vibhag* had met with Shri Virbhadra Singh ji who narrated the first-hand accounts of the passing of the bill and told them that if he could be instrumental in curbing conversion anywhere in Bharat outside Himachal Pradesh, then he would readily contribute.

Similarly, in 2008-09, when *Gau-Gram Rath Yatra* was organised, '*Sarvodaya*' workers participated in this *yatra* at many locations. In this way, issue-based cooperation with those who might not entirely share Sangh's worldview has been enabled by the *Sampark Vibhag*.

RSS has been and still continues to be at the receiving end of spiteful, organised efforts to malign its image through misinformation. To tackle this the *Prachar Vibhag* of RSS was formed in 1994. It aims to disseminate factual information of what Sangh really stands for and does in the society. It emphasises on RSS' national outlook toward various issues of national importance using different media and also counters the malicious, false propaganda built around RSS by providing accurate information.

Additionally, during the third phase, alarmed by certain burning social problems, key social reform projects were instituted. It was through the intervention of '*Dharmajagaran Vibhag*' that efforts to stop organised mass Hindu conversion operations and the project of helping those proselytised and desirous of connecting back with their roots were initiated.

Along similar lines, it was felt that the village dwellers could be mobilised to enable village development, instead of being dependent on the state alone. With a motto to usher in extensive rural development by empowering villagers in a way that they can accrue adequate benefits from the government schemes, '*gram vikas*' work was started.

Since antiquity our Hindu society has had members that identified with varied caste nomenclatures but those elements that have vested interests in dividing the society have consistently tried to instigate caste-oriented animosity. To create a consortium for all concerned to discuss common challenges and contemplate collective action, a series of meetings have been organised, known as "*Samajik Sadbhav*" (social harmony) meetings. Similarly, to eradicate untouchability and malpractices associated with it, by commemorating our common heritage, efforts have been made through "*Samajik Samarasata*" (Social Equality and Brotherhood).

The work of "*Gauseva – Gausamvardhan*" has flourished with thousands of new *gaushalas* coming up all across Bharat. Creating mass awareness about the medicinal value of products obtained from cows of indigenous breeds, conservation and promotion and breed improvement of these cows along with education programs to train farmers in cowdung-based natural farming are some of the programs undertaken.

While Western thought sees the individual as the smallest unit of the society, Bharatiya culture believes that it is the family. According to the Bharatiya spiritual worldview, family is the first step of the journey from "Me to We." In the present scenario, urbanisation and the fast pace of life have shrunk families and created a lack of opportunities to come together and celebrate our heritage, traditions, relationships, and festivals. Therefore, "*Kutumb Prabodhan*" (familial awakening through dialogue) was started wherein family members gather weekly to understand our civilizational heritage, traditions, culture and the prevailing social scenario from the national point of view and also discuss their duties in the light of the same.

In the last 500 years, the growth based on a Western paradigm of development has wrecked the ecological balance of our precious earth. With the aim to restore this equilibrium, *Paryavaran gatividhi* (environmental protection initiative) was started. It strives to bring in awareness and propel activism around the issue of 'environment,' by encouraging public participation.

Now we are in the fourth phase of our evolution wherein we expect every "earning young *swayamsevak*" to actively participate in and cooperate for social awakening and social change by choosing any one area for social transformation according to his interest and ability.

The founder of Sangh, Dr. Hedgewar in his address during a 1940 RSS training camp said, "Sangh work and values should not be confined to the *shakha* only but should be extended and established in the entire society." Earning the necessary income for our families, nurturing our families and attending *shakha* regularly would not suffice. To invest one's time in actively working towards social change and social awakening is the definition of a *swayamsevak*.

Sangh expects that its *swayamsevaks* - 1. will develop themselves to effectively execute Sangh's mission in the society. 2. Will uphold the holistic *Akhil Bharatiya* (All-India) perspective, that this entire nation from (Ram)

Setu to the Himalayas is one and is my own. 3. Will realise the feeling that all members of the society are equal. 4. Will regularly attend *shakha* so that the practice of putting the nation above oneself and leading the movement while remaining in the backdrop could be perfected. 5. Will actively channel the character traits built through *shakha* in one of the many areas of social transformation.

Simultaneously, *swayamsevaks* should be more active in the society and meet new people so that newer sections of the society can come into contact with Sangh, understand the Sangh and know the national ideals of the RSS. Being an integral part of the society they can also connect and contribute to protect *Hindu Dharma*, the Hindu culture and the Hindu society and remain devoted to the cause of all-round progress of the nation.

Along with this, the fundamental work of societal organisation and character building will go on. Social awakening is also a perennial task. With a view to bring about systemic changes, *swayamsevaks* are actively contributing in different areas through various organisations. It is time that each *swayamsevak* goes out with a renewed vigour for social change. Working towards these initiatives directed at the realisation of Sangh's goals would be the best way to celebrate the centenary.

किमन्यै: श्रमै: शुन्यै : *Kimanyaihi Shramaihi Shunyaihi* (All other efforts are pointless.)

Endnote :

This article first appeared in *The Sunday Guardian* on May 14, 2022.

2

RSS and the Freedom Movement

Some time back, a journalist came to visit me. During our conversation, he asked, "What role did the RSS play in the Independence struggle?" In response, I enquired what he meant by the "Independence struggle". He was caught by the hop. He could not speak anything. Perhaps he too was a victim of the propaganda against RSS. After a while, he replied in a low and hesitant voice, "The one which Mahatma Gandhi did". I asked, "So, nothing happened before Gandhiji? Did the trinity of Lal-Bal-Pal have no contribution? Did Subhash Chandra Bose and revolutionary movements like the *Anushilan Samiti* have no role in the Independence struggle?" He kept mum. Then I asked, "how many *satyagrahas* happened under Gandhiji's leadership?" He was unsure of that. I answered, three *satyagrahas* took place - in 1921, 1930 and 1942. He did not know it. I informed him that the founder of RSS, Dr. Hedgewar (who passed away in 1940), had participated in the *satyagraha* before (in 1921) and after (in 1930) he founded the RSS, for which he suffered imprisonment also.

I had to narrate this incident because for several decades now systematic attempts have been made to tell selective parts of history to the people of the country. The people of Bharat are being led to believe that independence was gained purely because of the Congress and the *Satyagraha* of 1942, and nobody else made any contribution to the cause. This is a propaganda. Of course, the *satyagraha* provided a simple and easy-to-adopt means for the common people to participate in the Independence struggle through *Charakha* and *Khadi.* However, to crown a particular movement or a party as the sole benefactor of the entire struggle is to play with history and an outright insult to the efforts of all others who attained martyrdom to free our motherland.

Now, if we want to discuss RSS in the freedom struggle, then we have to start with Dr. Hedgewar. Keshav Baliram Hedgewar was born in 1889. The fervour of the Independence struggle reached Nagpur in 1904-1905. Yet, in 1897, the 8-year-old Keshav threw away the sweets in a dustbin that were distributed in the school on the occasion of the diamond jubilee of Queen Victoria's coronation. This was the reflection of his anger and annoyance for being a slave to the British. In 1907, Keshav invited the wrath of his school management for making both sections of his matric class sing '*Vande Mataram*' in front of a government inspector in his school and was expelled from the school as a punishment for the same. This was against the tyrannical order called the Risley Circular which banned the public chanting of *Vande Mataram*. For his medical education, he chose Calcutta over Mumbai, even though the latter had the facilities, Calcutta was the hub of revolutionary activities. There he became a core group member of the top revolutionary organisation – *Anushilan Samiti*.

He returned to Nagpur in 1916 after becoming a qualified doctor. At that time, almost all the top leaders of the Independence struggle were married, leading a family life and had their own means to earn for the family. Even as family men, these people were actively involved in the Independence movement. Coming from a family that could barely make ends meet, it was expected that Dr. Hedgewar thought along the same lines. The family would've also expected him to lead a normal social life and support them financially. Nevertheless, he decided not to follow the medical profession and not to marry. Doctor ji could have very well emulated his contemporaries. However, his desire for independence was so intense that he gave no thought to his personal life. He felt such urgency for independence that he often said – till the time our country is enslaved, I don't have the time to think about myself. Therefore, he channelized all his energy towards the freedom movement. He dedicated all his might, time and ability to the nation and joined every type of movement for independence.

Dr. Hedgewar had unflinching faith in Lokmanya Tilak. All the responsibilities of logistics for the Congress session held in Nagpur in 1920, were given to Dr. Hardikar and Dr. Hedgewar, who inducted 1200 volunteers for the same. Dr. Hedgewar was the joint secretary of the Nagpur city unit of Congress at that time. He had proposed to the resolution committee of the Congress to come up with a resolution with a clear objective - "to have

Poorna Swaraj (total independence) in Bharat, turn it into a republic, and free the world from the clutches of capitalism." After nine years, in the Lahore session of 1929, the Congress accepted his suggestion of *Poorna Swaraj* or complete self-rule. Pleased with this, Doctorji instructed all the *shakhas* of the RSS to congratulate Congress on January 26, 1930. After Lokmanya Tilak's demise on August 1, 1920, all Tilak supporters in Nagpur were in mourning. Thereon, the Congress's independence struggle continued under Gandhiji's leadership. In 1921, Mahatma Gandhiji supported the Khilafat during the Non-Cooperation Movement with a view to expand the social base against imperialism and accommodate the Muslims that were hurt by the abolition of the Khilafat in Turkistan by the British. Many Congress leaders and nationalist Muslims were against this decision. Initially, the Non-Cooperation Movement was not very effective in and around Nagpur. However, Dr. Hedgewar, Dr. Cholkar, Samimulla Khan etc., changed this scenario. Even after disagreement with the decision of the Congress about Khilafat, he did not make the objection public. He took part in the movement with the sole purpose of opposing imperialism. He was indifferent towards the political atmosphere around him or the views of vocal Tilak supporters. He had to suffer one year in prison, charged with sedition.

Even after knowing the importance and priority of attaining independence, one question haunted Dr. Hedgewar – how could a handful of Englishmen, who came from 7000 miles away for trade, rule this large country? There must be some flaw within us. He realised that our society had forgotten its real self and got divided along the lines of castes, provinces, languages and faith, that it was unorganised and marred by bad practices. The British benefited from this and managed to rule over us. This history might repeat itself in the future as well if the society remained the same even after gaining independence. He would suggest this when he said "when Nagnath goes, Sapnath may come" (when one perpetrator leaves, another may show up). Hence, it is imperative to make our society proud of itself, become aware and organised, as well as liberate it from all bad practices and infuse national character in it. He realised that this work could be done only by staying away from politics and publicity and by working silently and consistently. He founded Rashtriya Swayamsevak Sangh in 1925 with this vision. He had cordial and intimate relations with all political and social movements, activities and leaders even after founding RSS.

The Civil Disobedience Movement was started by Gandhiji on April 6, 1930, in Dandi (Gujarat). The decision to support this movement was taken in November 1929 in the three-day meeting of RSS *sanghachalaks*. As per the RSS policy, Dr. Hedgewar decided to participate in this *satyagraha* in his individual capacity. Some other *swayamsevaks* also joined him. To ensure Sangh's work continued uninterrupted he handed over the charge of *sarsanghachalak* to his trusted colleague Dr. L.V. Paranjpe. Shri Babasaheb Apte and Bapurao Bhedi were entrusted to travel, ensuring unhindered Sangh work. Initially, 3,000-4,000 people accompanied him from Nagpur on July 21 during this *satyagraha*. By the time they reached the venue of the *satyagraha* in Pusad (Vidarbha) in 1930, 10,000 people had gathered. Dr. Hedgewar was sent to jail for nine months in this *satyagraha*. He resumed the responsibility of *sarsanghachalak* after his release and refocused on RSS work.

Hindu Mahasabha and Arya Samaj had given a call of *satyagraha* under the banner of Bhagyanagar Nihshastra Pratikar Mandal in 1938 to oppose Nizam's atrocities against the Hindus in Bhagyanagar (Hyderabad). Doctorji gave consent to those *swayamsevaks* who sought permission to participate in that *satyagraha*. But he clarified that they could do so in an individual capacity. When the organisers frequently mentioned in their press releases that RSS had participated in the Bhagyanagar *satyagraha*, Doctorji wrote a letter and asked them not to mention RSS.

Doctorji had deliberately devised this strategy with a vision and clear thinking. He understood the difference between the transitory, momentary and conflict-ridden political movements and the consistent, uninterrupted and constructive nature of RSS work. He wanted movements to be successful without hampering the perpetual work of RSS. Even during the jungle *satyagraha*, he participated with many other *swayamsevaks* after entrusting the responsibility of *sarsanghachalak* to Dr. Paranjape.

On August 8, 1942, Mahatma Gandhi gave the historic call of "British! Go Back" in the Congress session at the Gowalia Tank ground in Mumbai. From the next day itself, the movement caught momentum all over the country and arrests of leaders started in many places.

Agitations at Bawali (Amaravati), Ashti (Wardha) and Chimur (Chandrapur) in Vidarbha were remarkable. The news from Chimur was broadcast even on Berlin Radio. The agitations there were led by Uddhavrao

Korekar of Congress and RSS functionaries Dada Naik, Baburao Begade and Annaji Siras. The only death from a British bullet in that agitation was that of RSS *swayamsevak* Balaji Raipurkar. Congress, Shri Gurudev Seva Mandal of Shri Tukdoji Maharaj and RSS *swayamsevaks* collectively organised the agitation and *satyagraha* in Chimur. Cases were filed against 125 *satyagrahis* in this agitation which included many *swayamsevaks.*

Besides this, senior members and *pracharaks* of RSS at many places all over Bharat vehemently jumped into this movement, such as Shri Jaidevji Pathak (*pracharak* in Rajasthan), who was later active in Vidya Bharati, Dr. Annasaheb Deshpande at Arvi (Vidarbha), Ramakant Keshav (Balasaheb) Deshpande, who later founded the Vanvasi Kalyan Ashram in Jashpur (Chhattisgarh), Vasantrao Oak in Delhi who later became the *Prant pracharak* of Delhi, Krishna Vallabh Prasad Narayan Singh (Babuaji) in Patna and who later shouldered the responsibility of Bihar *Sanghachalak*, Chandrakant Bhardwaj (Delhi), whose foot was hit with a bullet that could never be removed. Dattatray Gangadhar (Bhayyaji) Kasture in Ujjain (Madhya Pradesh), Madhavrao Devale in East Uttar Pradesh were a few among many others.

Along with the tyranny of the British on one hand *satyagraha* was going on, while on the other many agitators went underground and worked for steering the movement. To give shelter to the underground workers during those times was not free from risk. Many Sangh *swayamsevaks* took that risk and sheltered many of them. Innumerable names can be cited like these. It was nearly impossible to collate and document these details in those days.

Dr. Hedgewar's life is a glowing example of total dedication to the independence of the nation. The path that he chose for the same was to organise a national-thinking, flawless, virtuous Hindu society. Until 1947, the main objective enshrined in the oath of RSS was "to make the Hindu nation independent."

Hedgewar's Vision – RSS' Vision

In Bharat, the society has displayed the tendency to take extreme positions. Even in Doctorji's lifetime, the society was divided into the binaries of Congress-revolutionaries, Tilak supporters-Gandhi supporters, violence-nonviolence, Hindu Mahasabha-Congress etc. The trend was of scoring political brownie points over each other. Sometimes, owing to their differences, they would fiercely oppose each other, instead of fighting against British imperialism. A resolution to condemn the revolutionaries was to come up in the provincial session of the Madhya Prant Congress presided by Loknayak Ane in 1921. Dr. Hedgewar intervened and convinced him that even though he did not believe in the path of the revolutionaries, their patriotism should not be doubted. The proposed resolution was withdrawn after his intervention. Thus, Doctorji's life was not determined by the narrow outlook of political views, philosophy and policies of violence-nonviolence, Congress-revolutionaries, etc. The fundamental aim of attaining independence was far more important than a personality or a particular path.

A class considering Bharat merely a political entity always tries to take credit for everything. It pursues unilateral propaganda to take the sole credit for Bharat's independence without recognising the role and contributions of others. The freedom that Bharat gained was a cumulative result of all-round efforts from armed revolutionaries to non-violent *satyagrahis*, Indian National Army and the rebels in the British Army, etc. The role of prevalent precarious situations in England after World War II and their inability and reluctance to rule the colonies cannot be completely ruled out either. The British eventually gave independence to other colonies too, where there was no freedom struggle like Bharat.

The *satyagraha* in 1942 was the last *satyagraha* led by Mahatma Gandhiji and Bharat attained independence in 1947. However, to say that independence was gained only because of the Quit India Movement in 1942 and the people who were arrested for participating in that movement is ridiculous.

I'm reminded of a story here that goes like this- A farmer was very hungry. The wife was serving rotis and he was eating. However, his hunger was not satisfied. He was satisfied only after eating the eleventh roti. The upset husband scolded his wife for not serving the eleventh roti earlier. His logic was the futile effort of eating so many rotis could have been avoided, and he would have experienced satisfaction earlier. The idea itself is laughable.

Similarly, giving credit for Bharat's independence solely to the 1942 Quit India Movement is laughable. If we go through some historical accounts, we get a clearer picture of this movement—

While granting independence to Bharat, British PM Clement Atlee said "Gandhi's nonviolence movement had next to zero effect on the British". The former acting Governor of West Bengal P. M. Chakraborty (CJ of Kolkata High court) opined, "When I was the acting governor, Lord Attlee, who had given us independence by withdrawing British rule from India, spent two days in the governor's palace in Calcutta during his tour of India. At that time, I had a prolonged discussion with him regarding the real factors that had led the British to quit India. My direct question to Attlee was that since Gandhi's Quit India Movement had tapered off quite some time ago and in 1947 no such new compelling situation had arisen that would necessitate a hasty British departure, why did they have to leave? In his reply Attlee cited several reasons, the main among them being the erosion of loyalty to the British crown among the Indian Army and Navy personnel as a result of the military activities of Netaji." He is further quoted as thus — "Towards the end of our discussion, I asked Attlee what was the extent of Gandhi's influence upon the British decision to leave India? On hearing this question, Attlee's lips became twisted in a sarcastic smile as he slowly chewed out the word, 'm-i-n-i-m-a-l'." [Ranjan Borra, "Subhash Chandra Bose, The Indian National Army, The War of India's liberation". Journal of Historical Review, Vol 20,(2001), No 1 ref. 46]

Ramesh Chandra Mujumdar, the famous historian also has echoed similar thoughts. He opines, ".... It was the cumulative effect of all three (revolutionary activities, non-violent *satyagraha* of congress and military efforts in the name of Azad Hind Sena) that brought freedom to India. In particular, the revelations made by the INA trial, and the reaction it produced in India, made it quite plain to the British, already exhausted by the war, that they could no longer depend upon the loyalty of the sepoys for maintaining their authority in India. This had probably the greatest influence upon their final decision to quit India." (Mujumdar, Ramesh Chandra, - Three phases of India's Struggle for Freedom, BVN Bombay India 1967. PP 58-59.)

After reading this, to think that the Quit India movement in 1942 had no contribution in Bharat's independence would be inappropriate. However, it isn't right to believe that suffering in jail is the only characteristic of being a patriot. Besides the people who went to join the freedom struggle, those who looked after the families of those who were in prison, who worked underground, who gave shelter to the underground activists, who aroused patriotism in the students through education that inculcated national character, and those who propagated and practised *"swadeshi"* and economic blockade of British goods, who provided reliable alternative through the *swadeshi* industries and all those who created national awareness through the folk art, journalism, stories, novels and dramas made contributions in their own way. We need to take cognisance of all those silent contributors as well.

Bharat is not a mere political entity. It is a cultural unit based on the enduring, comprehensive and integral vision built on spirituality-based eternal thinking and vision of thousands of years. This vision and the culture stemming out of it provides a unique identity to this varied society spreading from Hind Mahasagar (Indian Ocean) to the Himalayas. Therefore, whenever there is a political change, just before that or simultaneously, a process of cultural awakening by spiritual leaders takes place in Bharat. It is visible that if the situation is more critical, the manifestation of this spiritual force becomes stronger. Precisely owing to this, the Bhakti Movement spread all over Bharat during the 12th to 16th centuries during the Mughal rule. An uninterrupted chain of significant spiritual figures like sadhus, saints and sanyasis were seen in every region, from Swami Ramanand in the north to Ramanujacharya in the far south. The tradition of spiritual leaders like Swami Dayanand Saraswati, Shri Ramakrishna Paramahamsa and Swami Vivekananda is apparent during British rule. No political change has been successful or permanent in the history of Bharat without the spiritual and cultural awakening. Therefore, the impact of cultural awakening should not be undermined and evaluated by political parameters. It must be underlined that the spiritual and cultural awakening that goes on silently and calmly has much more significance for a nation like Bharat.

Endnote :

This article first appeared in *Organiser* on December 11, 2016.

3

Gandhiji and Sangh

The poll bugle has been sounded. All the political parties are busy campaigning, delivering speeches in line with their party culture and tradition. In one such speech, a party representative commented, "This time around the voters will have to choose between Gandhi and Godse." Through the years I have come to observe that those who are Gandhian in the true sense of the word are especially mindful of their conduct, they refrain from even uttering the name Godse. In Sangh gatherings as well Gandhiji is often discussed, but I haven't yet come across a discussion where Godse was mentioned. It is ironic that people whose actions and policies are in direct opposition to the Mahatma's life and legacy, who rely on deception and violence as a political weapon should insincerely use his name for petty political gains.

An editor of a news daily who also happens to be a Sangh *swayamsevak* shared that his daily was slated to publish articles written by a Gandhian. This editor added that the Gandhian thinker when talking about writing on the topic 'Gandhi's relation with Sangh' remarked, "I am aware of the nature of the relation between Gandhi and Sangh, yet I will write about some other aspects which are unknown to many." Upon hearing this my response was "Does this thinker really know what Gandhiji's relationship with Sangh was like!?" Like with most aspects of Sangh, when it comes to RSS' relationship with Gandhiji, people often make presumptions without the requisite examination of facts. Even the so-called scholars rarely attempt a holistic study of the subject before writing their commentary. More often than not their study is picky – drawing from material authored with a specific ideological perspective. The fact of the matter is that in most cases these thoughts are far from the 'truth'.

Regardless of the strong contention with certain opinions of Gandhiji, what sort of relationship Sangh and Gandhiji shared requires some serious clarification in light of the literature available on the subject. Even though RSS is steadfast in its belief that it was not wise of Gandhiji to surrender to the extremist and Jihadi elements among the Muslim community, RSS has also greatly admired and appreciated his ingenious efforts to broaden public support for Bharat's freedom struggle. The introduction of simple means like the *Charakha* (weaver's spinning wheel) and a foolproof method like the *satyagraha* (insistence on truth) clearly resonated with the common man and connected the masses to the ongoing freedom movement. These achievements are obvious demonstrations of his greatness. If one is perceptive then one cannot deny Gandhiji's contribution through his insistence on constructive programmes like *Gram Swaraj*, *Swadeshi*, cow protection and abolition of untouchability among many others. His affinity and perseverance for the eternal Hindu thought are invaluable. His own virtuous life inspired many young people to vow their lives in the service of the nation.

Dr. Hedgewar, the founder of RSS, participated in the Non-cooperation Movement of 1921 and the Civil Disobedience Movement of 1930 under the leadership of Gandhiji. For his involvement, he served two rigorous prison sentences, from August 19, 1921, to July 12, 1922, and then again from July 21, 1930, to February 14, 1931, respectively.

On March 18, 1922, Mahatma Gandhiji was sentenced to a six-year imprisonment. From then on the 18th of every month was celebrated as 'Gandhi Day.' Whilst Gandhiji was in prison, some of his self-professed followers were serving their own interests in the name of patriotism. Dr. Hedgewar flagged this discrepancy in his speech on the Gandhi Day of October 18, 1922, by saying "This day is extremely auspicious. It is time to listen and mull over the values and qualities found in the life of a noble soul like Mahatmaji. Those who are proud of being his followers have an additional responsibility to emulate the qualities championed by him."

In 1934, when residing at Jamnalal Bajaj's residence in Wardha, Gandhiji learnt about an ongoing RSS Winter Camp, which was being conducted nearby. Curious to witness the camp in person, Gandhiji reached the campsite where he was warmly welcomed by the organisers, and many *swayamsevaks* present there engaged in a dialogue with him. Through those conversations, he learnt that *swayamsevaks* from the Scheduled Castes were also participants of the camp and that everyone there mingled with each other with a sense of kinship. No discrimination was observed among the *swayamsevaks* present. Learning this fact deeply gratified him and he openly expressed his happiness about it. After independence when Gandhiji was staying in Delhi, in what was then called '*Bhangi Colony*' (sweeper's colony), an RSS morning *shakha* used to be conducted on the ground right in front of his residence. On September 16, 1947, upon Gandhiji's request, more than 500 *swayamsevaks* holding mandal-level responsibilities assembled there to hear Gandhiji's address. He started his address with these words - "I had visited the RSS camp years ago in Wardha. At that time the founder Shri Hedgewar was alive. The late Shri Jamnalal Bajaj ji had taken me to the camp, and I was impressed by their rigorous discipline, the complete absence of untouchability and simplicity. Since then the Sangh has grown. I have always believed that any organisation which is inspired by the ideal of service and self-sacrifice is bound to grow in strength." (Published in the *Collected Works of Mahatma Gandhi*, vol. 89, pp.193-94)

On January 30, 1948, RSS *Sarsanghachalak* Shri Guruji was in Madras when he got the news of Gandhiji's assassination, he sent a condolence telegram to Shri Devdas Gandhi (Gandhiji's son), Pandit Jawaharlal Nehru and Shri Vallabhbhai Patel. In that message, Guruji wrote - "Shocked at the news of the fatal cruel attack and tragic loss of the greatest personality. The country's loss is unbounded in these critical times. God help shoulder responsibilities that have grown heavier and fill the void caused by the loss of an incomparable unifier."

Shri Guruji issued instructions to all *swayamsevaks* of RSS to suspend all activities for 13 days in memory of Mahatma Gandhi and immediately concluded his journey and returned to Nagpur. On January 31, 1948, he wrote a letter to the prime minister and the home minister, saying, "Yesterday at Madras I heard the shocking news that some thoughtless perverted soul has committed the heinous act of putting a sudden and ghastly end to the life of Poojya Mahatmaji by a bullet. This vile act is a blot on our society in the eyes of the world." This entire correspondence is available in the book *Justice on Trial* and *Complete Works of Sri Guruji*.

Later on October 6, 1969, on the occasion of the birth centenary of Mahatma Gandhi, a statue of Gandhiji was unveiled by Shri Guruji in Sangli, Maharashtra. There in his address, he said, "We have congregated here on an important and a pious occasion. 100 years ago, on this day, a child was born in Saurashtra. Several other children would have taken birth on that day, but we don't celebrate their birth centenaries. Mahatma Gandhi was born like any other common man, but he attained the status of a great man due to his deeds and the love in his conscience. We should mould our lives along the lines of his life ideals. We should try and emulate his life as much as we can." He further said, "Mahatma Gandhi turned dust into gold, bringing out the extraordinary in ordinary men. This was the reason why Britishers had to leave. Mahatma ji used to say, "I am a hardcore Hindu; therefore I love every manifestation of life and not only humans." The primacy that *satya* (truth) and *ahimsa* (non-violence) held in his life and political ideology accrued to his adherence to staunch *Hindutva* only. The '*Hindu Dharma*' which we often discuss today, his thoughts on the destiny of this *dharma* have been expressed under the title, 'Future of Hinduism'. He writes, "*Hindu Dharma* is the one that does not stop, which grows with persistence and is a path for the enquiry of Truth. Today this *dharma* appears worn out, incapable of inspiring progression within us. This is because we are fatigued, not the *dharma*. The moment we will emerge from this lassitude will be the moment of a grand eruption of *Hindu Dharma*, unlike anything that has ever happened in the past—so large in magnitude that *Hindu Dharma* will be glowing in its own lustre in the whole world." It is our responsibility to fulfil this prophecy of Mahatma ji.

"The country needs political and economic freedom. Likewise, there is a need for religious freedom as well that no one shall disrespect anyone and people from different sects and religions can live together. There should also be freedom from the shackles of foreign thoughts. This is the essence of the preachings of Gandhiji. I have met Gandhiji several times. I have also had discussions with him. What I have said is my analysis after deliberating upon the thoughts expressed by him. Therefore, owing to the realisation of my conscience, I feel great respect for Gandhiji."

Guruji says, "My last meeting with Mahatma ji was in 1947. Having secured the reins of the government, political leaders were ecstatic. At the same time, riots had broken out in Delhi. Even those who were non-violent by tradition had become cruel, roguish and heartless. At that time I was in the same area, working to establish peace. Home Minister Sardar Patel was also trying to do the same, and to some extent he even accomplished it.

In the backdrop of this scenario, I happened to meet with Mahatma Gandhiji. Mahatma ji said, "See, what is going on?" I replied, "This is our misfortune. The British would say, when we leave, you people will slit each other's throats. Today, in reality, the same is happening. It is bringing us disrepute in the whole world. It should be stopped." That day in the evening prayer, Gandhiji illustrated my name using glorious adjectives and put my thoughts before the gathering, pleading for immediate action to stop acts that brought ignominy to the country. I was fortunate that the Mahatma personally honoured me by illustrating my name. These affiliations compel me to reiterate that we must all strive to emulate Gandhiji.

"If we act on Mahatma ji's thoughts we shall reawaken the great *Hindu Dharma* that imparts such lessons. Without *dharma*, human society will be like a society of animals, destroying each other. By awakening *Hindu Dharma*, its best qualities shall be entrenched in every individual of the society. We will have to decide that we will stand on the world stage as an ideal society, as a loving, harmonious country, that's why I keep expressing my feelings towards a venerable personality like Mahatma ji." (For further reference, refer *Complete Works of Shri Guru ji*, vol.1, pp. 208-21.)

When I was a *pracharak* in Vadodara (1987-90), I attended a lecture by *Sah-Sarkaryawah* Shri Yadavrao Joshi who talked about Gandhiji in highly reverential words. Later a *karyakarta* quizzed Yadavrao ji if he really spoke from the depths of his heart and actually meant all the reverential words he spoke to honour the memory of Mahatma Gandhiji. To which Yadavrao ji said, "I am not a political leader, so I do not say anything that I do not believe in my heart. Respecting someone does not imply blindly agreeing with all of their opinions, but to commemorate and idealise his special qualities." He further elaborated on his explanation to the inquisitive *swayamsevak* with an example of Bhishma Pitamah of Mahabharata. He said, "Bhishma is remembered for his strong commitment to the vows he had taken and not for his silence at the time when Draupadi was insulted by the Kauravas in the assembly. Similarly, despite a strong disagreement with Gandhiji's approach towards the fundamentalist and Jihadi Muslim leadership, his contribution in taking the freedom struggle to the common people, his ability to ignite the flame of disobedience in the common man's psyche, thereby infecting them with the desire for freedom, his insistence on many issues which are based in Bharatiya view of life, the embodiment of public outrage in the form of *satyagraha* – these contributions are both commendable and inspirational."

Commenting on the relationship of Gandhiji and Sangh without considering these facts is a disservice to the truth and absolutely undesirable. Sangh is carrying forward and embodying Gandhiji's ideals through its work on rural development, organic farming, cow conservation and protection, social equality and harmony, imparting education in one's own language, *swadeshi* economy and lifestyle and will continue to do so. That is more than can be said for those who only remember him when elections are around the corner.

This year is the 150th birth anniversary of Gandhiji. Humble tributes to his pious memories.

Endnote :

This article first appeared in *The Indian Express* on April 12, 2019.

4

Frank Dialogue for Confluence of Ideas

In his seminal work – "*Who Are We?*" Samuel Huntington states that "we have to know who we are before we can know what our interests are". Bharat is in the grips of a similar conundrum where the people of Bharat do not have one unifying idea of what Bharat is as a nation. Hence it is imperative that for a bright future "we, the people of Bharat" arrive at one idea of Bharat. This can be achieved by discussion and dialogue among the people of Bharat at large. Such discussions and dialogues are the soul of democracy and are an intrinsic aspect of our culture.

There seem to be two major streams of the "idea of Bharat" prevailing in Bharat. One looks for its inspiration from outside Bharat and the other believes its roots are entrenched in the age-old integral and holistic spirituality-based view of life which is the soul or chief attribute of Bharat. The former displays a reluctance towards dialogue and tries to compel or thrust a particular narrative, leaving no room for discussion over an alternative narrative. The latter believes and has facilitated dialogue and discussions with different viewpoints on numerous occasions through the years, with the sincere belief that by coming together and discussing each other's views, it is possible to achieve a point of confluence and a common understanding of the "idea of Bharat".

It is a unique worldview which has through ages believed and maintained that "Truth is One, sages describe it using different names – *Ekam Sat Vipraha: Bahudha Vadanti*. This view has facilitated and opened the door to an invaluable tradition of dialogue and acceptance of different views of life.

Hence 125 years ago, Swami Vivekananda proudly proclaimed that we go beyond tolerance and accept all ways to reach the Truth to be true.

This age-old tradition in Bharat has stemmed from the Hindu view of life, one that is based in spirituality and is practised by the people of Bharat for millennia. The history of Bharat is replete with examples of this exchange of ideas and assimilation.

RSS believes in the philosophy of *Hindutva* (Hinduness), the manifestation of a spirituality-based integral and holistic view of life. It is known as the "Hindu view of life" the world over. It has been a tradition in RSS to invite people of different points of view to one stage for discussions and better understanding.

RSS has conducted many mass contact campaigns (*jana sampark abhiyan)* to share the philosophy, views, activities and achievements of RSS with the public. The first countrywide campaign took place in 1985 on the occasion of the 60th birth anniversary of RSS. In 1989-90 during the birth centenary celebrations of Dr. Hedgewar – the great visionary and founder of RSS – the next one followed. At the turn of the century, in the year 2000, to mark the completion of 75 years of relentless work, expansion and achievements of RSS, *swayamsevaks* went to several thousand villages and cities to narrate the story, the philosophy and the work of RSS. During the commemoration of the birth centenary of the second *sarsanghachalak* of RSS, Shri Guruji (2006-07), yet again a mass contact campaign was undertaken that reached out to all sections of the society, including people from different political parties.

As a result of these efforts, the trust and support that RSS receives has multiplied and is growing consistently. Correspondingly, there is a growing curiosity and eagerness to know about RSS and its views on different issues among diplomats from various countries, bureaucrats, technocrats, industrialists, security personnel, educationists, academicians, intellectuals, religious leaders, political leaders, journalists, legal experts, management consultants and many others.

Today, we live in the era of new media and there are many more platforms for mass communication. So, it has become easier to reach out to a multitude of people with the click of a button. However, these same platforms are equally available to the detractors of the RSS and some anti-national forces which perpetually campaign to malign the image of RSS and spread targeted and false information. Nonetheless, the outreach, strength and positive influence of RSS and its all-encompassing Bharatiya philosophy are finding increasing resonance among the people of Bharat, especially the youth. RSS in keeping with the demands of the changing times and the internet age has opened itself up to innovative ideas and programmes in order to reach the masses through different platforms of mass communication.

The *Bhavishya ka Bharat* Lecture Series (2018) is one such attempt at outreach, to convey the views of RSS on different national and social issues. This is an effort to communicate directly with the people. This steady stream of communication and exchange will lead to a point of confluence.

Endnote :

This article first appeared in *Hindustan Times* on August 18, 2018.

5

Has RSS really distanced from Golwalkar?

The three-day lecture series (Future Bharat-RSS Perspective) of Dr. Mohan Bhagwat was an outright success, and as expected, conversations triggered by this first-of-a-kind interaction still continue. Opponents of RSS were numbed into silence – trying to pick apart the speech yet failing to come up with an incriminating utterance that confirmed their often repeated falsehoods. So whilst critics closed to new thoughts and engagement continued to rehash old accusations, the new dialogue that the *Sarsanghachalak's* outreach has triggered overwhelms past prejudice.

There seems to be some delight and even surprise about the clarification the *Sarsanghachalak* has given about the publication – *Bunch of Thoughts*, a collection of speeches and thoughts of Shri Guruji (the second *sarsanghachalak* of RSS). This analysis takes a further leap and goes so far as to assume that Dr. Bhagwat has distanced Sangh from Guruji! This couldn't be further from the truth. In fact, the entire lecture of the *Sarsanghachalak* on day two, about Hindu and *Hindutva*, was based on the intellectual articulation provided by Shri Guruji to the Sangh movement.

Bunch of Thoughts must be seen in the context of its times – also it must be emphasised that the period it is associated with is from 1940 to 1965 (not his entire tenure as *sarsanghachalak*), a specific time in pre- and post-independent history which had its own unique circumstances, leading to wide debate and discourse on nationhood, identity and belonging. Hence it is essential to view the opinions of that time as a subset of the larger dialogue around these issues and the creation of a new country – Pakistan – based entirely on religion.

When Shri Guruji took over as *Sarsanghachalak*, he was a mere 34-year-old. It was a daunting task for the young man to expand and guide this organisation, which had no other parallel to emulate and would need to forge its own destiny. At the time of his taking over as *sarsanghachalak*, the call for Pakistan had taken on a pervasive note and echoed across the country. The Quit India movement had also gained force and many *swayamsevaks* had been incarcerated and some condemned to death as well. It was a tumultuous time. In 1946 an election was held with the demand for Pakistan from the Muslim League and a promise of *Akhand Bharat* by the Congress. In Muslim-majority areas, Hindus were subjected to violence and persecution. As a result of Direct Action, Hindus in Bengal faced widespread violence. Bharat gained independence but it was also amputated. The largest displacement of humanity took place, Hindus sought refuge in Bharat, often after facing unspeakable violence and losing everything. The *swayamsevaks* were the only group who stood by this population, protecting them and playing witness to their trauma. The psychological impact of those years was profound and lasting on Hindu society and the nation.

On Gandhiji's assassination, RSS was targeted with falsehoods and a ban was imposed, even though the government was unable to prove the allegations. This was the beginning of the dirty politics of hate by the Congress party in independent Bharat. No doors were left open for conversation and Shri Guruji was incarcerated based on these false charges, *swayamsevaks* organised an unprecedented peaceful satyagraha against this injustice and eventually, the unfair ban was lifted. Correspondingly, communist ideology was expanding and divisive thought that undermined national identity was systematically mainstreamed. This impunity was so stark that in 1962 when communist China attacked Bharat and there was widespread despondency in the country, the communists openly praised the Chinese, clearly articulating their loyalty to their ideology over the nation. At the same time, conversions by Christians gained ground. Justice Niyogi Committee's report led the Congress-ruled states of Orissa and Madhya Pradesh to enact an anti-conversion law, leading to widespread protests amongst the Christian community.

During this time of upheaval, Shri Guruji addressed issues that plagued the national conscience. These contemplations and responses to the prevalent circumstances up to 1965 have been compiled in *Bunch of Thoughts*. However, Shri Guruji continued to be engaged in public discourse for eight more years beyond the time span of the book. Hence on his centenary birth anniversary in 2006, a 12-volume edition, an authentic compilation of his entire thoughts (*Shri Guruji Samagra Darshan*) during his time as *sarsanghachalak* was published. This compilation is worth reading for those who wish to understand Shri Guruji and the evolution of his ideas better, which were in many instances a response to the concerns of the day. No opponent of the Sangh has displayed the requisite intellectual rigour to study Guruji and his ideas entirely in depth before lifting the pen to write on him.

If twelve volumes are too expansive, then his ideas have been distilled into a book called *Shri Guruji – His Vision and Mission* (*Drishti and Darshan*) a book which provides a deep insight as well and is shorter. Dr. Bhagwat appealed to everyone to read this book. Now where does this stand against the allegation that he has distanced Sangh from its second *Sarsanghachalak*?

The answer given by Dr. Bhagwat to the query on the selectively quoted sections in *Bunch of Thoughts* is not any different from what Shri Guruji has himself said. There was an interview that Shri Guruji did with Dr. Jilani in the seventies, in which he answered a few direct questions. It is an interview that is rarely quoted either because critics develop selective amnesia or it doesn't suit their campaigns and narratives.

Below enumerated are the relevant sections of the interview-

Dr. Jilani: Much has been said about 'Indianisation' and a lot of confusion has arisen over it. Could you please tell me how to remove the confusion?

Shri Guruji: 'Indianisation' was of course the slogan given by Jana Sangh. Why should there be such confusion? 'Indianisation' does not mean converting all people to Hinduism. Let us all realise that we are all the children of this soil and we must have our allegiance to this land. We belong to the same society and our ancestors are common. That our aspirations are also common. Understanding this is Indianisation in the real sense.

Indianisation does not mean that one should be asked to quit his religious system. We neither said this nor are we going to say so. Rather we believe that a single religious system for the entire human society is not suitable.

Dr. Jilani: You said it right. It's 100 percent right. Therefore, I am thankful to you for this clarification. You have clarified it from your side quite well. Any thinking person and gentleman wouldn't disagree with you.

Don't you think it is high time that a meeting took place between you and such Muslim Indian leaders who would cooperate with you in finding ways and means to remove this communal discord once and for all? Would you like to meet such leaders?

Shri Guruji: I would not only like it, but I would also welcome it.

Eminent journalist Khushwant Singh also interviewed Shri Guruji in 1972 and if you were to read that interview, then the protracted effort to malign and misrepresent Shri Guruji by the communists who exercised control over most of the media and academic disciplines will become clear.

In the beginning, he writes- "There are some people against whom you build up malice without knowing them. Guru Golwalkar had long been at the top of my hate list. However, as a journalist, I could not resist the chance of meeting him." Towards the end, he writes- "Was I impressed? I admit I was. He did not try to persuade me toward his point of view. He made me feel that he was open to persuasion."

Both the interviews are worth reading in their entirety. However, communists have made it an art form to discuss and defame Guruji without going through the vast literature on him, it is a style of propaganda that they have "excelled" in across the world.

In *Bunch of Thoughts*, the concerns raised by Shri Guruji are the same that the world today is vexed with and are specific to an ideology (within the faith) that propagates fundamentalism and the jihadist mindset that leads to horrors and oppression. In addition, forced and illegal conversion in violation of the law by missionary bodies, urban Maoism as well as international support for such activities have once again in the recent past been highlighted through some incidents but have a long history of spreading disquiet and violence in society. Though it is necessary to take the Muslims and Christians of Bharat along in the nation-building process, it is also important to be cautious about the extremists, Jihadi and divisive elements active in the name of so-called minorities. In this sense, Shri Guruji's caution about the threats to the nation is relevant even today.

As the Hindu way of life manifests itself with the changing times, the same is true with the nature of Sangh's work. In the 92-year journey of Sangh, many attempts of opposition, suppression and venomous propaganda have been made. Despite all this, Sangh's thought and work has been growing with an all-inclusive and all-pervasive approach. Perhaps the inherent qualities of the basic Hindu philosophy characterised by 'flexible rigidity' and transformation with the changing times are its strengths.

Endnote :

This article first appeared in *Hindustan Times* on October 16, 2018.

6

RSS Doesn't Need Glasnost

It was anticipated that the three-day lecture series (Future of Bharat: An RSS Perspective) by Dr. Mohan Bhagwat would trigger conversation and debate. Most people welcomed this unique outreach. However, some people expressed doubts over the sincerity of the program, while others wondered if these ideals would filter down to the ground level.

The *Sarsanghachalak's* lectures were perceived as groundbreaking and even revolutionary by some people. In fact, one journalist commented that it was surprising to note that the *Sarsanghachalak* answered so many diverse questions with candour.

However, I found nothing "new" in there. No views expressed were such that haven't been discussed at some level in Sangh before. Along with the *Sarsanghachalak* national office-bearers routinely tour the country extensively and engage with all sections of society, addressing their curiosities and queries about the RSS.

Sangh has been maligned with negative propaganda for decades, so it was but natural for people outside Sangh circles to assume that there is no room for open debate in the organisation, and that this outreach was a "new" way. Now that these ideas were welcomed by the general public and the lecture series was received positively, others decided to call this a "*Glasnost*" moment. The lexicon of foreign concepts that is a part of the vocabulary of the opponents of Sangh can be so misleading that one may unknowingly use those inaccurate terms to emphasise a point. One such word is *Glasnost*. *Glasnost* and *Perestroika* are two Russian words that are related to openness with regard to social and economic issues. These words gained currency at the time of the downfall of the oppressive communist regime in the former Soviet Union. These two words articulated freedom from the harsh, violent and closed regime of the communists and ushered in an open social and economic era that had survived the oppression.

Semitic thought processes are unique in their stance of imposing the 'principle' that, "thinking is the work of a chosen few". For the rest, complete submission to that viewpoint is mandated, and any digression is "blasphemy", which is punishable. The communists borrowed extensively from this playbook. The Church was the progenitor of this iron-clad system of thoughts, drawing legitimacy in the name of the Christian faith. Bruno was burnt alive, Galileo was persecuted because he spoke in contradiction to the Church's position by stating that the earth revolves around the sun.

In Communist Russia and China, way too many people lost their lives and were subjected to unspeakable brutality for rejecting or merely questioning the ruling ideology, yet several others fled to remain alive. In these countries, where there was no right to free speech and even thought, *Glasnost* was an awakening - the emergence of a new dawn - a landmark for these societies that had spent decades in the darkness of oppression.

However, the oppression brought on by rigid ideologies was unheard of in Bharatiya history. Our history witnessed great philosophers, saints and social reformers, and so will our future. This is what makes Bharat exquisitely unique. In the modern era, people are familiar with Swami Dayanand Saraswati, Ramakrishna Paramhansa, Swami Vivekananda, Narayana Guru and many others. Bharatiya society has always acknowledged and respected social reformers. It is for this reason that a woman of European origin and the daughter of a Christian Priest, Swami Vivekananda's disciple Sister Nivedita wrote, had Bruno been in India, he would not have been burnt alive. Hence in countries where Semitic ideologies dominate, *"Glasnost"* must be welcomed.

The foundation of the philosophy of Sangh is rooted in Bharatiya *darshan* (view of life), and hence its doors have always remained open for lively and engaging debate.

I was born in a Sangh family. My father, at the age of 18, in 1941, took the vow to dedicate his life to Sangh. Today, at the age of 95, he continues to live out that vow. Since childhood, I have been a regular at the *shakha*, and have never heard any negative remarks about Muslims and Christians being made. However, anti-national elements are strongly condemned (not hated). In 1971, I was entrusted with the responsibility of conducting a local *shakha* in Nagpur (near Ajni Station). On one of the days little over ten children came and joined the *shakha*.While introductions were being made, two brothers introduced themselves as Amil Khan and Feroz Khan, from seventh and fifth grades respectively. This was my first chance interacting with Muslims. A couple of days later I went to their home to meet with their father, Bashir Khan, who was an ambulance driver at the nearby government hospital. In Sangh, it is a ritual to meet and to remain in touch with the family of *swayamsevaks*. After introducing myself I informed him that his sons had been attending *shakha* for the last two days, and he in turn offered me a cup of tea. At the time I was not in the habit of drinking tea, but feared the refusal might be wrongly perceived as declining the hospitality of a Muslim family. Hence I drank half a cup (my first taste of tea!). Up until grade 10 those two brothers were regular *shakha* attendees, in fact, I clearly remember Amil as a very good kabaddi player, - a popular *shakha* game. It is nothing but false propaganda and a targeted defamation campaign orchestrated by those who are in the business of peddling hate that confounds Sangh's stance on Muslims.

From 1996 to 2006 in the capacity of a *prant pracharak*, I had the opportunity to attend many national-level meets. The then General Secretary Sheshadri ji and *Sarsanghachalak* Rajju Bhaiya would always encourage me to participate in discussions and put forth different viewpoints.

Another incident comes to mind that elucidates Sangh's stance on and practice of free speech. Once a *vibhag pracharak* entrusted with the responsibility of Hindu Swayamsevak Sangh (HSS) brought an oversight to the notice of a senior Sangh functionary. He reported that while RSS and HSS conduct identical activities, the routine prayer at HSS *shakha* was missing two important renditions of the RSS prayer sung in Bharat. He demanded those words be included, to which he was informed that the said prayer had been penned by Bhideji, was approved by Shri Guruji and had been in circulation for many years. Dissatisfied with that explanation and the approach he raised the matter with veteran *pracharak* and thinker Dattopant Thengadi ji. Thengadi ji said that if such was the case, the prayer should be amended by adding those important aspects. Emboldened by Thengadi Ji's response, when he voiced this matter to the *Akhil Bharatiya* RSS office-bearers, they discussed and decided to include the relevant sections in the prayer. In the year 2000, after being in use for 50 years the prayer was amended as Sangh concluded that it must be amended. The fact that a *vibhag pracharak's* observation was heeded, raised to the highest level and finally acted upon is indicative of an open flow of feedback in the organisation.

Sangh is a living organisation and cherishes the tradition of encouraging and accepting change with time, hence there is no need for a *Glasnost* moment in RSS. However, it is true that being a large organisation, the letter and spirit of any change has to be communicated and understood by the rank and file in the organisation. This process takes effort and time.

Post-1990 the *Sewa, Sampark* and *Prachar Vibhags* (wings) of Sangh were created to reach out, communicate with and transform the society at large. This was a time-consuming process and took as long as five to ten years to communicate and convince the ranks. There is no opposition to new ideas, however, there are discussions and questions are answered, this is the way of Sangh. In 2015, when after 85 years the uniform of RSS was changed from shorts to full trousers, the decision came after five long years of debate and deliberation, which was subsequently accepted and embraced by all.

Glasnost and *Perestroika* are landmark moments and necessary processes for societies seeped in Semitic traditions that shun new ideas and use blasphemy as a tool to enforce and ensure conformity. However, an organisation that celebrates intellectual novelty and dialogue through its fundamental processes has no need for a *Glasnost* or *Perestroika*. I am reminded of a poem by the famous Gujarati poet, Shri Dhruv Bhatt.

"It is the earth that experiences the darkness of the night but for the Sun, the night and subsequent darkness never occur." In the same vein, for Semitic ideologies, *Glasnost* is a reckoner. However, where the openness of thought is routine, where modifications and innovations are welcome – the word *Glasnost* is irrelevant.

Endnote :

This article appeared in *The Indian Express* on October 17, 2018.

7

Hindutva In Essence Isn't Exclusivist

During the 'Future Bharat-RSS perspective' themed lecture series conducted by Dr. Mohan Bhagwat, the *Sarsanghachalak* said, " 'Fraternity' or *'Bandhu Bhav'* is the essence of the activities carried out by the Sangh, and it is this sense of fraternity and affinity that is exemplified in our country's 'unity in diversity'."

"It is this tradition of fraternity that is referred to as *'Hindutva'*," Dr. Mohan Bhagwat continued. "And that is why we say that Bharat is a Hindu *Rashtra* (a '*rashtra*', for us, meaning the 'people'). But this does not mean that we do not want Muslims in it. The day it will be said that there is no room for Muslims, then it will not be *Hindutva*, for *Hindutva* thinks of the entire world as one family – *Vishwakutumb*." Many eyebrows were raised at this. And some questions erupted in many minds.

When we take particular positions because of prevailing conditions, these positions influence how people see our intrinsic nature and sometimes the original spirit that defines who we are falls into oblivion in people's eyes. The same is true for the soul of Bharat and the speciality and identity of Bharat which is *Hindutva*. *Hindutva* is the spirituality-based, integral and holistic view of life that is naturally all-inclusive. Not only is this view truly global but it is also a perspective that prays and wishes for the good of not only the human race but the creation in its entirety.

This is why Hindus never named themselves 'Hindu'. When our people went outside the country for purposes of trade, they were called 'Hindus' by others. This was meant to indicate, for the outsiders, those coming from beyond the river Sindhu. The outsiders who invaded Bharat also called us Hindu, meaning, again, people living in the region beyond the river Sindhu. Thus Hindu became the name and identity ascribed to all of us living in this region beyond the Sindhu. All of us shared a world-view based on *Ekam Sat Viprah Bahudha Vadanti:* 'Truth is one'. The sages describe this further in various ways, but it essentially entails unity in diversity and a spiritual view of life.

While opposing British rule, be it during the first War of Independence in 1857 or the protests against the unjust partition of Bengal in 1905 – Hindus and Muslims worked together with a sense of solidarity. Subsequently, however, political masters planted the seeds of dissension and hatred between Hindus and Muslims, which eventually led to the partition of the country. The basis of partition itself was the division between Hindus and Muslims. In those tumultuous years, the Muslim view was one that completely negated what is Hindu and what is Bharat. Subsequently, the Hindu opposition to partition evolved into an articulation that was against Muslims. If in those years Hindu leaders reflected anti-Muslim sentiments, it was a consequence of those times: the looming threat of suppression and the eventual partition of the country and its gruesome aftermath. It was a reaction that, nevertheless, did not reflect the eternal inclusive thought that defines Bharat.

It should be kept in mind always that the Hindu view is not exclusivist and does not believe in excluding others or "otherising". This is why Swami Vivekananda said in his famous speech in Chicago that he was proud to belong to a faith in which its ancient Sanskrit language has no equivalent or substitute for the English word "exclusion".

Traditionally the Semitic thought or religions have divided humankind into two groups: those who are believers and those who are not. Hence those who are outside the realm of the Semitic faiths are siding with the devil and are *kafirs* who have no right to even be alive. This exclusivist conception of the world even influences ideologies like Communism that have their roots in such societies and view those different or differing from it as 'others'. If you do not subscribe to Communism, then you are a right-winger and must be shamed. The people who subscribe to such thought have hence represented Hindu"ism" as an "ism"– something that is ironclad and discriminatory towards those outside its fold. Hence in our opposition to this ironclad misrepresentation of an all-encompassing faith, we have also drifted towards this understanding of being Hindu and started using a derivative lexicon and reference points.

Independence came to Bharat alongside a partition of British dominion and a transfer of population that was not intended. The people of this subcontinent had been one since ancient times. In one part of Bharat, Bharatiya Muslims comprised a minority and in the other, what became Pakistan, the Hindus were the minority. Both were promised equal rights and were assured equal treatment. Both constitutions were written at the same time. Pakistan's constitution stayed true to Semitic thought and a delineation between Muslim and Non-Muslim citizens was written in and equal rights were denied. However, in Bharat's constitution, keeping with the Hindu view of life, all religions were given equal rights. This is the *Hindutva* (Hinduness) of the Bharatiya Constitution. Earlier, the entire populace was one. The part that became the Muslim majority Pakistan followed the Semitic traditions, introducing the concept of minorities and denying equal rights to them. However, Bharat, being a Hindu-majority nation, preserved a tradition of not discriminating among people on the basis of religion. Hindu society has always upheld the individual's right to practice the faith of his choice. This has been Bharat's view and history. Hence the concept of "religious minorities" is irrelevant in the context of Bharat.

In post-independence Bharat, unfortunately, the selfish tactics of opposing *Hindutva* and appeasing Muslims and Christians became a norm in party politics. At times, Hindu society had to counter the aggression by violent, Jihadi, fundamentalist Muslim elements. As a result, anti-Muslim sentiment sprouted up in the Hindu minds. However, it must be borne in mind that all the Muslims and Christians of Bharat have a Hindu origin. Because the Hindu society was weak, the circumstances were such that they had to or were compelled to change their faith but they are as much a part of this country as Hindus are. Muslims may forget their origins but Hindus must never do so. They must not be influenced by the exclusivist narrative of Semitism that has been mainstreamed. Instead, they must focus on the *Hindutva* in Bharat's tradition that makes us inclusive. The true identity of *Hindutva* or *Bharatiyata* is to take along our Muslim brethren and together plant the seeds of a prosperous Bharat.

The Sangh's second *Sarsanghachalak* Pujaniya Shri Guruji articulated this thought in an interview with the famous journalist Saifuddin Jilani many years ago. Here is an excerpt :

Dr. Jilani: Much has been said about 'Indianisation' and a lot of confusion has arisen over it. Could you please tell me how to remove the confusion?

Shri Guruji: 'Indianisation' was of course the slogan given by Jana Sangh. Why should there be such confusion? 'Indianisation' does not mean converting all people to Hinduism. Let us all realise that we are all children of this soil and we must have our allegiance to this land. We belong to the same society and share common ancestors. We also share common aspirations. Understanding this is 'Indianisation' in the true sense. Indianisation does not mean that one should be asked to quit his religious system. We neither said this nor are we going to say so. Rather we believe that a single religious system for the entire human society is not suitable.

During his lecture series Dr. Mohanji Bhagwat said, "As a *rashtra*, the people, we all have a Hindu origin and identity. Some people take pride in referring to themselves as Hindus and there are others who do not feel that same sense of pride. Due to some material considerations or political compulsions, some may not want to say they are Hindus publicly but do so in private. And there are those who have simply forgotten. All these people are our own, they belong to Bharat. Just like in exams, we attempt easier questions first before proceeding to the difficult ones, it is the same with our work. We have first chosen to approach those who consider themselves Hindus (culturally). This is because we consider no one as our enemy in the country, or in the world. There may be those who have declared us their enemies, but whilst we may defend ourselves, we have never wished to finish them, on the contrary, we aspire to take them along with us. This is the reality of *Hindutva*."

Freedom fighter Veer Savarkar once said, "You are a Muslim, hence I am a Hindu, else I am a '*Vishwa Manav*', a global human". To articulate the essence of *Bharatiyata* or *Hindutva* here are a few lines from a poem that I am reminded of :

> "He drew a circle and shut me out—
> Heretic, rebel, a thing to flout.
> But love and I had the wit to win.
> We drew a circle and took him in".

Endnote :

This article first appeared in *Hindustan Times* on November 21, 2018.

8

Welcome to Nagpur, Pranab Da

There has been unseemly outrage amongst certain sections of the political class on former President Dr. Pranab Mukherjee's acceptance of an invitation to be the chief guest for the concluding ceremony of the RSS' *Tritiya Varsh* training programme in Nagpur.

Dr. Mukherjee is a seasoned politician who has spent decades in public life. He is well-informed on matters of social and national significance. The invitation has been extended to him with the view that this will be an invaluable opportunity to get a glimpse into his nuanced views and understanding. Also, he will have the opportunity and first-hand experience to listen to the views of Sangh. This exchange of views and ideas is at the heart of the Bharatiya concept of discourse. This invitation and its acceptance are but a continuation of that democratic tradition enshrined in our cultural ethos.

So why then the dissonance and negative commentary? Why the opposition to this exchange? The resistance has surprised many, but if we were to delve into the ideological basis of this opposition it would be unsurprising. Most vocal voices of the prevalent, so-called intellectual spectrum of Bharat are those of a Communist persuasion, an ideology that is entirely alien to Bharat and has been rejected the world over for its infamous intolerance and bloody violent means to ensure conformity. Its compulsion for "thought conformity" necessitates this approach that not only rejects healthy exchange among diverse stakeholders but absolutely abhors it.

Then there is a lazy assumption that if you are not of a leftist persuasion, then by default you are a "right-winger" – their view of the ideological world exists in strict binaries, and consequently you become someone who ought to be criticised, publicly shamed and protested against. This is the communist tradition, verifiable with human experience or rather oppression the world over. And yet despite the repeated display of intolerance, they adorn the mantle of human rights and free speech advocates.

A few years ago, at the same programme, an invitation was extended to renowned social activist and Magsaysay Award winner Dr. Abhay Bang. At that time as well the left-leaning socialists in Maharashtra were up in arms against his decision to accept the invitation. Their pressure politics to discourage engagement led to opinion pieces and articles in their Marathi weekly *Sadhana* criticising his decision. Dr. Bang responded to the pressure tactics by stating that he was going to present the same views at the function that he does elsewhere, so why the opposition? He went on to praise the open-mindedness of RSS, which invited him as an honoured guest despite knowing his views. It was in fact the leftists who were exhibiting intolerance despite all their claims to the contrary. He remained firm in his decision to participate in the function and furthermore submitted the text of his speech to *Sadhana* for publication after the event. However, the magazine that claimed to be the vanguard of free speech refused to publish his speech regardless of the fact that he had been a past contributor.

In 2010, I met with Shri Keshavan Nair, a CPM Trade Union leader from Kollam in Kerala. He had been expelled from the Communist Party for writing two articles in a local paper on “Science in the Vedas”. Singed by this hypocrisy, Shri Nair decided to write extensively on communists and even published a book – *Beyond Red* (which he gifted to me). On the blurb of the book, it is quoted, “The only freedom Communists give you is to praise them”!

During one of my visits to Kolkata as *Prachar Pramukh* (in charge of media relations), whilst CPM was in power there, the local unit of RSS attempted to schedule appointments with the editors of *Statesman*, *Indian Express*, *Times of India*, *Vartaman* and a Communist-leaning newspaper. All granted time for the meeting but the Communist newspaper. The editor of the left-leaning newspaper declined to give an appointment saying he doesn’t want to waste his time. This is their democratic nature and commitment to free expression. The meetings were a success. We had no expectation that those who met with us would agree with Sangh on every issue, but all were open to understanding and engaging with RSS’s views. About the undemocratic attitude of the newspaper that declined the appointment, I asked our local *karyakarta* to get an appointment with them every time I came to Kolkata.

A few years ago Shri Dattatreya Hosabale (Joint General Secretary of RSS) and I were invited to the Jaipur Literature Festival to put forth the views of RSS about different social and national issues in an interactive open session with a journalist. We decided to accept the invitation and attend. At JLF as well there was opposition by the leftist forces. Individuals like Sitaram Yechury and M.A. Baby boycotted the festival only because RSS was given a platform to share its views despite the fact Sangh is increasingly finding acceptance, engagement and support from the society all over Bharat. Their elitist definition of free expression excludes even an attempt to understand such an organisation. But what precipitates these protests? Is it their fear that should the RSS be given an opportunity to reach out to a larger audience, the veil of misunderstanding will fall off-and their lies will be exposed? People will know the truth and that is the biggest fear of them all.

The Communist ideology and such fascist opposition to free speech are entirely against the Bharatiya thought. There is, however, another example that is in contrast to the ones elucidated so far. A few years ago, a delegation from the Chinese Communist Party (CCP) visited Bharat. They were interested in meeting with Sangh and were invited to Keshav Kunj, the Delhi headquarters of RSS. I happened to be in New Delhi and received the delegation, they also gifted me a memento of the Great Wall of China. I was curious about their interest in RSS. CCP being a political party, it was obvious that they meet leaders of different political parties here. But why meet Sangh? They responded to the query by saying that they were a cadre-based political party and Sangh was a cadre-based organisation, this motivated them to reach out for an exchange of ideas. To which I responded and underscored a distinction, "It is true but there is some basic difference between us. CCP is a political party that works for a state power and through a state power, whereas RSS neither works for a state power nor through state power. Rather we work directly in society, with the support of the people." Despite this articulated difference, we had a gracious meeting. We did not refuse to meet with them since having an exchange of views and ideas is the Bharatiya approach.

Advocates of Communist ideology have dominated Bharat's intellectual space for some decades now. Perhaps the choice of a dynastic, regional and caste-based model of politics has left Congress and all other parties except BJP with no original thinkers and hence they rely solely on left-leaning, communist ideologues as party thinkers and intelligentsia. And though they preach liberalism, democracy and freedom of expression, they invariably exhibit communist ideological intolerance and exclusion.

Their reaction to Pranab Da's decision to attend the RSS function has yet again exposed their "liberal" hypocrisy.

The fourth *Sarsanghachalak* – Shri Rajju Bhaiya – shared a strong friendship with Lal Bahadur Shastri ji – a senior Congress leader from Uttar Pradesh and the country's former prime minister. Once when Shri Guruji was visiting Prayag for an interaction with prominent citizens of the city over tea, the Congress politician was also invited. However, he regretfully declined stating, whilst he wanted to attend, his presence would lead to unnecessary and unpleasant chatter amongst his colleagues in the party.

Rajju Bhaiya was startled by this reticence and asked Shastri ji if they would indeed make him the point of discussion. To which he responded dolefully, "you have no idea how politics works". Rajju Bhaiya underscored, "In Sangh it is quite different. If a *swayamsevak* spotted us together he wouldn't doubt my intentions at all, in fact, he would assume that I might be explaining Sangh to you!" Why did Congress fail to trust a stalwart leader of its own?

History repeats itself! All these years later, a towering and veteran leader who is also the former president of this nation is being questioned by junior leaders, some of whom regretfully possess dubious reputations and not half his experience.

How is it that not one *swayamsevak* has questioned why the former president of Bharat and Congress stalwart has been invited? Herein lies the difference between the thought process of RSS and those who claim to be vanguards of free expression, but are all too often bald-faced in exposing their intolerance.

It is Bharatiya tradition to exchange ideas with a diverse set of people, to reject and oppose such an exchange is non-Bharatiya and an assault on our democratic traditions as a culture and the largest democracy in the world.

However, this debate over Pranab Da's presence at the *Tritiya Varsh* concluding ceremony in Nagpur has revealed the true face of these so-called proponents of free speech. Furthermore, Pranab Da has resisted these attempts to publicly shame him and has been statesmanlike in his response, stating that he will answer them with his speech in Nagpur, emphasising thus, that his decision to attend is unwavering. We welcome him and his statesmanship.

Endnote :

This article first appeared in *News18* on June 06, 2018.

9

Thank You Pranab Da For Resisting Intolerance

Despite the staunch protest by his own party men, Dr. Pranab Mukherjee remained resolute in his decision to participate in the closing ceremony of the *Tritiya Varsh* Sangh *Shiksha Varg* of RSS in Nagpur. His conviction in the democratic principle of open engagement is worth acknowledging with gratitude. During his visit to Nagpur, the former President visited Dr. Hedgewar's ancestral home and offered homage to a man he considered "a great son of India".

He also paid his respects at the "Smriti Mandir", dedicated to the memory and service of Dr. Hedgewar and Shri Guruji at the RSS headquarters and went on to place his thoughts before the gathered audience with unflinching honesty. Before the program and away from the camera lens there was a meet and greet program with senior RSS functionaries and the special invitees, in which he participated with endearing simplicity. At the time of personal introductions, he suggested having self-introductions. Leading by example he stood up and offered a simple introduction, "I am Pranab Mukherjee". For a man who needs no introduction, his simplicity was heartwarming.

Pranab Da had come with a written speech in English whilst RSS *Sarsanghachalak* Dr. Mohan Bhagwat spoke in Hindi, however, both speeches met at the confluence of – *Ekam Sat Vipra: Bahudha Vadanti* – each articulating the same principle in different words. Furthermore, Pranab Da explained very clearly that the concept of nation-state in the West was totally different from the Bharatiya concept of people as a nation, based on a unique integral view of life of Bharat. He emphasised on our 5000-year-old civilizational history with eloquence; highlighting the beliefs embedded in our view of life – *Vasudhaiva Kutumbakam* and *Sarve Bhavantu Sukhinah* -

values of diversity, secularism and tolerance, which are further enshrined in our constitution.

Dr. Bhagwat also expressed the same views in different words. Instead of 'tolerance', he used 'acceptance of all'. He emphasised that no Bharatiya can be treated as 'other' or alien as we all come from the same ancestors.

Both the stalwarts emphasised in their speeches that the national life of Bharat did not flourish on the basis of one religion, language or race but on the basis of the spirituality-based integral and holistic view of life and the values stemmed from it which became the foundation of our national life.

Dr. Bhagwat also clearly articulated that the Sangh would remain the Sangh and Pranab Da, Pranab da as this is the Bharatiya tradition of acceptance – neither imposition nor appropriation but acceptance.

In their speeches, both Pranab Da and Dr. Bhagwat proudly recalled the 5000-year-old civilizational history of Bharat as plural, diverse and one that considers the entire world as one family. This very view of life and value system is reflected in our constitution. This humane worldview is also our greatest inheritance.

Our neighbour Pakistan (which was once a part of Bharat) also wrote its constitution around the same time. However, their constitution does not speak of these inclusive values, it does not take note of the inherent diversity, nor does it celebrate it. Now the obvious question that arises is that when both were one country and one people why did this distinction in going forward emerge?

The answer lies in the spirituality-based integral and holistic view of life that we inherit. Former President Dr. Sarvepalli Radhakrishnan and Gurudev Rabindranath Thakur, have described it as the "Hindu View of Life". Pakistan rejected it and Bharat accepted it. In fact, our constitution is not the reason for the liberal and inclusive values enshrined in it but our constitution is the result of our age-old integral and holistic view of life.

These liberal, plural values have come to us not from our constitution but through our constitution.

Kahlil Gibran in his famous poem "Children" says—

> *"Your children are not your children.*
> *They are the sons and daughters of Life's longing for itself.*
> *They come through you but not from you,*
> *And though they are with you, yet they belong not to you."*

Similarly, we are traditionally liberal and inclusive and treat everyone equally not because of our constitution but our constitution has enshrined these values because we have been like this for ages, at least 5,000 years. Hence it is our duty to honour and follow the Constitution. The RSS has stayed steadfast in this pursuit. Despite the unfair, unjust two-times ban on the RSS, the *satyagraha* that was carried out in protest was literally countrywide, disciplined and peaceful, a unique example of protest in the history of independent Bharat and one that was constitutional. No other organisation or party can claim such a history. But consider the dissonance, those who violate every tenet of the constitution, take the path of violence, attack our own armed forces, and those who support such divisive, unconstitutional activities are the first to preach the constitution to the RSS.

On April 2, 2018, the "Bharat Bandh" in six BJP-ruled states witnessed despairing scenes of unprovoked violence. It was actively supported by Rahul Gandhi and the "secular-liberal" lobby with no consideration of the constitutional values of peaceful protest.

After Pranab Da's speech, those who had been anxious about what this engagement might reveal were quick to come up with sanctimonious summations that "explained away" this engagement. These reactions exposed that the Left still influences the political and intellectual space of our country. This very Left ideology being non-Bharatiya obviously lacks dissent, liberty and tolerance. They discarded analysis and commented with farcical haste that Pranab Da had shown the RSS "a mirror" by speaking of secularism and Nehru on an RSS platform etc.

However, it is important to note that critics of Pranab Da's visit to Nagpur had nothing to say about Dr. Bhagwat's speech. It is quite possible that they didn't hear his speech, maybe it wasn't worth their time, after all this was in sync with their elitist definition of "free speech" – which prescribes that all they say is correct and all else is false. We are right and you are wrong just on the lines of "Four legs good, Two legs bad" described by George Orwell in his famous novel exposing the authoritarian tenets and hypocrisy of communists. Hence listening to "two legs" would obviously be blasphemy!

The inclusiveness of "*Vasundhara Parivar Hamara*" (The song recited before the speeches in Nagpur) includes everybody, even those who practise intolerance. But those who believe "four legs only are good" would prefer to reside in their darkness of ignorance. In all those negative articles that followed, not one spoke of their own experience. But to be in conversation with the RSS is considered blasphemous, and results in instant ostracisation amidst the "liberal left" (an oxymoron). Under such pressure, paying heed to what the RSS chief says is not even an option.

A few months ago, I met with a Christian family from Agra. The husband asked a lot of straightforward questions about the RSS. I answered every one of his queries. In the last, he asked, "Sir, I don't believe in idol worship and I am a Church-going practicing Christian. Can I become a member of RSS?"

I replied, "Why not." The family attended some RSS programs and had first-hand experience. Now when they meet a co-religionist who claims that RSS is anti-Christian, they pose three questions to them:

— Is your opinion based on your own experience?

— Have you ever met with a Sangh functionary?

— Have you read any literature from the RSS?

They invariably get answers in the negative to all these questions. During my routine tour when I was in Agra, this couple insisted that I stayed with them. They also arranged my meeting with the Bishop there. We went to the Bishop's office and the meeting went well. But we can't expect such openness from the Left-inspired-RSS-haters.

There is a Marathi poem :

सरावाच्या होकाराला नकाराचे भान नसते
सरावाच्या नकारात होकाराला स्थान नसते

Those who are habituated to saying "Yes" do not want to hear any 'No"
And those who are habituated to saying "No" have no place for a "Yes"

In the same vein:
In our "inclusion" of all, we also include these "intolerants".
But in their (intolerant) tolerance they cannot tolerate us, the "inclusive".

During his tours, the *Sarsanghachalak* often meets influential people from all walks of life. During one such interaction, he met with a famous industrialist, who suggested that in place of using the word "Hindu" the Sangh should use the word "Bharatiya".

To this Dr. Bhagwat replied, "In our understanding, there isn't much difference between the two terms. However, the term Bharat has a territorial connotation and the term Hindu has a value-based resonance. This is the reason why Pakistan-born Tarek Fateh, refers to himself as Hindu. Hence, you can say Bharatiya and we can say Hindu. Some others may say Indic, and we would understand that we are speaking of one and the same thing. This is what is meant by: *Ekam Sat Vipra: Bahudha Vadanti.*"

But in the dogmatic and fascist worldview of communists these values, so Bharatiya in their essence, hold no significance. Their tribe insists that the *lingua franca* permits only words like secularism, Nehru and Marx whilst *Hindutva* is a pejorative. Should you deviate from this language, you are not worthy of being tolerated, let alone be engaged with. Even your right to live is denied. In Kerala, the red bastion of Communist intolerance, over 233 RSS workers have been killed (from March 1965 till May 2017) for the only reason that they were working for the RSS. 60 per cent of these RSS workers killed were ex-communists.

As many times as you may try and explain the idea of *Hindu Rashtra* and its true meaning, the communists and left-leaning "intellectuals" sans engagement and debate will define it as only narrow, divisive and exclusive. They will quote some years old letters, or an article - cut, copy, paste and reproduce, without historical context or deliberation. They will never see what RSS leaders have been saying during these years till today. The reason is simple – "Two legs bad"!

However, just because they choose to look away and obfuscate at every given opportunity, the irrefutable fact remains that there are Muslims and Christians in the RSS. As Hindus, we do not believe in conversions. These *swayamsevaks* for years together keep following their religious practices as Christians or Muslims.

In 1998 there was a three-day camp of the Vidharbha Prant (a part of Maharashtra) where 30,000 *swayamsevaks* participated in full uniform and stayed for three days in tents. These camps normally take place over the weekend. For those who observed fast on Saturday, a headcount was taken to make arrangements for special food. And it was only then that it came to our notice that it happened to be the holy month of Ramzan as well and 122 *swayamsevaks* among the participants were keeping Rozas and needed to break their fast late at night. Arrangements were immediately made to facilitate this. Had there been no Ramzan, no one would have noted that there were Muslims among *swayamsevaks* in the camp.

These are stories drawn from real-life experiences, which do not make it to the hallowed pages of mainstream publications, however, if you observe carefully and eschew the rhetoric that is peddled, the stark, intolerant and fascist approach to the heterogeneity of ideas is clearly visible and increasingly stands exposed.

They say Pranab Da has shown the RSS a mirror, however, the Sangh is quite open to looking in the mirror and does so every year at the *Chintan Shivirs* and *Pratinidhi Sabhas*.

In these meetings a careful examination of activities is undertaken and where required course correction is implemented. One such meeting took place this year as recently as in the month of April in Pune. But when will the left-liberals, who stake claims on the progressive values of inclusiveness but display every aspect of intolerance in their actions, look in the mirror?

Whether they choose to look in the mirror or not, their truth is reflected in their actions and the public continues to take note of their rampant hypocrisy, between words and actions.

On a lighter note – one must express gratitude, had it not been for their shrill display of intolerance, the media would not have turned the lens on a program that is an annual event and always invites distinguished guests as speakers. Thanks to the intolerance of communists and those inspired by their hollow rhetoric, the general public got to witness a live transmission of the program on all media channels. From the 1st to the 6th of June 2018, the official RSS website had received 378 requests per day to join RSS, however, on the day of the program, in a single day, there were 1779 requests. Need one say more?

Endnote :

This article appeared in *The Indian Express* on June 26, 2018.

10

Swaraj through Social Transformation

Dr. Keshav Baliram Hedgewar, the founder of Rashtriya Swayamsevak Sangh (RSS), was a born patriot, organiser par excellence and a far-sighted visionary. Though he looked like a very common man, he possessed unparalleled qualities, which made him uncommon. He was deeply rooted in the philosophy, culture and history of Bharat and simultaneously had a farsighted vision for its future. That's how he was a visionary.

His aversion to British rule in Bharat was deep-seated and was exhibited since his childhood. For the vaulted purpose of freedom, in whatever way it can be achieved, he actively participated in all paths available for freedom, from non-violent *satyagraha* to armed struggle and revolutionary activities. However, he also believed that for freedom to be realised it was essential that psychological, spiritual and social awakening needs to take place alongside. Hence, he commenced his endeavour to organise the entire society for the purpose of freedom. In 1921, though he participated in the first *satyagraha* he used to say, "going to jail alone is not being patriotic, awakening the society and inspiring an invigorated spirit and renaissance are equally important."

Swami Vivekananda, after two years of extensive travel around Bharat, embarked on a journey to the United States in 1893. Four years later in 1897 when he returned to Bharat after his extensive travels in the USA and Europe, he advised three things of importance to the Bharatiya people. Firstly, he said, "it is the 'organisation' that we must learn from the West". Secondly, "we need to have a 'man-making machine.'" And thirdly, "for the coming 50 years let us all Bharatiyas put aside our personal deities and worship only one deity, that is 'Bharat Mata.'"

The work of Sangh to organise the entire society by inculcating national character and discipline through the methodology of daily gathering centres called *'Shakha'* is the embodiment of Swami Vivekananda's advice.

In his book *'Annihilation of Caste'*, Dr. B.R. Ambedkar states that- "History bears out the proposition that political revolutions have always been preceded by social and religious revolutions.

"The religious reformation started by Luther was the precursor of the political emancipation of the European people. In England, Puritanism led to the establishment of political liberty. Puritanism founded the new world. It was Puritanism which won the war of American independence, and Puritanism was a religious movement.

The same is true of the Muslim Empire. Before the Arabs became a political power, they had undergone a thorough religious revolution started by the Prophet Mohammad. Even Indian history supports the same conclusion. The political revolution led by Chandragupta was preceded by the religious and social revolution of Buddha. The political revolution led by Shivaji was preceded by the religious and social reform brought about by the saints of Maharashtra. The political revolution of the Sikhs was preceded by the religious and social revolution led by Guru Nanak. It is unnecessary to add more illustrations. These will suffice to show that the emancipation of the mind and the soul is a necessary preliminary for the political expansion of the people."

With this principle in mind, Dr. Hedgewar thought of starting a movement to free the soul and mind of Bharatiya society from the colonial hegemony that would simultaneously help strengthen the political movement to free Bharat from colonial rule. It was with this awareness of history that Dr. Hedgewar embarked on this endeavour of organising the society.

Rabindranath Thakur in his book *'Swadeshi Samaj'* wrote that a welfare state is not a Bharatiya concept. Barring defence and security, judiciary and foreign affairs the people had their autonomous systems for all other matters like education, healthcare, industry, trade & commerce, temples, fairs, art & aesthetics, music, dance, drama, pilgrimage, etc. that did not depend on the state. *Sanatan* Bharat did not rely on the state treasury to fund these activities of the society. The society had its independent arrangement which had *dharma* as its guiding principle. This *'dharma'* does not imply religion or worship. To give to the society as one would to one's own family, to give back, is considered *dharma.* Swami Vivekananda's disciple Bhagini Nivedita has noted, "the society, whose members instead of withholding their remuneration with themselves share it with the larger society, with the accumulated remunerations (the social capital) build a wealthy and prosperous society, which in turn makes each individual of the society wealthy and prosperous. But in a society where people hoard their remuneration with themselves, instead of sharing it with the rest of the society, only a few individuals become wealthy and prosperous, while the larger society remains poor." A tent-like structure that is supported by but one pole is grounded in case the pole is broken whereas the tent-like structure that is erected with the help of three-four poles will not be grounded in case any one of the poles breaks, moreover it can be internally reconstructed. Bharat has traditionally been working in the same way.

Hence, Islamic conquests and the Christian crusades were able to convert almost all people when they conquered lands where all such systems of welfare were dependent on the state and with the defeat of the state in bloody wars the dependence of the populace naturally shifted onto the new conquerors.

However, in Bharat, despite 500 years of Islamic rule and 150 years of British or Christian rule the society - the *rashtra* - could not be destabilised. They were not able to convert more than 15 percent of the population to Islam and 3 percent to Christianity. The reason for this was that Bharatiya society was not dependent on the state alone, like the one-pillared structure. Independent from the construct of a 'welfare state' society it had its own structures that withstood foreign invasions.

The RSS also has these same principles at the base of its foundation. The work of the Sangh is self-dependent and is not dependent on the machinations or patronage of the state. The Sangh *swayamsevaks*, inspired by the RSS run over 1.5 lakh service *(sewa)* projects that work in diverse aspects of social life and about 90 percent of these *sewa* initiatives are not dependent on government funds.

When I was *prant pracharak* in Gujarat and Keshubhai Patel got elected as chief minister, the BJP workers thought of giving some portion of funds allocated for tribal welfare through *Vanvasi Kalyan Ashram* (VKA) -a tribal welfare initiative by the *swayamsevaks*. However, the VKA workers refused to apply for the state funds. A few years later, a *swayamsevak* asked me why those workers had refused help from the state. I gave a response in the manner Vinobha Bhave spoke, "Where does the government get money from? It gets from the society, which gives its money to the state in the form of taxes. Which means the government is the 'servant' and the people are the 'master'. Instead of the 'servant', we are hence asking for contributions directly from the 'masters' and they are giving as well."

In the book *"The Starfish and the Spider"* the author mentions a study by Professor Navin, a specialist in Latin American history. Navin had recounted an interesting sequence of events from the 16th century when European and Spanish mercenaries set sail in the pursuit of gold and lands. A part of these fortune seekers was a contingent of Spanish mercenaries who took to the high seas in 1519 and headed for Latin America. On reaching the shores where the Aztec tribe was living, they captured the ruler and placed a gun on his head, asking for all the gold in the land. This he readily parted with but was killed anyway. By 1521, in only two years, all the indigenous Aztec tribes were under Spanish rule.

In 1534, one such Spanish flotilla reached the land of the Incas and subjugated them as well by 1536. After this, one by one the Spanish army subsumed regional kingdoms in Latin America. However, in 1618 the Spaniards met their match in the Apaches, whose chieftain they killed as well. However, the Apaches were not wealthy, hence the Spanish converted them and put them to work in the fields, but the resistance from the Apaches continued to grow even though they had no leadership, this conflict between the two continued for 200 years, finally the Spanish left.

Professor Navin says that the Apaches did not have an army that was stronger than Incas and the Aztecs armies, nor the Spanish army this time around, was weaker than the armies that invaded Incas and the Aztecs. Then how was it possible that they eventually triumphed over the Spanish? He explains that the Apaches were differently organised and were not dependent on the state, so even though their chief was killed, all power was not concentrated in him, hence they survived his demise. Society had its own preparedness, which was independent from the state. Hence, even though the state was defeated, society was not and it continued to resist the colonial occupation of the Spanish. It is essential to understand this difference.

Hence, Dr. Ambedkar had said that for any nation to achieve freedom, it is essential that society first achieve freedom of the mind and soul. Swami Vivekananda's message was that we need to get organised as a nation.

Rabindranath Thakur's belief that a *'swadeshi samaj'* was vitally important in ensuring lasting freedom, which can be accomplished by creating social leadership.

Dr. Hedgewar was deeply inspired and moved by this need to create a society that was capable of protecting and enriching its freedoms, the need for national consciousness would be imperative to ensure that the desire to uphold national character and soul persisted among people. It was with this objective that he founded the RSS. Dr. Hedgewar was one of the great visionaries of the twentieth century, his organisational skills were highly regarded and his vision of repurposing Bharatiya society to be the custodian of freedom has remained invaluable in a free Bharat.

Endnote :

This article first appeared in *Organiser* on August 14, 2019.

We : Soul of Bharat

11

Hindutva : Reality, Essence and Strength

Once a second-year college student while introducing himself shared that he writes short stories. "What kind of short stories?", I asked. He narrated a recently penned story. Those were election days, and the subject of his short story was 'elections' too. The story went something like this:

The election dates were announced in a state and four candidates filed their nominations. The candidates were Air pollution, Soil pollution, Water pollution and Food pollution. Interestingly all of them insisted on having the same election symbol, "Human Being". The electoral officials were puzzled. Why would they want the same symbol? Logically and legally, it could only be allocated to only one of them. They were summoned to discuss the issue with the electoral official. The official explained his predicament to all of them. To find a way out, he said the candidates will have to justify why each one of them deserves the symbol. The most convincing answer will win the right over the symbol, while others will have to choose another symbol. Every candidate put forth the same argument. Each one expressed gratitude and considered the human being as their creator and nurturer, making them strong contenders. Thereby implying that each one of them alone deserved a right over the symbol!

It is such a heart-rending truth that the story unfolds so effortlessly. Today not only the entire humankind but also Mother Earth is getting diabolically devoured by the problems of air, land, water, food pollution and the consequent global warming, all in the name of development.

It is, therefore, a matter of great concern for all of us. At the same time, it is ironic that the societies that are progenitors of these problems are not uneducated, undeveloped and backward, but on the contrary, are (so-called) developed, advanced, educated and modern societies. Why did we end up like this is a question worth pondering over. It is now being realised that this (so-called) modern, developed human civilisation's outlook towards nature and humankind is fractured, incomplete and flawed. In the name of progress, they went full-throttle towards destruction, rather than development.

How the pursuit for unlimited material growth has resulted in unethical behaviour of human beings with our fellow beings and nature is well articulated by renowned management professor, Dr. S. K. Chakraborty from IIM Kolkata. He notes:

"The march of modern science and the technology derived from it coincided with an era when the human race was beginning to snap its ties of personal feeling-level-relationship with earth and nature. One need not stop for a moment to consider the right or wrong of any action regarding something to which there is no relatedness. Undoubtedly, numerous aspects of external physical life benefited from the sci-tech combination through control and subjugation of matter, air, water, time, distance, and so on. Yet, the keynote has been the shift from harmony to high-handedness, from awe and reverence to petulance and arrogance. If man-nature alienation has been the chief cause of unethicality towards ecology and environment, this same alienating ethos began to evade all dimensions of human society. This process leads to a gradual weakening of ethical sentiments, which are seen to be soft and fuzzy. Not only has nature come to be treated as a resource, as a means, but man too unethically emerges as an inherent property of this clever techno-centric outlook.

From tool to machine to automation to chip -- this progression seems to have made the human race increasingly less human. Because of this attitude, man is getting distanced and detached not only from nature but also from society and his fellowmen. Hence, he is becoming more arrogant, cruel and more violent in his dealing with surrounding nature, aliens and fellow beings. And the societies that hold this mindset are the (so-called) developed, modern societies and human communities."

Considering the background, insufficient knowledge and comparatively minimal experience of life in the aforementioned "progressive-developed" society, it can be concluded that their inferences are erroneous, fragmentary and self-contradictory. But their proclivity to blatantly claim an exclusive right over the ultimate truth, especially when they have achieved or known only a little, indicates sheer immaturity.

This tendency of imposing one's unbaked, inexperienced half-truths and inferences as final conclusions has created the predicament folklore of the premature birth of 'Arun,' narrated by philosopher-writer Sai Makarand Dave. He writes-

"In our Puranas, we have a story about the birth of 'Arun,' the charioteer of Lord Sun. Sage Kashyap had two wives: Kadru and Vinata. Kadru bore many serpents. Vinata laid two eggs. Vinata was told that two luminous and valiant sons would be born out of the eggs after a prolonged period. Since nothing happened for quite some time, she broke one egg. The premature baby 'Arun' was born. A luminous and valiant Garuda was born from the other egg at the appropriate time. Arun cursed his mother for taking him out of the egg prematurely."

'Arun' symbolises the brightness of premature light. It is a situation in the life of humankind when the darkness of ignorance has not vanished completely, and the sunrise of revelation has yet to appear on the horizon. Suppose a man impatiently begins to believe that he has achieved everything when he is yet to see the full luminance of divine light and realise spiritual blessings. In that case, he may be reverted to confinement instead of experiencing liberation. Therefore, dawn (*Arunodaya*) is the time for serene and deep contemplation. It is a moment of quiet and composed rumination. It is not the time to dance around in ecstasy of "I have achieved everything in life". Thus at this juncture, if one starts hopping and shouting from one's rooftop with self-complacency that "I have realised the ultimate truth", then his plight will be like that of 'Arun'. Either he will fall into the pit of illusion or lead people in an entirely wrong direction.

The (so-called) "progressive-developed" societies or nations which, despite not having found the whole truth – having just the glimpse of it – and yet bragging and foisting upon the world that "they" have found the ultimate truth, remind us of premature, crippled 'Aruns'.

This know-it-all attitude of the frontlines of these "progressive societies" is still bearable, but what adds to the enormity of the issue is the obstinacy and vehemence in their insistence that their incomplete and incorrect doctrine is the ultimate truth and must be universally accepted. Their hankering for the social, political, economic, religious and other related systems based on this partial truth and justifying the oppression and violence to make it universally acceptable, to be able to establish its hegemony is the real issue.

The history of how the Western mindset used technological and scientific inventions to invade and exploit new territories is illustrated in '*Global Parasites- Five Hundred Years of Western Culture.*' In this book, Winin Pereira and Jeremy Seabrook wrote:

"The Western technological and scientific system that developed in symbiosis with its colonial expansion underpinned and made more efficient the process of expropriation. The unsustainability and injustice of this project can now be seen, though at the time of the "discovery" of distant lands and new trade routes, neither moral nor ecological limits to the accumulation of wealth occurred to them, mainly as a result of the cultural imperatives embedded in the fabric of European society.

"The West now claims the moral high ground as it castigates other countries for their failings in human rights, their inability to control population growth, and their corruption and mismanagement. But the West has attained its apparent pre-eminence only after passing through brutal and merciless phases of human rights abuse, the widespread practice of tyranny and genocide, slavery and colonialism. Without the exploitation of occupied territories, the Industrial Revolution would have been aborted before takeoff. The West's enormous structure of affluence has been constructed upon the sands of unsustainability and injustice.

"It should be noted that the term "West" does not refer solely to any geographical region, nor does it include all the people there. It refers mainly to the agents of Western-style development, in the West or elsewhere, particularly the TNCs, the politicians and academics. Their beneficiaries encompass much of the populations of the West, knowingly or unwittingly, except perhaps the impoverished."

By following the above agenda, have these "progressive-developed-modern" societies solved all of their problems? No. That's not even in sight. Despite all round prosperity and affluence of all kinds, there is no peace, happiness, or contentment. The mind is in turmoil. They are experiencing the heat of its social, familial and psychological adverse outcomes. But they are unable to find the way out because their very conception of the universe, nature, society and human beings is incomplete, distorted, superficial and incorrect.

How the 'West' created such a ruckus is well-explained by famous thinker and particle physicist Prof. Fritjof Capra when he writes—

"The paradigm that is now receding has dominated our culture for several hundred years, during which it has shaped our modern Western society and has significantly influenced the rest of the world. This paradigm consists of a number of entrenched ideas and values, among them the view of the universe as a mechanical system composed of elementary building blocks, the view of the human body as a machine, the view of life in society as a competitive struggle for existence, the belief in unlimited material progress to be achieved through economic and technological growth, and - last, not least - the belief that a society in which the female is everywhere subsumed under the male is one that follows a basic law of nature. These assumptions have been fatefully challenged by recent events. And indeed a radical revision of them is occurring.

"The new paradigm may be called a holistic worldview," he writes, "seeing the world as an integrated whole rather than a dissociated collection of parts. It may also be called an ecological view if the term 'ecological' is used in a much broader and deeper sense than usual. Deep ecological awareness recognises the fundamental interdependence of all phenomena and the fact that, as individuals and societies, we are all embedded in (and ultimately dependent on) the cyclical processes of nature.

"Ultimately, deep ecological awareness is spiritual or religious awareness. When the concept of the human spirit is understood as the mode of consciousness in which the individual feels a sense of belonging, of connectedness, to the cosmos as a whole, it becomes clear that ecological awareness is spiritual in its deepest essence. It is, therefore, not surprising that the emerging new vision of reality based on deep ecological awareness is consistent with the so-called perennial philosophy of spiritual traditions."

SATYA: The Reality

Now this new alternative paradigm that is coming forth is the same that the Bharatiya (Hindu) seers and thinkers propounded thousands of years ago. The salient features of this age-old paradigm are :

ईशावास्यमिदं सर्वं यत्किञ्च जगत्यां जगत् तेन।
Eeshaavaasyam Idam Sarvam Yatkincha Jagatyaam Jagat

Whatever is moving (and non-moving), every form of manifestation - living or non-living, pleasant or otherwise, planets, stars and even our Self, the *Aatma* is pervaded by the same divinity. This perspective shines a light upon its omnipresence, which can further allow one to experience Oneness with all and everything- oneness in multiplicity, unity in diversity.

एकम सत, विप्रा बहुधा वदन्ति।
Ekam Sat Vipraah Bahudhaa Vadanti

Truth is one and it can be called by different names and can be reached by various paths by the seekers and the knowers.

वसुधैव कुटुम्बकम।
Vasudhaiva Kutumbakam

This creation is one living organic unit which is interconnected and interdependent. There is mutual coherence, not conflict. Everything is mutually complementary.

माता भूमि: पुत्रोहं पृथिव्या:।
Mata Bhoomih Putroham Pruthivyaah

The Earth is our mother and we are its offspring. Therefore milking nature is alright, but exploitation is not.

तेन त्यक्तेन भुञ्जीथा मा गृध: कस्यस्विद्धनम्।
Tena Tyaktena Bhunjeethaah

Since the entire creation is pervaded by Divinity and encased within Divinity, one can easily "let go," "rejoice" or experience "bliss," and detach oneself from worldly desires. As per the principle of '*dharma*', earning wealth and enjoying sensual desires is one of the four major principal objects of human endeavour and should be pursued in righteous ways. However, by limiting our needs and wants, one should strive to lead a simple and disciplined life. Here our attention is drawn to the virtues of non-stealing, controlling and overcoming jealousy and abstaining from greed and deceit. The residual wealth and energy should be used for the welfare of the society and the humankind.

वयम् अमृतस्य पुत्रा:।
Vayam Amrutasya Putraah

Divinity is omnipresent. It is more prominently manifested in human beings. This divinity within can be manifested completely by one's efforts.

It can be done by controlling nature, both internal and external, to become "free". Revealing the omnipresent divinity and being "free" is the ultimate goal of human life and pursuit. This spirituality is the foundation and the essence of social systems, dispositions and human life.

Man and woman are complementary to each other. Both are equally important and responsible for the betterment of the society. Both of them have equal rights and opportunities to evolve spiritually and get liberated.

Based on this Hindu or Bharatiya worldview, highly advanced, educated, cultured and affluent life – individual as well as social – prospered here in Bharat for thousands of years. Many foreign travellers noted and recorded this. Hindus (Bharatiyas) were the first to reveal, comprehend, and understand this mystery of creation and life. Therefore, it came to be known as the "Hindu worldview". Hindus are naturally pleased and feel proud that the modern Western scientific world has begun to reveal, experience, appreciate and accept this *"Satya"* or reality, this Hindu view of life.

SWATTVA : Self Identity

In the light of this holistic, integral, interconnected and spiritual worldview, a way of life evolved here in Bharat and became the norm through the ages. Systems, virtues and policies were developed to practice and firm up this worldview in individual and social life. And in order to propagate and establish this value system many people dedicated their entire life and performed penance, thus creating ideals in the society. As an aggregation of all these developments, a unique culture – the Hindu culture –evolved here. The sages, saints, and cultural ambassadors of Bharat travelled throughout the world, sharing this view and way of life with the sole intention of enlightening people all over. The practice of virtues of affection, love, compassion and patience and the ways adopted by these cultural ambassadors to disseminate their knowledge and to share their experiences are the salient features of the Hindu culture. These Bharatiyas (cultural ambassadors), never adopted coercion, force and violence to disseminate this knowledge, anywhere. This culture has become the identity, the expression, the soul (*Swattva*) of Hindu society. If one desires to have a world living together in peace, free from conflicts, with mutual understanding and cooperation, with harmony among diverse people, while sustaining the ecological balance, one has to resort to this holistic, integral, interconnected, spiritual view and way of life or the Hindu view of life.

Hence it is the foremost duty of the Hindus spread all over the world, to protect, nourish and nurture this Hindu way of life and their own expression *(Swattva)* of it, by putting it in regular practice and presenting a live example of the "global and noble" culture.

Salient features of Hindu Culture or self-identity are best captured in the following verses and aphorisms:

मातृ देवो भव।
पितृ देवो भव।
आचार्य देवो भव।
अतिथि देवो भव॥

Maatru Devo bhava
Pitru Devo Bhava
Aachaarya Devo Bhava
Atithi Devo Bhava

Mother, Father, Teacher and Guest should be revered like *Deva* (deity).

त्यजेदेकं कुलस्यार्थे ग्रामस्यार्थे कुलं त्यजेत् ।
ग्रामं जनपदस्यार्थे आत्मार्थे पृथिवीं त्यजेत् ॥

Tyajedekam Kulasyaarthe, Gramsyaarthe Kulam Tyajet
Graamam Janapadasyaarthe, Aatmaar the Prithiveem Tyajet

Personal gains can be relinquished for the sake of family; family's gains for the sake of the town; town's interests for the sake of the country and everything can be renounced for the freedom of the soul.

रुचीनां वैचित्र्यादृजुकुटिल नानापथजुषां
नृणामेको गम्यस्त्वमसि पयसामर्णव इव॥

Rucheenaam Vaichitryaat Riju Kutila Naanaa Pathajushaam
Nrunaameko Gamyastvamasi Payasaamarnava Iva

As the different streams having their sources in different places all mingle their water in the sea, so, O Lord, the different paths which men take through different tendencies, various they appear, crooked or straight, all lead to Thee. (Translation as narrated by Swami Vivekananda in 1893, at the Parliament of World's Religions in Chicago.) A variety of religions, that which entail worshipping the formless Almighty to a deity with a specific form, all lead to the same realisation. Even in one family, the members may adhere to different forms of worship.

मातृवत् परदारेषु, परद्रव्येषु लोष्ठवत्।
आत्मवत् सर्वभूतेषु, यः पश्यति सः पण्डितः

Maatruvat Paradaareshu, Paradravyeshu Loshtavat
Aatmavat Sarvabhooteshu, Esha Dharmah Sanaatanah

The utmost reverence one can have is for one's mother. A cultured person sees all women as his mother, except for one's own wife. One should know how to put one's wealth to good use, but at the same time should not be greedy for wealth and should consider others' wealth as immaterial to one's own self. Lastly, one should behave with others the way he/she wishes they would behave with you. If one remembers that no one wants to be treated badly then they will treat everyone as one's own. Worshipping the Earth, Water, Fire, Air, Space, Trees, the Sun, and the Moon as divine manifestations and worshipping the machines, tools, weapons, and our family deity with a feeling of larger connectedness gives birth to the feeling of interconnectedness. One's orientation to these values inspires one to spend for the betterment of others and be noble. One who sacrifices his self-interest is elevated. To work, toil, spend, and share for the betterment of others in the society is *'dharma'* and is virtuous. *dharma* constitutes the very basis of Hindu or Bharatiya society. This *dharma* is not to be confused with religion *(Upasana)*.

Women and Bharatiya Culture:

Worshipping the female form of divinity, the Goddess, as a symbol of *'Shakti'* comprises one of the major ancient religious traditions of the people of Bharat. There have been innumerable women contributors to Vedic hymns that speak of mundane and spiritual knowledge and wisdom. Man and woman are complementary to each other. One is incomplete without another. To perform any religious ritual, the wife is an inevitable companion by the side of the performing husband. The highest and the ultimate gratitude lies in the reverence of the many forms of "Mother" (goddess or provider) - *Gomata* (The Cow), *Bhoomata* (The Earth), *Lokamata* (The River), *Tulasi Mata* (The holy plant).

Rebirth and Karma Siddhaant (principle):

Belief in the Rebirth (of the soul or the *Aatma*) and the principle of Karma *(Karma Siddhaant)* are the causal effects underlying all cultural practices of Hindu culture. Unique concepts of *Tirtha Yatra* (Pilgrimage), *Punya* (Auspicious actions) and *dharma* are the civilizational best practices that Hindus have consciously engaged in for eons. The practice where one takes food only after feeding the birds and animals living in one's surroundings emanates from these very principles.

SATTVA: Core Strength

Bharat – the abode of *Hindutva* – has a role to perform to help the Hindus spread all over the world, protect their self-identity and self-expression *(Swattva)*. This role is in augmenting its core strength (*Sattva* or essence). This *Sattva* lies in:

Bharat is militarily strong and invincible. It has been a universal experience to date that if any nation in the world grew in its military strength, it utilised its power to invade other nations, fight wars, expand its territory, exploit and plunder. Bharat is the only honourable exception which never used her strength for territorial expansion. Bharat did fight wars, but only in self-defence, for cultural protection and to establish *dharma*. That is why Shri Ram and Shri Krishna are the ideals and apostles of Bharatiyas. They fought and won wars, but not for territorial expansion.

Bharat is economically prosperous and self-reliant. We may surely undertake trade and business with the world around us, but not at the cost of our self-reliance. The purpose and content of our school and university education are based on the Bharatiya philosophy that reflects our soul. New ideas and achievements around the world shall be welcome if they stand true to the test of our extensive, rich experience.

Our social systems are founded on our holistic, spiritual, interconnected Hindu vision where the standard of life is not determined by economic parameters only, but by one's life values and quality of life.

Hindutva's "Sattva" is augmented by establishing a social value system, promoting simple living, moderate spending and relinquishment despite abundance of resources. Having socio-centric, multi-power centred social systems instead of politico-centric, mono-power centred social systems help protect *Hindutva's "Swattva,"* facilitating the influence of the holistic Hindu worldview i.e. *"Satya"*, bringing happiness and betterment to everyone throughout the world.

सर्वे भवन्तु सुखिनः। सर्वे सन्तु निरामयाः।
सर्वे भद्राणि पश्यन्तु। मा कश्चित् दुःख भाग्भवेत् ॥
ॐ शान्तिः शान्तिः शान्तिः ॥

Sarve Bhavantu Sukhinah Sarve Santu Niraamayaah
Sarve Bhadraani Pashyantu Maa Kashchit Duhkhabhagbhavet
Om Shanti. Shanti. Shantih.

May all beings be happy and prosperous; may all remain free from illness. May all see what is auspicious, may no one suffer. Om. Peace. Peace. Peace.

Endnote :

This article first appeared in VSS (*Vishwa Sangh Shivir*) souvenir on December 31, 2010.

12

Bharat & Hindutva : Eternal and Intrinsic

For ages, Bharat has offered a unique view of life because it is based on spirituality. Bharat believes that Truth can have various forms, names and paths to reach it. Though diverse, all these paths are equal. Bharat sees unity in diversity and has the capacity to establish unity amongst such expansive variety. It doesn't see diversity as a difference: This brand of spirituality teaches us that every soul is potentially divine and the same divinity pervades all things, animate or inanimate, and hence we all are connected with each other. To realise this connectedness, to expand its ambit, and to work accordingly towards the betterment of the connected is the basis of *dharma*. *Dharma*, which is different from religion, is not exclusivist; it includes, connects and benefits all.

This spiritual view of life is known as the Hindu view across the world, and all those who live in Bharat, irrespective of their caste, region, religion or language, subscribe to this view of life. Hence, being Hindu or *"Hindutva"* has become the identity of all Bharatiyas. The founder of RSS, Dr. K.B. Hedgewar, made this *Hindutva* the tool to awaken and rekindle the sense of unity among all Bharatiyas — connecting them with each other irrespective of their caste, region, religion and language. He started organising the entire society by binding them together with this thread of *Hindutva*.

The activities of the Sangh built on the foundation of *Hindutva* kept expanding despite the ill-will directed at it. Those with vested interests continued dividing the society on the lines of caste, region, religion and language. *Hindutva* and Sangh were labelled as communal, regressive, divisive and anti-minority. Then, the same ill-intentioned critics started saying that *Hindutva* is alright, but there is a demarcation between soft-*Hindutva* and hard-*Hindutva*. The *Hindutva* of someone like Swami Vivekananda is soft, but RSS practices hard *Hindutva*, which is condemnable. Books such as *Why I Am Not a Hindu* and then *Why I Am a Hindu* have been written by such naysayers, but irrespective of such attempts, the acceptance of *Hindutva* has grown exponentially. This is because it is the soul of Bharat and an expression of its consciousness and cannot be countered by books that seek to compete with the epics.

Elements with vested interests started creating confusion by calling Hinduism a virtue and *Hindutva* an evil. A media house recently asked me, "What is the difference between 'Hinduism' and '*Hindutva*'?" I told them that it is one and the same. One is in Hindi whereas the other is in English. Dr. S. Radhakrishnan wrote a book in English, titled *The Hindu View of Life* and used the term "Hinduism". Had he written it in Hindi, he would have used "*Hindutva*". If Savarkar had written his book, *Hindutva*, in English, then he might have used the term Hinduism. That said, it is my personal belief that an apt translation of *Hindutva* should be "Hinduness" instead of "Hinduism". RSS *Sarsanghachalak* Dr. Mohan Bhagwat has clearly enunciated the meanings of "Hindu" and "*Hindutva*" in his three-day lecture series (Future Bharat-RSS Perspective) in Vigyan Bhavan. But propagandists won't refer to it because it does not suit their malafide intentions. The real ideological battle is between the two different ideas of Bharat. One is the Bharatiya concept with roots going back to age-old spiritual traditions of the nation, and the other is an alien or foreign conceptualisation.

A journalist-turned-politician recently stated that in this election, the choice to be made is between "Hindu India" and "*Hindutva* India". The only reason people like him talk of Hindu India is because of the growing influence of "*Hindutva*". It doesn't reflect their conviction but convenience. Given that Bharat is coming together and uniting due to "*Hindutva*", their casteist, communal and regional politics is weakening day by day and their support base is eroding. For their petty politics, it is imperative for them to divide the society — if not in the name of caste, language or religion, then on the basis of Hindu and *Hindutva*. But today, the common Bharatiya is smart enough to not fall into their trap. Their sense of entitlement has, thus, been challenged.

Another term that is being used to spread confusion is "*Hinduvadi*" or Hinduist. There are capitalists, communists and socialists in the world that subscribe to capitalism, communism and socialism respectively but in Bharat, there is no place for any "-ism" like in the West. The "-isms" in the West have a hegemonic tendency to impose their worldview on others, even by force. In Bharat, "*Hindutva*" (Hinduness) refers to people living and leading their personal, familial, social and professional life in the light of this spirituality-based holistic view of life, called "Hindu".

It is, therefore, imperative to expose the conspiracy to divide and confuse, and to establish the eternal philosophy of *Hindutva*, by dedicated action and practise. This will result in the unfolding of Bharat's identity, known to the world for centuries, and Bharat's *purusharth* will manifest in every sphere of social and national life. In his essay, *Swadeshi Samaj*, Rabindranath Thakur rightly says — "We have fully understood today that just by lying low we cannot protect ourselves. The only way of self-protection is by evoking and directing our innate strength in every possible way. This is the rule of the divine. The English would continue to control our mind, until we come out of our comfort zone and start toiling. Sitting on the fence and constantly ruing imminent ruination would yield no fruit. Aping the English in every sphere and disguising ourselves in an attempt to survive is analogous to disregarding ourselves. We can never be true English and even by mimicking the English we cannot bring them to a halt. Our intellect, our heart, our taste are auctioned off at very low rates every day. The only way to prevent it from happening is by becoming what "we" are consciously, strongly, actively and completely."

Endnote :

This article first appeared in *The Indian Express* on May 08, 2019.

13

A Rashtra named Hindu and Sanatan its Adjective

Sanatan or eternal is the adjective ascribed to Bharat as Bharat is *Anaadi* (beginningless) and *Anant* (unending). There are two reasons for the same. One the philosophy that has shaped Bharat is eternal, and two, the society which lives it, that is the embodiment of this philosophy, is also eternal.

The unique worldview of Bharat is eternal because it is based in spirituality, therefore it is integral and hence holistic. Owing to this world view Bharat sees the entire creation to be connected as one single unit. Hence it believes in *Vasudhaiva Kutumbakam*- the entire earth is one family.

Bharatiya view of life has four facets central to its civilization. First, Truth or God is one, it can be called by various names and realised through different paths and religious practices. Second, to see unity in seeming diversity, to appreciate it and to celebrate it is the very essence of Bharatiya way of life. Third, every soul (man & woman) is potentially divine and the goal of life is to manifest the divinity within by controlling nature external and internal and to liberate oneself from the cycle of birth and death by merging into that supreme consciousness *(Moksha)* is the ultimate goal of human life. Fourth, one's innate divinity may be manifested by walking different paths (referred to as religion or *upasana*) as conducive to one's unique nature and constitution and all paths are equal, acceptable and respectable. These paths may be referred to by different names and with time newer paths may emerge. The old and the new are all welcome here. This is the defining feature of Bharat. This is why Swami Vivekananda in his 1893 Chicago address referred to Bharat as the "mother of all religions". What makes this philosophy eternal is the fact that it is based in spirituality.

Now a philosophy alone cannot be a good enough indicator for such a claim. A timeless tradition of living that philosophy has been established by the people here. Having suffered innumerable attacks and blows this society, which is referred to as the '*rashtra*,' continues to exist. The interminability of this society also makes Bharat *Sanatan*. Two main factors responsible for the continuity and *sanatan* tradition of this *rashtra* are spirituality-based view-of-life and the society not being based on a welfare state. Gurudev Rabindranath Thakur in his essay '*Swadeshi Samaj*' writes "welfare state is not a Bharatiya tradition. Barring defence and security, judiciary and foreign affairs the people had their autonomous systems for all other matters like education, healthcare, industry, trade & commerce, temples, fairs, art & aesthetics, music, dance, drama, pilgrimage, etc. that did not depend on the state. *Sanatan Bharat* did not rely on the state treasury to fund these activities of the society. The society had its independent arrangement which had *dharma* as its guiding principle. This '*dharma*' does not imply religion or worship. To give to the society as one would to one's own family, to give back, is considered *dharma*. Swami Vivekananda's disciple Bhagini Nivedita has noted, "the society, whose members instead of withholding their remuneration with themselves share it with the larger society, with the accumulated remunerations (the social capital) build a wealthy and prosperous society, which in turn makes each individual of the society wealthy and prosperous. But in a society where people hoard their remuneration with themselves, instead of sharing it with the rest of the members of the society, only a few individuals become wealthy and prosperous, while the larger society remains poor." This is called *dharma;* that which enriches the social capital. *Dharma* does not discriminate.

A tent-like structure that is supported by but one pole is grounded in case the pole is damaged whereas the tent-like structure that is built with the help of three-four poles will not be grounded in case any one of the poles gets damaged, moreover it can be possibly internally be reconstructed. Bharat has traditionally been working in the same way. Hence though the foreign attacks on Bharat defeated the kings, the foreign rule could not destabilise the society, the *rashtra*. It remained undefeated and each time swaraj has been restored through suitable awakenings. This design is also at the heart of the secret of Bharat being *Sanatan*.

The unique spirituality-based view of life of this *rashtra* is known by the name *Hindu* across the world, which is why this *rashtra* is Hindu and its adjective *Sanatan*. We did not coin this name because we never considered ourselves separate from the rest of humanity. *Vasudhaiva Kutumbakam* (the whole *vasudha* or earth is one *kutumba* or family) has been our belief. But those who viewed us from outside christened this uniqueness of ours in order to single us out as Hindu (those who hail from the other side of the Sindhu). Between 1935-1940 the ghee shops in Nagpur bore boards flanked by the name of the neighbouring villages, viz, *Boregaanv*, *Dahegaanv* or *Aamgaanv* followed by the suffix "ghee shop." At around the time when WW-II was going on a product called 'Dalda' made an appearance in the market, which looked like the ghee but wasn't actually ghee. It was then that the boards of those shops began to be renamed as "*shuddha ghee shop*" suffixed after the name of the village. Now the word '*shuddha*' (pure) was added later but that cannot be interpreted as what was being sold earlier was not pure. It was added to differentiate it from the imitative article. This applies to Hindu too. Living by the dictum of *aatma vat sarva bhuteshu* (to consider everyone as oneself) the necessity to define ourselves with a name or a label was never felt, therefore we did not consider doing it. With time, in the natural course of events, every society undergoes changes. While remaining steadfast in the eternal principle, discarding obsolete practices in the light of the timeless principles and adopting concurrent, new practices comes naturally to Bharat. On these lines Bharat has had a culture of adopting certain values and systems from outside after refashioning those as per the local lore. This is yet another hallmark of Bharat that makes it ancient and antiquated (*chir puratan*), yet ever so young (*nitya nutan*). Many treatises or *smritis* (code of conduct) were created here from time-to-time as this process of aforementioned integration of eternal values and knowledge systems in the light of the changing society took place. This text here is the panacea of knowledge and that there will be none beyond this - Bharat has never proclaimed this.

For the Bharat of current times our constitution is the latest *Smriti*. The provisions for modifying this constitution are enshrined within the constitution itself. The tact of periodically renovating the structure while retaining the base of the foundation is what Bharat has championed. It has ensured our civilisational continuity and renewal and it is this which makes it *Sanatan*.

Yet another peculiarity of Bharat is that it has held both *abhyuday* (material prosperity) and *nihshreyas* (salvation or liberation) as equally important. To live a life that strikes a balance between these two inseparable pursuits is what is *dharma* - 'यतोऽभ्युदय नि:श्रेयस सिद्धि: स धर्म:' This is another definition of *dharma*. Because of this view in the first seventeen centuries of the current era Bharat's share in world trade was over 30% (highest in the world, then). Despite trade relations with several countries we did not attempt to colonise them, plunder their riches, 'convert' the natives or enslave the people and rob them of their dignity by trading them as labour. This also was possible because of the eternal global view - *Vasudhaiva Kutumbakam* - held by Bharat. Bharat is an ancient civilization. In the long journey of its existence it has seen periods of oblivion which led to a passivity in the attitude of its people. In such situations to awaken and strengthen the society many saints incarnated in all segments of the society who were instrumental in reinvigorating the consciousness of the people. This timely intervention through directives of many such saints and sages also gives Bharat its adjective – *Sanatan*.

Today when the whole world has moved in closer, newer speed and efficiency have dawned upon the mediums of transportation and communication, to balance the diversity manifested in languages, lineages and religions with the finite resources available on the earth is the challenge before all of humanity. When the need of the hour is the aspiration to live a truly prosperous life but in harmony, Bharat has the worldview, the philosophy, the experience and also a history that illustrates a similar achievement.

Famous physicist Fritjof Capra's this illustration illuminates the same idea—

"The paradigm that is now receding has dominated our culture for several hundred years. During which it has shaped our modern western society and has significantly influenced the rest of the world. This paradigm consists of a number of entrenched ideas and values, among them the view of the universe as a mechanical system composed of elementary building-blocks, view of human body as a machine, the view of life in society as a competitive struggle for existence, belief in unlimited material, economic and technological growth, and last not the least, the belief that a society in which the female is everywhere subsumed under the male is one that follows a basic law of nature. These entire assumptions have been fatefully challenged by recent events. Indeed a radical revision of them is occurring. The new paradigm may be called a holistic world view, seeing the world as an integrated whole rather than a dissociated collection of parts. It may also be called an ecological view, if the term ecological is used in a much broader and deeper sense than usual. Deep ecological awareness recognizes the fundamental interdependence of all phenomena and the fact that as individuals and societies we are all embedded in (and ultimately depend on) the cyclic process of nature. Ultimately, deep ecological awareness is spiritual or religious awareness. When the concept of the human spirit is understood as the mode of consciousness in which the individual feels a sense of belonging, of connectedness, to the cosmos as a whole, it becomes clear that ecological awareness is spiritual in its deepest essence. It is therefore not surprising that the emerging new vision of reality based on deep ecological awareness is consistent with the so-called perennial philosophy of spiritual traditions."

Therefore, preservation of this uniqueness of Bharat along with its prosperity, continuity and security is a global necessity. And for Bharat to remain *Sanatan* this *Sanatan* spirituality-based Hindu view-of-life must continue to thrive. Continuity of a close-knit, strong, active and victorious society that embodies this view-of-life is equally important. Honouring the essence of the word *Hindu* by consolidating the *Hindu samaj*, remedying it and instilling the virtue of the *rashtra*, our *Sanatan* Bharat will be strengthened and its continuity (*sanatanta)* remain.

Endnote :

This article first appeared in *The Sunday Guardian* on March 18, 2023.

14

Bharatiya Consciousness is National, Not Nationalistic

Bharat and the entire world are witnessing Bharat's metamorphosis. Fundamental changes brought about in foreign, defence and economic policies of the country have made this possible. Amendments in defence and foreign policies have instilled renewed vigour among Bharatiya defence forces. The world is now looking at us as a credible voice. Consequently, more and more countries are stepping up to support our views and join collaborative hands with us. Recently, Bharat was elected as a non-permanent member of the United Nations Security Council, but what makes this honour especially rewarding is the fact that 184 countries among the 193 countries voting supported us.

Bharat's appeal to adopt International Yoga Day with the aim to further the holistic well-being of mankind was welcomed by all member countries at the United Nations General Assembly in 2014. We have spearheaded the movement for the International Solar Alliance. Bharat's leap towards development, growth and empowerment will prove to be a boon to all of mankind and even nature because our worldview values dialogue – not contention and competition, but integration. Not merely human life, our ancient philosophical foundation encapsulates views of the well-being of man as well as all other life forms, small or big. "*Vasudhaiva Kutumbakam*" (the world is one family) and "*Sarve Bhavantu Sukhinah...*" (may all be happy) are the guiding values of our way of life since time immemorial. The fact that overvaluing self-interest is not a component of our DNA is what sets us apart from other civilizations.

The economic policy of the country requires further reforms, however, altering the scenario while the wheel is still spinning is not a simple task. Bharatiya government's efforts to bring in economic reforms in the background of the pandemic-induced economic slowdown have become evident. But the resolution to realign a 70-year-old system requires courage, foresight and decisiveness on the part of the overseers, and patience and consistent collective efforts on the part of society. Conceived in the light of our all-encompassing worldview of oneness with all and integration, these schemes must take into account the current global context and be flexible to incorporate the developments of the modern era. Our country's resolute march in this direction has commenced. Bharat is now expressing itself as it truly is in its essence and the whole world is observing this rising phenomenon. This move is natural in our eyes but offbeat to the rest of the world.

Decades-long efforts that were instrumental in ushering in this country-wide awakening have been consistently opposed and labelled as "nationalism" by the communist-minded self-proclaimed intellectuals, liberals and journalists. In the true sense of the word, the movement leading to this mass awakening is "national", not "nationalistic". The word "nationalism" featured neither in Bharatiya vocabulary nor in Bharatiya consciousness. It is the byproduct of the concept of the "nation-state" of Western liberal democracies. Those countries are nationalistic. They forced two world wars upon the world. Their nationalism is rooted in their capitalistic ideological past. And the now-often-discussed "super-nationalism" is a manifestation of communism. Russia's unsuccessful, coercive attempts of slapping its half-baked communist economic model in the faces of Eastern European and Central Asian countries are etched in the human memory. Along similar lines, China's expansionist agenda and dictatorial tendencies have become common knowledge, with Chinese troops audaciously barging into Hong Kong and other South Asian countries. An estimated 41 lakh sq km area belonging to six different countries has been annexed by China and it is involved in border disputes with 18 countries across the world. Increasingly, more and more countries of the world are mobilising to tackle Chinese imperialism or super-nationalism.

Bharatiya consciousness holds a "national" (*Rashtriya*) sentiment, not "nationalistic" (*Rashtrawadi*). We are national, not nationalistic. For this very reason, Sangh (RSS) is "Rashtriya Swayamsevak Sangh" and not

"Rashtrawadi Swayamsevak Sangh". Setting nationalism in motion is not our motive. The Bharatiya concept of *"Rashtra"* is based on our view of life, where people *(Lok)*, not the state, define the *"Rashtra"*. People of this country, who speak different languages and dialects, wear separate caste titles as their identities and worship diverse deities, all subscribe to a spirituality-based, holistic and integral view of life. The deep entrenchment of this view of life in our psyche gives rise to a feeling of affinity with all members of society and fosters a bond with the whole landmass that we inhabit. Adopting and adapting to this time-tested eternal view of life, appropriating it according to the present-day scenario and manifesting the "self" in all walks of social and national life is being "national" about Bharat. To rekindle the adherence to this heritage of ours and to invoke the bonds of brotherhood to motivate selfless service to the society is the key to awakening the national sentiment of Bharat. Seamless expression of this nationality in all social domains is akin to rearrangement and self-expression of the country. Realising and promoting the emergence of the "self" of a country should not be misconstrued as "nationalism".

The recent clashes between China and Bharat where the Bharatiya Army's gallant efforts successfully ousted the enemy from our rightful land, were dubbed "super-nationalism" by the Communists. The fact of the matter is that the Communist lobby has time and again failed to comprehend the heart of the "self" of Bharat. And that which is becoming apparent in this current context is not some form of nationalism. It is the true identity of our country that has been long denied and suppressed. With *"Vasudhaiva Kutumbakam"* (the world is one family) and *"Sarve Bhavantu Sukhinah..."* (may all be happy) as the bedrock of our civilization, the resurgence of our identity and the emphasis on self-reliance and self-sufficiency ought not to be perceived as the clarion call for war. It is the plain reawakening of a long-established consciousness.

Vehement opposition to the emergence of this selfhood of Bharat within the country of its origin is not new. Upon completing the merger of the Junagadh princely state into the newly independent country of Bharat, the then Home Minister, Vallabhbhai Patel visited the Somnath temple. He was deeply saddened to see Somnath [one among the twelve revered Jyotirlingas (symbol of eternal radiance)] in ruins. Free from the clutches of foreign rule and rulers he resolved to resurrect the site and restore its glory in independent Bharat. He appointed Kanhaiyalal Munshi, a cabinet minister in the Nehru-led government to translate the idea into action. When Patel confided his plans to Mahatma Gandhi he supported the plan on the condition that the project be funded by people and not be state-funded. Obligated by this condition the project was accomplished using only people's funds. Dr. Rajendra Prasad, who was the president of the country at the time, presided at the *prana pratistha puja* of the temple. His address to the country from the ceremony is noteworthy.

However, Pandit Nehru was against this move. An event in our history which to illustrious leaders of the country like Sardar Patel, Mahatma Gandhi, Kanhaiya Lal Munshi and Dr. Rajendra Prasad was a proud moment, was antagonised in the name of "Hindu revivalism" by Prime Minister Nehru. This illuminates the fact that the suppression and denial of the true identity of our country date back to a bygone era. However, leaders with a national mindset were well represented in the Congress party then. It is for this very reason that this task of restoration could be accomplished. But gradually a strategic methodology to push such people to the fringe of the political leadership of the country was adopted and the Congress party became an apparition of Communism. Communism discarded the very notion of spirituality. Not only spirituality, but it is also opposed to the idea of a nation. Since its inception, communism has been a materialist ideology like capitalism. The erstwhile Soviet Union and the modern-day Chinese regimes too are reflections of the same expansionist, dictatorial psyche; therefore, they are unable to comprehend the self-expression of Bharat. They may want to push their agenda of countering the unifying process of the entire nation resulting in the bickering of the people in small groups, ultimately weakening the country.

How do we discharge our moral obligation towards our country in such a scenario? A clear and succinct guide to this inquiry emerges from the essay *"Swadeshi Samaj"*, penned by Gurudev Rabindranath Thakur in 1904. Gurudev Thakur was indeed unsympathetic to the idea of nationalism. However, his opposition was directed at colonialism and the Western nation-states that erupted as a consequence of the two world wars. However, his motion of favour for the self-expression of Bharat as a nation is evident in his writing. He writes: "We have fully understood today that, just by lying low, we cannot protect ourselves. The only way of self-protection is to evoke and direct our innate strength in every possible direction. This is the rule of the Creator. The English would continue to control our minds until we come out of our stagnancy and start working for ourselves. Sitting on the fence and constantly ruing imminent ruination would yield nothing.

"Aping the English in every sphere and disguising ourselves in an attempt to survive is nothing but self-treachery. We can never become truly English by mimicking them, nor can we stall them by becoming their inauthentic clones. Our intellect, our heart, and our values are all being auctioned off at throwaway prices every day. The only way to prevent it from happening is by embracing who we actually are – consciously, strongly, actively, and completely.

"Our stored vigour will be unleashed in the face of the blows from a foreign nation because the time has come for it to fulfil its purpose in this world. The potency created by ancient seers through austerities is priceless, and it is not destined to lie unused. That is the reason why God has ordained the indolent Bharat to undergo difficulties, so that it may be awakened.

"To experience unity in diversity and to establish unity amongst variety—this is the inherent *dharma* (the spirit) of Bharat. Bharatvarsh never interpreted diversity as hostility and, neither considers the outsider as an enemy.

"As Bharatvarsh possesses this trait, we would never get frightened by visualising any society as our opponent. With every new dissension, we inevitably will grow. The Hindu, Bauddha, Muslim and Christian would not fight with each other and die in Bharat. Rather they would find a balance, a meeting point here. This balance will not be non-Hindu, but very specifically Hindu. However foreign maybe its body parts, its life and spirit will be Bharatiya.

"If we believe that this arrangement for Bharat is divinely ordained, we will be able to focus our vision, overcome our embarrassment, as well as locate the undying force in Bharat. We will have to remember that we will not be obliged to forever be in the position of a learner concerning European erudition and science. The stream of knowledge in Bharat is going to integrate these divergent strands of knowledge and their mutual conflicts and contests, and develop them into a lotus of hundred petals; thereby removing their separateness. The renowned scholar of Bharat Dr. Jagadish Chandra Bose has made a tremendous contribution in bringing physics, biology and botany within the same disciplinary fold. It is only a matter of time before he could bring in psychology and consciousness within the same scientific fold too. The principal goal of the Bharatiya mind is to bring about this integration. Bharat does not support the doctrine of leaving anyone behind. One day, Bharat will show the way to the world characterised by feuds and distance, how to acknowledge all, accept all, as well as accord and preserve a distinct significance of each part in the larger integrated whole.

"Before the dawn of that glorious day, do call out to the nation once, as Mother! She is the mother who is always engaged in bringing all the countrymen closer to each other, dispelling their differences, nurturing and protecting us; and tirelessly infusing the wisdom preserved in her treasure to protect our souls from deprivation during the long nights of subjugation." (*Swadeshi Samaj*- Essay by Rabindranath Thakur)

The time to rekindle the spiritual essence of Bharat and to allow its blossoming has come. This divinely ordained process has commenced with the blessings of the Almighty. No matter how hard the deniers of this identity push or how much Bharat-opposing foreign forces try, the Bharatiya people have made their resolution explicit a few years back. "We are silent worshippers of the idea of global welfare" (विश्वमंगल कामना के हम हैं मौन पुजारी) is how successive generations of workers who have been tirelessly invested in the task of reawakening our consciousness, devoid of temptations of fame, are addressed. Their efforts will undoubtedly reap the sweet fruits of success. Setting aside our political and other vested interests and contributing to the re-emergence and re-establishment of the true identity of Bharat is what the nation expects of us in this historic moment.

Endnote :

This article first appeared in *The Sunday Guardian* on July 18, 2020.

15

Temple, Somnath and Ayodhya

Though the nature of the land disputes over the Ram Mandir issue of Ayodhya and that of the Somnath temple in Gujarat are totally different, the Supreme Court's decision to not speed up the Ram Mandir case reminded me of a debate that took place in 1948 about the reconstruction of the *Somnath Mandir*- a magnificent temple destroyed by the Islamic invaders.

This debate, between K. M. Munshi and Jawaharlal Nehru, has been recorded by Munshi in his book, '*Pilgrimage to Freedom*'. Munshi writes: "In December 1922, I went on a sort of pilgrimage to the broken shrine. Desecrated, burnt and battered, it still stood firm. I can scarcely describe the burning shame which I felt on that early morning as I walked on the broken floor of the once-hallowed Sabhamandap..."

"At the end of October 1947, I was with Sardar (Patel)... when a telephone message was received... that Sir Shah Nawaz Bhutto had invited the Indian Army to take over Junagadh. When Sardar conveyed the news to me, he said "So it is Jaya Somnath".

The reconstruction of the Somnath Temple was initiated by Sardar Patel, then home minister of India, executed by K. M. Munshi, a cabinet minister in the central government and inaugurated by Dr. Rajendra Prasad, the then president of India. But it was also met with opposition. Munshi further writes: "In November 1947, Sardar... visited the temple. At a public meeting, Sardar announced: 'We have decided that Somnath should be reconstructed. You, people of Saurashtra, should do your best."

Munshi expresses his belief when he writes, "The temple of Somnath is not just an ancient monument; it lived in the hearts of the whole nation and its reconstruction was a national pledge." He goes on to add, "Jawaharlal called me and said: "I don't like your trying to restore Somnath. It is Hindu revivalism."

The difference of opinion between Patel, Munshi and Nehru is illustrative of two different ideas of Bharat. Pandit Nehru was not anti-Bharat but his idea of Bharat was rooted in a Eurocentric school of thought. On the other side was an idea of Bharat rooted in its land and tradition.

Munshi also wrote a letter to Nehru where he says, "When the whole scheme was discussed by Sardar with Bapu (Gandhiji), he stated that it was alright except that the funds necessary for reconstructing the temple should come from the public. Thereafter, the idea that the Government of India should finance the reconstruction of the temple was given up."

"You pointedly referred to me in the cabinet as connected with Somnath. I am glad you did so; for I do not want to keep back any part of my views or activities, particularly from you who have placed such abundant confidence in me all these months. If I am now helping to build Somnath as a centre of religion (*dharma*) and culture, a university and a farm, it is only as a humble task to which I have been called. I can assure you that the 'collective subconscious' of India today is happier with the scheme of reconstruction of Somnath sponsored by the Government of India than with many other things that we have done and are doing."

"Yesterday you referred to 'Hindu revivalism.' I know your views on the subject; I have always done justice to them; I hope you will equally do justice to mine. Many have been the customs which I have defied in my humble way through literary and social work to shape or reintegrate some aspects of Hinduism, in the conviction that that alone will make India an advanced and vigorous nation under modern conditions."

"It is my faith in our past which has given me the strength to work in the present and to look forward to our future. I cannot value freedom if it deprives us of the Bhagavad Gita or uproots our millions from the faith with which they look upon our temples and thereby destroys the texture of our lives."

Shri V. P. Menon, who was then advisor to the states ministry, replied to Munshi's letter saying, "I have seen your masterpiece. I for one would be prepared to live and, if necessary, die by the views you have expressed in your letter". And so the reconstruction went ahead.

When the time came to install the deity, Munshi approached Dr. Rajendra Prasad and asked him to perform the ceremony, but added a rider, "that he should accept it only if he was prepared not to fail us."

Munshi says, "He promised that he would come and install the deity whatever the attitude of the Prime Minister, and added: "I would do the same with a mosque or a church if I were invited" but "when it was announced that Rajendra Prasad was to inaugurate the Temple, Jawaharlal vehemently protested".. Still, "Rajendra Prasad kept his promise. However, his speech delivered at Somnath was published in all the papers, but was cut out from the official organs."

It is ironic that Nehru, the Bharatiya icon of liberalism and freedom of expression, should ensure that the speech of the president is censored. In this manner, despite opposition, Somnath was rebuilt and today the shrine attracts lakhs of devotees. However, because of 60 years of rule by one regime, the proponents of the Nehruvian idea of Bharat with the support of the government, have proliferated in academia and media. Hence, history is repeating itself and the opposition to the Ram Mandir is even more vocal. But that does not take away from millions and millions of *Bharatwasis* who believe in the integral and holistic spiritual tradition of Bharat ; which is in tune with the idea of the "collective-subconsciousness of Bharat" that Sardar Patel, K.M. Munshi, Dr. Rajendra Prasad, Mahatma Gandhi, Dr. Radhakrishnan, Pandit Madan Mohan Malaviya and many such stalwart architects of modern independent Bharat believed in. The curious should read the correspondence in its entirety in the monumental book *'Pilgrimage to Freedom'* by K.M. Munshi (page 559 to 566).

Endnote :

This article first appeared in *The Indian Express* on December 1, 2018.

16

Ram Mandir for a Strong Bharat

On 5 August 2020, the foundation stone of the soon-to-be-constructed Ram Mandir was laid in Ayodhya. People living in Bharat and people of Bharatiya origin across the world witnessed this dazzling event with a sense of contentment. To scores of men and women, it was a dream come true. A sense of achievement was evident as the event was a result of a centuries-long battle. The glow of satisfaction and tears of joy could be seen bejewelling innumerable faces. It was a day of accomplishment for many, but in reality, it is the beginning of a new task.

For many people, it was the mere inauguration of the temple construction. However, the Bharatiya view of tradition and philosophy is holistic and integral. Bharat never segregated religion from social life but considered them as complementary pursuits. The Bharatiya view has maintained that every soul is potentially divine. With this view, it sets the goal of manifesting this divinity within, thereby attaining *Moksha* (to become one with the Supreme being) as the ultimate goal of human life. This process can be pursued by controlling nature, internal and external, by everyone. Bharat accepts and believes that according to the potential, nature and taste of the person there can be various ways and means to accomplish this and all these multiple ways (religions) of manifesting divinity are equal. We are the shining example of this tradition as *Bharat Mata* is known to have cradled and nourished various religious legacies that continue to shine and thrive here in Bharat. Several other cultures that had a brush with our rich religio-cultural heritage at various points in the past have experienced this truth. While treading the spiritual path, Bharat hasn't devalued material affluence or prosperity, ever. It is for this reason that *Artha* (that, which is related to material wealth) and *Kama* (that, which is related to fulfilling desires) find a place alongside *Dharma* and *Moksha* in the four broad goals enlisted in *Purusharth Chatushtya* (which give meaning to human life).

"*Ubuntu*", a Zulu-African conceptualisation translates as "I am because we are". This phrase also resonates with one of the concepts of *dharma* in Bharat. Me, my family, village, state, country, humanity and all living creatures and the nature are units progressively spiralling out towards a larger whole and thus integral *(ekatma)*. These units are not in conflict, but there is harmony amongst them; not in competition but complementary to each other. Human life is a cumulative togetherness of all these forces. We are what we are because these units are what they are. Striking a balance between the myriad units that compose human life is *dharma* and to strive for this balance is to establish *dharma*.

It is unfair to box our view of *dharma* under the category of religion; to label it worship is insufficient too. In our meditation on the spiritual goal of human life, material prosperity was neither opposed nor deemed futile. One of the definitions of *dharma* is:

यतो अभ्युदय निःश्रेयस सिद्धिः स धर्मः
"Yato Abhyuday Nihshreyas Siddhih Sa Dharmah"

Here *Abhyudaya* stands for material prosperity and *Nihshreyas* stands for *Moksha*. As per the teachings of *Ishavasya Upanishad*, the knowledge that enables the creation of wealth is called *Avidya* and the knowledge that enables the achievement of *Moksha* is referred to as *Vidya*. The creators of the *Upanishads* suggested *Avidya* paves the way for comfortable navigation through this mortal plane *(Mrityu Lok)* of existence. At the same time, *Vidya* aids the journey beyond, to the eternal abode of the supreme entity:

विद्याञ्च अविद्याञ्च यस्तद् वेदोऽभयम् सह। अविद्यया मृत्युम् तीर्त्वा विद्ययाऽमृतमश्नुते।
"Vidyaancha Avidyaancha Yastadvedobhayam Sah, Avidyayaa Mrutyum Teertvaa Vidyayaa Amrutmashnute"

Meditating and balancing the pursuits of material prosperity and *Moksha* is *dharma*.

Understanding this concept of *dharma* is essential. The Sangh prayer that sprouts from the hearts of millions of RSS *swayamsevaks* each day is also a meditation on the balance between elevating one's material self *(samutkarsh)* and one's spiritual self *(nihshreyas)*. In fact, the suffix "*Asya*" used to express possessive case in a singular noun *(Shashthi Vibhakti, ek vachan)* in Sanskrit has been used here, indicating these are two facets of one and the same concept, hence not disparate. This implies that the holistic Bharatiya view of life placed material (physical) and spiritual (meta-physical) progress on the same continuum.

For the longest time, affluence was the hallmark of Bharatiya civilization. Enamoured by the lore of its material and spiritual glory, seekers of trade and knowledge are known to have set out in search of Bharat from distant lands. Despite its riches, Bharat did not bully other human settlements and countries by waging wars on them. Having traversed long trade routes and engaged in trade with varied people from far-off lands, we never formed colonies. Neither was our behaviour undignified nor did we plunder their wealth. We didn't attempt to convert them either or push them into cycles of slavery. Instead, Bharatiya people were agents of economic, social and cultural elevation in places where they went. Even today, remnants of that splendid exchange are found in the languages, art and literature, temples and cultural practices of many South Asian countries. This civilising barter that enabled and enriched those natives and brought about prosperity on both ends is revered as "*Mahalakshmi*" in Bharatiya scriptures. We are no venerators of money, we worship "*Dhanalakshmi*" and "*Mahalakshmi*". Therefore, it is fair to conclude that the primogenitor of our pursuit of material wealth and dignity for human life is our concept of *dharma* (balance, not religion) and for time immemorial our temples have been the seat of meditation over different facets of this all-encompassing *dharma*. Given the spirituality-based view of life, the temples in Bharat are centres of worship and inner guidance on one hand and precursors of our material and cultural civilisation on the other.

In 1951, while performing the *prana pratishtha* pooja at Somnath Temple, the first president of independent Bharat, Dr. Rajendra Prasad, illustrated this point vividly. An excerpt from his speech is enlightening. He said, "On this holy day, we should learn from the *prana pratishtha* of this Somnath Mandir, and all of us should vouch for the re-establishment of the influence of Bharat in terms of prosperity in the world. Our country was an industrial pioneer in ancient times; the products which were made here were exported all over the world. Our export was higher than our import, and thus Bharat became a land of wealth. The gold and silver which are stored in the treasury of the developed nations were once stored in the temples of Bharat, an example of which is the temple of Somnath. I think that this *prana pratishtha* will be complete only on the day we reclaim that dominance and do justice to the Somnath Mandir. Moreover, we should also strive to achieve the level of cultural brilliance which we had in the ancient times so that when people judge us by today's culture, they should know that we are still far better than them."

The struggle for reinstating Ram Mandir on Ram Janmabhoomi was a movement to reinstate the *dharma* of Bharat which was being systematically distorted in the name of secularism.

In his address at Ram Mandir *Bhoomi Pujan*, RSS *Sarsanghachalak* Dr. Mohan Bhagwat mentioned three keywords: आत्मनिर्भर/*Aatmanirbhar* (self-reliant), आत्मविश्वास/*Aatmavishwas* (self-confidence) and आत्मभान/*Aatmabhaan* (self-awareness). Self-reliance was referred to for our knowledge (Bharatiya knowledge—*Vidya* and *Avidya*, both) and economy. Self-confidence is in the context of a resolute aim to march towards newer heights with a firm belief in our ancient yet evergreen and eternal spirituality-based integral, holistic and all-encompassing view of life. And self-awareness implies demonstrating our Bharatiya worldview in all spheres of one's life—individual, familial, social, professional and national—to the best of one's ability and knowledge. Rabindranath Thakur in his essay *"Swadeshi Samaj"* was drawing our attention to this fact when he wrote, "We should aim to become who we are. Finding our true self by embracing our identity consciously, deliberately, strongly and completely."

Re-establishing a deeper connection with our spiritual, cultural and historical roots is the assured path to reclaiming trade dominance and cultural brilliance. In turn, it will allow Bharatiya people to profess once again the civilising values of peaceful communication, solidarity, patience and congeniality to a world plagued by competition, struggle, violence, war, exploitation and torture. By exercising our "*dharma*" we will be able to shepherd diverse humanity onto a path of peaceful, prosperous and harmonious coexistence. This line from Dr. Prasad's speech holds the key to unlocking that path: "Temples were the epicentres of our material and cultural progress. I hope for this temple to be the centre of excellence once again. Until that happens, I will not believe that the reinstatement of the temple is complete."

This approach is relevant in the context of the Ram Mandir in Ayodhya today. For this reason, the celebration is of both- an end of one long struggle and the beginning of a new journey.

Recently, a few other issues of paramount national significance seem to have reached their conclusive ends one after another. Why is it so is another issue that deserves some attention here. In 1987 *Ram-Janaki Rath Yatra* was underway when one Sangh *swayamsevak* quizzed Shri Balasaheb Deoras, then *sarsanghachalak* of RSS: "Our pleas to ban cow slaughter and repeal Article 370 from Kashmir seem to have fallen on deaf ears. Nothing seems to move. Will Ram Mandir have a similar fate?" To which Shri Balasaheb Deoras replied, saying, "Let's work towards awakening people's consciousness toward this issue. In fact, efforts to stir people's consciousness to causes of national significance must be consistent and perpetual. At present, the general level of national consciousness of the Hindu samaj is very low, which is why these problems surround us. The day when the general level of national consciousness of the whole society will get elevated, it will be a time when the resolution to most problems may come about simultaneously."

In his book, *Tipping Point: How Little Things Can Make a Big Difference*, Malcolm Gladwell defines "Tipping Point" as "the point at which a series of small changes or incidents become significant enough to cause a larger, more important change." In hindsight, one is compelled to reflect if Shri Balasaheb Deoras was hinting at this "tipping point" when he talked about the consistent efforts for elevating national consciousness.

Shri Dattopant Thengadi, one of the luminaries and visionaries of Sangh would often remark, "A handful of nationally conscious and active workers cannot bring about lasting social change. But when the common man becomes even slightly more conscious about matters of national significance, then a huge difference comes about. Therefore, unwavering attempts at bringing causes of national consequence to the fore and stirring a discourse over those in the society will gradually boost the general level of national consciousness. As a cumulative effect, small and big issues of national significance will be conclusively addressed. So, it is imperative that some people must dedicate their lives to the task of augmenting the general level of national consciousness."

It seems the tipping point of Balasaheb Deoras and Dattopant Thengadi's imagination is nearing. Rabindranath Thakur's *Swadeshi Samaj* is coming alive. Several overdue decisions in matters of great national significance are now being made. The world has taken note of the shifts in the defence and foreign policies of the country. We have started our journey towards self-reliance by adopting decentralised, agrarian economic policies. The new education policy that will empower young minds to remain true to our roots, our true identity, while spreading their wings far and wide has been recently announced. An atmosphere that is nurturing the entrepreneurial spirit and innovation is emerging. Since all these developments are coinciding with one another after 2014, it is but natural that they are attributed to the change of government at the Centre. However, I would like to cite a line from the editorial dated May 18, 2014, of *The* Guardian, published from London, commenting on the election results of May 16, 2014. It read: "It should be obvious that the underlying changes in Indian society have brought us Mr. Modi and not the other way round." This observation is important. All these changes are a consequence of a boost in the general level of national consciousness and not the other way round. Overthrowing the old regime and electing a new central government is one among those changes.

Fuelled by its timeless wisdom *Bharatvarsha* has sought a new ground to fulfil its divinely ordained duties. A senior Sangh *pracharak* defined RSS as "the evolution of the life mission of this Hindu nation." Previously impeded essential reforms of national consequence have begun to take shape. It is the time for conscious and careful consolidation of nation-building efforts. This consciousness will inevitably pave the way to the desired self-confidence and self-reliance.

> "अरुणोदय हो चुका वीर अब कर्मक्षेत्र में जुट जाएँ,
> अपने खून-पसीने द्वारा नवयुग धरती पर लाएँ।"
>
> "*Arunoday ho chuka veer ab karmakshetra mein jut jaayen,*
> *apne khoon-paseene dwara navyug dharti par laayen.*"

As mentioned in one of the Sangh songs, "Colours of the dawn are inviting us to march into the field and usher in a new era by watering the ground with our blood and sweat."

Endnote :

This article first appeared in *The Sunday Guardian* on August 29, 2020.

17

The Nation Must Stand for the People

After the 2019 Lok Sabha elections, a senior journalist associated with the Left asked me what brought Congress to its present condition of decline. It was an unanticipated query. In response, I presented a counter question: What is the full name of Congress? He thought for a while and answered, "Indian National Congress".

I said, "Indian" means Bharat and encompassing all of it. What should be the meaning of "National" then? He couldn't come up with a response. I told him that here "Indian" has a geographical connotation and "National" has a qualitative connotation.

Taking the conversation forward, I said that in the Bharatiya context, "Nation" means "people". A few special traits of the Bharatiya society have become its identity after a journey of thousands of years. Being 'national' means connecting with this identity, taking pride in it, and preserving and strengthening the same by practising it in day-to-day life. It also involves efforts to reform society in accordance with changing times while keeping the eternal values of Bharat as its base.

Twenty years after its foundation, Congress took the shape of an anti-British freedom movement. At that time, all the Congress leaders were of "national" thought and stood proudly with this nation's special identity that had taken shape after a collective journey of centuries and survived despite numerous invasions and conflicts.

Personality of Bharat: Four Characteristics

The core of Bharatiya society is spirituality, which has been formed after a journey of thousands of years. This spirituality has granted a different temperament and innate nature to Bharat. People living in this large territorial expanse, inhabited by different castes, religions and languages, share these intrinsic traits of Bharat.

There are four aspects to Bharat's being. First is, *Ekam Sat Vipra Bahudha Vadanti*—the Almighty or God is one and can be called by various names and can be reached by different paths and all these paths are equal. Bharat has established this by its conduct. Hence, Swami Vivekananda, in his famous Chicago address, proclaimed "We go beyond tolerance and accept all ways to be true." He further said that he was proud to represent a country in whose language Sanskrit, there is no synonym for the term "exclusion".

The second aspect is realising "unity in diversity". In Rabindranath Thakur's words, "To experience unity in diversity and to establish unity amongst variety—this is the inherent *Dharma* (the spirit) of Bharat. Bharatvarsh neither interpreted diversities as hostility and, nor did it consider the alien as an enemy. Thus, without sacrificing our own, without destroying others, Bharat aspires to assign a distinct place to everyone in one vast ecosystem. Thus, it is willing to accept all ways of life and acknowledges the greatness of each in its own way".

The third feature is that Bharat believes that every soul, man or woman, is potentially divine and the goal of human life is to manifest the divinity within by controlling nature, internal and external. Do it either by work, worship, meditation or psychic control—any of these four or more or all and be free. Therefore, four *purusharthas* of *Dharma*, *Artha*, *Kama* and *Moksha* have been conceptualised and practised in Bharat. "*Artha*" and "*Kama*" are not negated, instead, life is considered complete and meaningful when all are fulfilled by following *dharma*.

The fourth aspect is that there is liberty and freedom to choose one's path to *Moksha* (being one with the Divine). Depending upon one's interest, taste, capacity and nature, the composition of their path can be a mix of paths such as the *Karma, Bhakti, Dhyan* or *Jnana marg*. Hence, we say that there is spiritual democracy in Bharat.

Intrinsic Nature of Bharat is '*Dharma*'

The intrinsic nature of Bharat is *dharma*. Here, *dharma* does not mean religion or worship or rituals. If you open your eyes and close your "I" you will expand your circumference of "we" to progressively include family, relatives, village, district, state, country, the entire humanity, and all animate and inanimate creation. Expanding our sphere of belonging and working for the well-being of those whom we consider our own is called *dharma*. *Dharma* is not about wearing symbols of identity but about righteous conduct. For instance, going to the temple or any place of worship, observing fasts or performing rituals is not *dharma*. Rather, it is *Upasana* (religion) or worship that helps you to tread on the path of *dharma* which is nothing but giving back to society in order to enrich the "social capital". Hence, such "worship" or religion is for *dharma* and not *dharma* by itself.

This idea of "*dharma*" is purely Bharatiya. It is described and discussed consistently through the ages in classical and folk literature in all Bharatiya languages and dialects. There is no synonym for *dharma* in any language outside Bharat. Hence it is apt and correct to use "*dharma*" even in English. Translating it as religion would be wrong, though different modes of worship or *Upasana* can be called religion.

> ईशावास्यमिदं सर्वम् यत्किञ्च जगत्यां जगत्।
> तेन त्यक्तेन भुञ्जीथाः मा गृधः कस्यस्विद धनम्॥
> *Ishavasya idam sarvam yatkincha jagatyam jagat,*
> *Tena tyakten bhunjeethah maa gridhah kasyasvid dhanam.*

Meaning : This entire changeful creation is inhabited by the Supreme Spirit or *Isha*. We are called on to be free of all desires and let go of any impulse to possess that which is not rightfully ours. This way, through renunciation, one can rejoice in the omnipresent Bliss.

At the root of this very idea is experiencing oneness stemming out of spirituality. It is this expression of spiritual oneness which leads us to feel related to all humanity, and the animal and plant kingdom. To impart knowledge to a seeker, give water to the thirsty, food to the hungry and shelter to the homeless—each of these is a *Dharmic* act. Hence, terms like *Dharmshala* for inns, *Dharmarth aspataal* for charity hospitals are widely used in practice. Constructing ponds or lakes, planting trees on pathways, helping physically challenged people and doing all this with a sense of duty is called *dharma*. Doing *dharma* leads to societal enrichment or prosperity which takes care of everybody without any discrimination.

Sister Nivedita has said that in a society where people, instead of keeping the remuneration of their work to themselves only, share it with others in the society, the accumulated collective wealth of the society makes everybody prosperous. But when people keep the remuneration of their work to themselves without giving it to society, some people may become rich, but the society at large remains poor. *Dharma* lies in the enrichment of social capital on the whole. This is the basis or foundation of *dharma. Dharma* does not discriminate. It connects with everybody and everything. One who discriminates while helping cannot be a follower of *"dharma". Dharma* connects, binds and holds all in the society together hence *dharma* is defined as "one that beholds, connects, binds together and helps to prosper."

धारणाद् धर्ममित्याहु: धर्मो धारयते प्रजा: ।
Dharnaad dharmmityahuh dharmo dharyate prajah.

Dharma prospers when we give back to society more than what we receive. Hence, the Vivekananda Kendra's prayer says:

जीवने यावदादानं स्यात् प्रदानं ततोऽधिकम्।
इत्येषा प्रार्थनास्माकं भगवन् परिपूर्यताम्॥
Jivane yavdadaanam syat pradanam tato'dhikam
Ityesha prarthanasmaakam bhagawan Paripuryatam

Meaning- "Whatever we receive in life let us give far more than that. O Almighty! Grant our wish."

Rabindranath Thakur elaborated on this in his seminal essay titled *"Swadeshi Samaj"*, saying that the welfare state is not a Bharatiya tradition. Barring defence and security, judiciary and foreign affairs the people had their autonomous systems for all other matters like education, healthcare, industry, trade & commerce, temples, fairs, art & aesthetics, music, dance, drama, pilgrimage, etc. that did not depend on the state. *Sanatan* Bharat did not rely on the state treasury to fund these activities of the society. The society had its independent arrangement which had *dharma* as its guiding principle. This *'dharma'* does not imply religion or worship. To give to the society as one would to one's own family, to give back, is considered *dharma.*

Dharmachakrapravartanaya (Let the Wheel of *Dharma* Keep on Moving)

It clearly appears that while working on Bharat's Constitution, the members of the constituent assembly were clear about the concept of "*dharma*". Hence, it is reflected in the motto of the Supreme Court as "*Yato Dharmastato Jayah*".

"*Dharmachakrapravartanaaya*" has been embedded on the walls of the Lok Sabha and in Rajya Sabha it is "*Satyam Vada, Dharmam Char*". Not only this, the *chakra* or wheel on our national flag is "*Dharma Chakra*". The *Chakra* or wheel is meant to keep on moving. Every task, no matter how small it may seem, when undertaken as a way of giving back to society, helps in keeping this wheel of *dharma* moving and everyone should play their role in it.

In 1988 when I was a *pracharak* in Vadodara, there was a severe drought in one part of Gujarat. *Sukhdi*, a nutritious meal, was being collected from families in the Sangh *Karyalay* to be distributed in the drought-stricken areas. An old lady who appeared to be a street beggar came to the *karyalay* and when the *karyakartas* present there enquired, she said in her weak voice, "*sukhdi*". The volunteer tried telling her that "*sukhdi*" was for distribution in drought-stricken areas and not for people in the same locality to which she replied by saying, "Son, I am not here to take *sukhdi* from you but to give you some." *Dharma* is strengthened by such small actions of individuals and the wheel of *dharma* keeps moving.

A couple of years ago in Tirupur city of Tamil Nadu, a camp for the persons with disabilities was organised by the organisation *SAKSHAM* with the help of the Central government. *SAKSHAM* is an RSS-inspired organisation that works among *Divyangjan* (persons with disabilities). Medical tests were being conducted and scores of persons with disabilities were making their way to the camp alighting at the bus stand. An auto driver who ferried one such individual was so struck by the purpose of the camp that for the entire day he let go of his earnings and provided free rides from the bus stand. A photographer whose studio was near the campsite realised that people required photographs for their identification cards when many of them struggled to make it to his studio to get clicked. He put in his share of efforts to make things less difficult for them by temporarily shifting his studio to the campsite and serving for free. All such acts contribute to keeping the *Dharma Chakra* moving.

This philosophical foundation of Bharat and its intrinsic nature stemmed out of it is known to the world as *Hindutva* (Hinduness). The national identity of Bharat and Bharatiya society is Hindu. "Hindu" is the identity of this nation, meaning, the people of Bharat. That makes us the people or *rashtra*, a *Hindu Rashtra*. *Hindutva* has always been about connecting and uniting everyone and doing away with discrimination. Being national means this personality. *Hindutva* (Hinduness) finds expression in the personal, familial, professional and social life of the people of Bharat.

Being national is respecting our ancestors, great men and women of the past, reformers, sages and seers, who inspired and guided this nation to counter foreign onslaughts and invasions and kept the spirit of nationhood unhindered.

Being national is worshipping this holy land, where this noble thought was conceptualised and rooted deeply and a great culture and civilisation took shape. The fundamental and essential task is to keep everyone in tune with this national identity and spirit. This cannot be accomplished by any political or state power but by the people themselves.

> सर्वेऽपि सुखिनः सन्तु सर्वे सन्तु निरामयाः।
> सर्वे भद्राणि पश्यन्तु मा कश्चित् दुःखमाप्नुयात्॥
> *Sarvepi sukhinah santu sarve santu niramyah*
> *Sarve bhadrani pashyantu ma kashchid dukhamapnuyat.*
>
> Meaning- "May all beings be at peace,
> may all remain free from illness,
> May all see what is auspicious, may no one suffer.
> Om Peace. Peace. Peace."

Here, "*api*" includes all—children, senior citizens, ill, weak and others deprived of any means. It is *dharma* that guarantees happiness to all who are vulnerable, which is to be followed by all in their conduct.

The belief that the people of Bharat are one and my own, that everyone is equal and that one has to give back to society with a purposive sense of duty, is being "national' or Hindu. It is a timeless truth that all the people living in Bharat believe in this doctrine and are known as "Hindu". This is what we mean when we say that ours is a *Hindu Rashtra* (nation). There does not arise any question of disrespecting anyone.

The "national" people of Bharat, full of diversity, speaking different languages and following different modes of worship have been living in harmony and peace together for centuries by accepting this diversity not as difference but as our special characteristic.

The world has gotten closer with modern means of transportation and communication. The diversity of language, race and religion is there to stay and Bharat has the vision to look at the underlying unity in the apparent diversity. The reason being, *Isha Vaasyamidam Sarvam* is Bharat's motto, *Tenatyakten Bhunjitha* and *Ma Gridah* are its codes of conduct. Through this, *dharma* can be strengthened and happiness for all can be accomplished.

Bharat has lived these principles for centuries, hence it has conceptualised the idea of *Vasudhaiva Kutumbakam* (the entire world is one family) and *Vishwam Bhawatyek Needam* (Let the entire world become one nest). Bharat will once again exhibit how human society can live in harmony in this diverse world by following its *Hindutva* code. This is the duty of Bharat and the need of the hour in today's world. Creating such a Bharat is what makes Bharat a "*Vishwa Guru*". It is not a matter of announcing one to be the "*Vishwa Guru*", but exhibiting so with our conduct. Rashtriya Swayamsevak Sangh (RSS) has been engaged in this noble task. This is the purpose and goal of RSS.

An insightful expression was given by a veteran *pracharak* of the RSS when he said, "RSS is the evolution of the life mission of this Hindu Nation."

Being "national" is sometimes described as being "nationalist" which is not correct. Nationalism is not a Bharatiya concept. The concept of a nation which took shape in the 16th century in the West is completely different from the Bharatiya concept of *rashtra* which is loosely translated as 'nation' in English.

Where the "nation-states" in the West have led to wars, oppression and violence, the Bharatiya concept of *rashtra* is "people-oriented", who share a unified culture, view of life and history. Hence, despite there being various political authorities or state powers here, this *rashtra* (the people) has been and is "one" in its view of life and culture. This is about nationality and not nationalism. We are national and Hindu, not nationalists.

During the freedom movement, almost all leaders of the Indian National Congress were of this national character. Gradually with the increasing influence of Communists within the Congress, this "national" leadership was marginalised. After the Congress split of 1969, this process of marginalisation was complete and the Congress fell completely under communist influence. Moreover, the reason for the party's existence was limited to striving to be in power by hook or crook.

At the same time, with the efforts of the Rashtriya Swayamsevak Sangh, mass leaders, saints, sages and social reformers, the awakening of the national consciousness happened and the result is visible throughout the country. On one hand, there was a national awakening due to which the society was rising above caste, religion, region and language barriers and was starting to think with a single national vision. On the other hand, the Congress party was entangled in its scheming and plotting to stay in power by arousing narrow sentiments of caste, religion, region and language. As a result, the nationally awakened people began marginalising the Indian National Congress which had marginalised those who were "national". This is the answer to the question asked by the senior journalist at the beginning of the conversation as well.

Endnote :

This article first appeared in *The Sunday Guardian* on December 21, 2019.

18

Time for Bharat to Unite

In the midst of fighting the thickening coronavirus pandemic situation, Bharat got the news of the Chinese attempt to encroach into Ladakh's Galwan region. Twenty warriors of our army made a heroic sacrifice of their lives to safeguard our motherland. This damage garnered many headlines in the media with a few news features touting this bloody struggle to be one of its kind since the Indo-China war of 1962. Some elements have questioned the gallant efforts of the Bharatiya Army and blamed Bharatiya leadership for lacking alertness and rigour. A microscopic examination of the history of these very elements reveals an interesting pattern. Coincidentally, it comprises the same elements that went all out to prevent the BJP from securing a majority at the centre and defeating Narendra Modi. The fact is, including this crisis, many other geopolitical and socio-economic challenges faced by Bharat are due to poor leadership, myopia, impracticality and a lack of cohesive understanding of the concept of *Rashtra*.

Perhaps, till now, China had not experienced the kind of rigour, courage and forbearance displayed by Bharatiya leadership in the recent past in Doklam and Galwan. After 1962, China has been regularly exerting encroachment efforts that were not met with planned and forceful opposition until recently. Such resistance cannot be staged by isolated displays of valour by the armed forces. It is a synchronous effort of the political leadership and the armed forces, wherein strategic thinking at the leadership level is paramount. This fact became apparent when Bharat conducted a successful nuclear weapon test in 1998. Bharatiya nuclear atomic scientists had developed the capability to conduct nuclear tests way back in 1994. Still, they failed to conduct the same as the then leaders of the country could not show the same courage as the late Atal Bihari Vajpayee displayed (in 1998).

This decision won Bharat a new position in the world, both as a country and people. Since 2014, along with China, there has been a fundamental change in the way Bharat has been dealing with state-sponsored terrorism by Pakistan. The Uri airstrike, Balakot, Doklam, Galwan and resistance of Pak-supported terrorism in Kashmir—all these events evidently testify to the same change. Speedy border construction in previously ignored border regions and display of wisdom in reclaiming the rightful Bharatiya areas of the Aksai-Chin landmass that were formerly usurped by Pakistan, and lately by China are indicators of a firm, courageous and far-sighted national leadership. All these factors may have infuriated China, and therefore, it is not surprising that the anti-national forces within our country are feeling unsettled with Bharat's current treatment meted out to China.

In the Indo-China war of 1962, despite the incomparable bravado and sacrifice of the soldiers of the Bharatiya Armed Forces, we lost. Critical analysis of that defeat points out two evident reasons — first, the lack of foresight on the part of the then Bharatiya top leadership; and second, unpreparedness for war. Well aware of China's expansionist tendencies, the then *Sarsanghachalak* of Rashtriya Swayamsevak Sangh, Guruji Golwalkar and several other prudent political leaders of the country had warned of the impending danger of embracing the enemy and chiming "*Hindi-Chini Bhai-Bhai*" slogans (Bharatiya and the Chinese are like brothers). They feared China might deceive Bharat, and this strategy would backfire. We had to face the disgraceful defeat due to complete neglect of those warnings, failure to prepare for the war and continuation of hobnobbing with a deceptive China. In the aftermath of the defeat, military reforms were contemplated. However, the mere strengthening of the military base alone was insufficient. Mature and determined national leadership is essential in dealing with such conflicts.

Recently, a video surfaced where the then Defence Minister A.K. Antony was addressing the parliament on December 6, 2013. He is noted as saying, "China is much more advanced in the area of building infrastructure in comparison to India. Their infrastructure development is superior to India's. We are only catching them. That is also history. What is it? Independent India had a policy for many years that the best defence is not to develop the border. Undeveloped borders are safer than developed borders. So, for many years, there was no construction of roads or airfields in the border areas. By that time, China continued to develop their infrastructure in the border areas. So, as a result, they have now gone ahead of us. Compared to us infrastructure-wise, capability-wise in the border areas, they are ahead. I admit that. It is a part of history."

Soon after Independence, Bharat's foreign, economic and defence policies were headed in the wrong direction. The lag in defence policy has been illuminated through the aforementioned examples. Talking of economic policy, instead of emphasising a rural-centric development model, and decentralised policies, the state favoured urban-centric development policies that were centralised in nature and proposed to build metropolitan centres around which human life would revolve. It is a consequence of such policies that Bharatiya villages, where about 70% of the country's population lives remain underdeveloped and ill-equipped. Compelled to uproot themselves from their villages, innumerable people relocate to large towns and cities to pursue education, to seek health facilities and employment opportunities. Post-Independence economic policies grossly ignored the farmer and agriculture. We have experienced the outcome of these policies during the corona pandemic crisis when lakhs of inter-state labourers felt alienated at their metropolitan workplaces. At the same time, we should remember that the process of mindless urbanisation and development also alienates them from their families, their land and even their culture. Even today, agriculture and agro-based industries have the potential to generate the highest employment, which is being explored through the *Aatmanirbhar Bharat Abhiyan*.

Talking of foreign policy, non-alignment was flagged as the country's foreign policy consistently. Adopting non-alignment as a tactical tool until Bharat becomes globally influential is reasonable enough, but that alone cannot be the cornerstone of our foreign policy. The two superpowers, concerning whom non-alignment was being deliberated, were comparatively young nations. Their ideological basis, the experience of individual, social and community life were amorphous, underdeveloped and partial in comparison to the well-developed, complete and holistic Bharatiya view about the nation, society and philosophy of life. The very idea of basing our policies on those views is a sign of a colonised mentality. America and Russia — the two power centres of the time — had been less than 500 years into their existence. Their ideological bases had been in use for less than 100 years. On the other hand, Bharat's history, its life as a unified civilisation predates at the very least 10,000 years.

The spirituality-based Bharatiya view of life is inherently holistic, integral and universal. For this very reason, even in times of power and prosperity, it did not burden other countries with war. Having traversed extensive distances and engaged in trade with far-off lands, we did not form colonies in those lands. Neither did we exploit those places and people nor plunder their wealth, or attempt to convert or enslave them. Instead, our people enabled those people to elevate their economic and social life by becoming prosperous, capable and civilised. This inclusive worldview is the hallmark of Bharat. For the same reason, this very view of life should have guided our foreign policy as well.

However, the first prime minister of Bharat was under the spell of communism. In the name of modernisation, and enticed by fancy Western terminology, the spirituality-based holistic Bharatiya view of life was disregarded, setting a different tone for our country's policies. With the passage of time, Communist influence grew within the Congress Party. Eventually, Congress was cast in the mould of Communism as a whole. Consequently, Bharat was alienated from its "self," i.e. Bharat. Overriding the core identity of Bharat, a spiritual, unifying and universal image was swapped for titles like progressive, liberal, and intellectual, which became something like a fashion. However, due to the perennial awakening of social and national consciousness, which was simmering below the surface all along, the BJP won majority support in the 2014 general elections and was elected to power. This development was historic, as post-Independence, this was an isolated instance of a party, which was not Congress, forming a government with a full majority. The significance of the 2014 results was not just a victory of the first non-Congress majority government, but also the victory of proactive and committed people who thrived on national rejuvenation based on positive contextualisation of the ancient roots, as well as a rejection of colonial intellectual imposition, which became a symbol of "progressive thinking".

This movement bloomed with the repetition of the success story of 2014 in 2019, this time only with a greater majority, marking a milestone in Bharat's journey towards revival.

On May 16, 2014, the Lok Sabha election results were announced and the Narendra Modi-led Bharatiya Janata Party was invited to form the National Democratic Alliance (NDA) government with an absolute majority. Describing this incident, the editorial of Britain's *The Guardian* dated May 18 began with, "Today, 18 May 2014, may well go down in history as the day when Britain finally left India. Narendra Modi's victory in the elections marks the end of a long era in which the structures of power did not differ greatly from those through which Britain ruled the subcontinent. India under the Congress party was in many ways a continuation of the British Raj by other means." The commencement note of this editorial itself captures the essence of the change described earlier.

At around the same time, Shiv Viswanathan's write-up was published wherein he made a notable confession. The title itself gives away the message encased in his confession. The title reads: "How Modi defeated liberals like me".

Shiv Vishwanathan goes on to explain: "What secularism did was, it enforced oppositions in a way that the middle class felt apologetic and unconfident about its beliefs, its perspectives. Secularism was portrayed as an upwardly mobile, drawing room discourse they were inept at." "On May 17, Narendra Modi revisited Varanasi to witness a pooja performed at the Kashi Vishwanath temple. After the ritual at the temple, he moved to Dashashwamedh Ghat where an *aarti* was performed along the river. The *aarti* was more than a spectacle. As a ritual, it echoed the great traditions of a city, as a performance it was riveting. As the event was relayed on TV, people messaged requesting that the event be shown in full, without commentary. Others claimed that this was the first time such a ritual was shown openly. With Mr. Modi around, the message claimed 'We don't need to be ashamed of our religion. This could not have happened earlier'.

"At first, the message irritated me and then made me thoughtful. A colleague of mine added. "You English-speaking secularists have been utterly coercive, making the majority feel ashamed of what was natural." The comment, though brutal and devastating, was fair. I realised at that moment that liberals like myself may be guilty of something deeper."

This is the new Bharat, and Bharatiya people alongside the whole world can sense this phenomenon rising. Yet if truth be told, this Bharat is not new at all. It is in fact the outmoded, cast-off Bharat. Shrouded in the shadows of propaganda and false titles, this antiquated yet evergreen and eternal entity that favours self-reliance and collective strength is our very own

"Bharat". Since "*Vasudhaiva Kutumbakam*" (the world is my family) and "*Sarvepi Sukhinah Santu*" (may all be blissful and happy) are the bedrock of our civilisational foundation, the resurgence of Bharat's identity and its emphasis on self-reliance and self-sufficiency should not be perceived as a threat. It is in fact an invitation to the whole world to come to dive deep into the bliss of the revival of our reverential view of life because it is the same Bharat that is reawakening.

At a time when the entire country is determined to defeat the coronavirus pandemic, the challenge posed by the expansionist and dictatorial Chinese regime requires Bharatiya society to unify as one unit and set an example for the enemy. So far we have been successful in doing so. It is essential that all the people and the leaders of all political parties have credence for the armed forces and the decision-making ability of the government in matters of national security and defence strategy by showing maturity. This is not the time to do a cost-benefit analysis or to plot for wins or losses at the political level.

Endnote :

This article first appeared in *The Sunday Guardian* on July 11, 2020.

19

Are Tribals Non-Hindu?

The Jharkhand state government recently passed a bill with a majority that deems Sarana Dharma followers as non-Hindu and claims "Sarana" to be a separate religion. At around the same time, the Andhra Pradesh government declared that the Scheduled Tribe will be listed not as Hindus but just "Scheduled Tribe" in the 2021 census with the view that they are non-Hindus. These developments are an indicator of a lack of realisation of Bharat and a correct understanding of *Hindutva* (Hinduness), which is combined with an insatiable hunger for political power on the part of these decision-makers. *Hindutva* is not some religion. Even the honourable Supreme Court of the country honoured and established the fact that it is a view of life. One hallmark of this view of life is that it is based in spirituality. Notwithstanding language and worship-related differences, countless lineages of people born in the Bharatiya sub-continent have identified themselves as Hindu from time immemorial. Deep identification with this view of life has led to a distinct outlook and personal character of these people.

"एकं सत् विप्राः बहुधा वदन्ति।"(*Ekam Sat* Vipraha: *Bahudha Vadanti*) "Truth is one, but the wise call it by different names." This shloka from the *Rig Veda* means the Truth or God is one but there may be many paths to its realisation and all paths are equal. This tenet of the Hindu view of life has been well ingrained in the Hindu psyche and the people here have been practising this for long. Jews, Parsis and Syrian Christians fleeing religious persecution and conversion in their countries of origin sought asylum in different kingdoms of Bharat, at various points in time. The itinerants, though ethnically, religiously and linguistically alien here, were given equally liberal and respectful treatment by the kings and the locals who granted them asylum. They were welcomed, accepted and nurtured within each of those geographies. This behaviour was an outcome of their adherence to the

Hindu view of life. To see unity in diversity is the hallmark of this view of life. We've held that one Spirit *(Chaitanya)* manifests in different life forms and therefore the ability to see the underlying oneness among seemingly apparent diversities is the default view of Bharat. This is why 'diversity' is not perceived as 'difference' here. Bharat has the unmatched capacity to take all the apparently diverse expressions together while protecting the uniqueness of each of those units while assimilating them into one cohesive whole. The third uniqueness of Bharat is the recognition of the fact that every soul (man or woman) is potentially divine. The very goal of human life is to manifest the divinity within to ultimately be one with the Supreme Divinity *(Moksha)*. Different people may walk different paths to manifest their divinity and each of those paths may be called their religion or faith. The body of thought with an amalgamation of these unique qualities has been popularly perceived as "*Hindutva*" around the world. Whether someone refers to it as Bharatiya, *Sanatan*, Indic or any other name, the essence is the same.

Now the question is which among these unique features is un-relatable or offensive to the Sarana people or other Scheduled Tribes?

The first president of independent Bharat, Dr. S. Radhakrishnan referred to *Hindutva* as the "Commonwealth of All Religions". Swami Vivekananda in his 1893 Chicago address at the World's Parliament of Religions described *Hindutva* as the "Mother of all religions".

The view that sees diverse people as one, that accepts and assimilates different paths and faiths is what *Hindutva* is. This civilisation that predates more than 10,000 years has seen people worship different deities at varied points in time. To be able to keep pace with evolving faith-based norms and to accept changes is what *Hindutva* is all about. Swami Vivekananda propounded this very fact by reciting this shloka in his famous 1893 Chicago address.

> त्रयी साङ्ख्यं योगः पशुपतिमतं वैष्णवमिति प्रभिन्ने प्रस्थाने परमिदमदः पथ्यमिति च।
> रुचीनां वैचित्र्यादृजुकुटिल नानापथजुषां नृणामेको गम्यस्त्वमसि पयसामर्णव इव॥

Meaning: O Almighty! Innumerable paths lead one to you—Sankhya, Vaishnav, Shaiva, Vedic ways of life, etc. As per their orientation, people choose any one path, but like many rivers eventually converge into one sea, all these paths lead to the same, Eternal Truth. It is true that regardless of the path we choose we can all realise the Divine.

The beauty of this Bharatiya view of life is that it recognises the fact that in tandem with man's continuous evolution, he is sure to discover and worship newer deities. Nurturing the old while making space for newer deities is *Hindutva.*

Gurudev Rabindranath Thakur explicitly stated: "To experience unity in diversity and to establish unity amongst variety—this is the inherent *dharma* (the spirit) of Bharat. Bharatvarsh neither interpreted diversities as differences nor considered the outsider as an enemy. Thus, without sacrificing our own, without destroying others, Bharat aspires to assign a distinct place to everyone in one vast ecosystem. Thus, it is willing to accept all ways of life and acknowledges the greatness of each in its own way.

"As Bharatvarsh possesses this trait, we would never get frightened by visualising any society as our opponent. With every new dissension, we inevitably will grow. The Hindu, Bauddha, Muslim and Christian would not fight with each other and die in Bharat. Rather they would find a balance, a meeting point here. This balance will not be non-Hindu, but very specifically Hindu. However foreign may be its body parts, its life and spirit will be of Bharat."

This holistic approach and assimilation are intrinsic to the Hindu view of life. Given this definition, what deems Sarana and Scheduled Tribe members as radically distinct from *Hindutva* is a mystery. Because *Hindutva* does not emphasise the Almighty to be one definitive form, rather appreciating the common thread underlying all manifestations of the Divine is *Hindutva.*

Some years ago, a survey was conducted in North-Eastern states in the Assam region which has a sizable population of the Scheduled Tribes. Representatives of 18 Scheduled Tribes present at the conference expounded their responses over: 1. Their concept of God. 2. Their view of Earth. 3. What do they pray for? 4. Their concepts of virtue and sin. 5. Their opinion over faith based practices of those from other religions. And lastly, 6. If they wish to compel followers of other faiths and religions to forcefully convert to their religion.

Their responses were consistent with the views of a common Hindu living elsewhere in the country. It was surprising for the surveyors to note that despite apparent language differences their beliefs are more or less similar and reflective of the age-old spiritual tenets of the Hindu belief system. That which unifies the diverse religious and faith-based beliefs and practices of this geo-cultural unit of Bharat is *Hindutva* and our spirituality-based holistic, unifying and all-encompassing Hindu view of life.

The Semitic basis of Abrahamic religions like Christianity and Islam prevents those religions from having a similar view of human life. In fact, those religions divide the human race into binaries, which cannot coexist in harmony. It is for the same reason that these religions have a bloody, violent, deceptive and greed-ridden history of conversion. Among the tribals of the North-Eastern states of Bharat also the Christian Church propaganda to impose the view that those tribes are non-Hindu has been underway for a long time now, first with the support of the British colonial ruler and later by those in power after our Independence. This is the direct cause of the emergence and strengthening of separatist militant groups in the region. As part of their agenda, they lured the people of the land with the temptation of a new and separate identity and uprooted their cultural roots to start "soul harvesting". But the tribals of the region have understood that this barter with the Christian missionaries may be too costly. It can lead to the complete disappearance and annihilation of the rich, faith-based realisations of their ancestors. They also realise assimilating with the Hindu society will prevent such a fate, and in this way, they can preserve and pass on their unique customs and traditions to future generations. This belief is taking a firm hold over their consciousness with each passing day and has resulted in the emergence of indigenous faith movements like "Donyi Polo" and "Seng Khasi" in those areas. Leaders of groups like the Sarana and other Scheduled Tribes must learn from the experiences of the organisers of these indigenous faith movements reconnecting to their roots so as to preserve their unique cultural and faith-based practices and further enrich their culture and people.

With "ईशावास्यं इदं सर्वं यत्किञ्च जगत्यां जगत्" meaning, "the entire creation is inhabited by the Supreme Spirit or *Isha*" as the basis of faith mankind invoked, venerated and worshipped the formless Divine Truth even at the time when gods and goddesses hadn't yet been personified. Thereafter that same Truth began to be pursued by the means of worship of various gods with a definite form. However, the worship of nature and that of the five basic elements is eternal. Many self-realised men and women *(avatar)* added newer paths to the list of faiths, yet the worship of nature in the form of worship of earth, water, fire, air and space continued. Therefore, nature-worship is eternal, only newer practices and dimensions emerged with the march of time. Nature worship also features in several forms in the Hindu culture. It is for this reason that Hindu society sees itself as one with those who strictly worship only nature. But certain elements are bent on projecting the variations in practices as differences and disillusioning people.

In fact, it is not only true of the Sarana or the Scheduled Tribes. For the last several years, organised drives to brainwash members of many communities are underway across Bharat into believing that they are not Hindu. Operations to splinter Hindu society are being carried out at an international level by distorting and erasing from people's memory the propensity of *Hindutva* to appreciate oneness in diversity. Instead, they highlight and misrepresent the diversities among different faiths as differences among people. If Hindus remain united, society remains united and hence the country remains united. And the country will progress only if it is united. All those elements who have a vested interest in preventing the country from progressing are engrossed in the fragmentation of Bharat.

Several fact-based, well-researched books that illuminate the details about such efforts (breaking India forces) and drives are available in the market. One key player in that scheme is the church. Their aim—to increase the number of believers in Bharat by converting more people—finds an explicit mention on the websites of all their proselytising agencies. Some agencies that have assumed fake identities are working to first create illusion, then opposition and then fragmentation in the society, which would ultimately result in separatism. They connote conversion as "harvesting". These organised efforts of "harvesting" have been ongoing since the British era. But Bharat's cultural roots run deep and are strong. Many ascetics and enlightened people took to reigniting the spiritual and cultural conscience of our society from time to time. No tribe or caste is devoid of the inheritance of such knowledge, as such ascetics were born in every tribe and caste that ever lived on this land to share the nectar of their realisations. It is for this reason that the conversion efforts of missionaries have been comparatively less fruitful in Bharat, thus compelling those agencies to adopt newer tactics to fulfil their agenda. The elements that aim to fragment Bharat work closely and cohesively to actualise each of their agendas. Incessant efforts of the ascetics and social reformers to facilitate socio-religious and spiritual and cultural enlightenment generation after generation have resulted in a firm cultural foundation of the society. Therefore, successful conversion requires uprooting the deep religio-cultural roots of the potential converts. Where the foundation is weak and roots bare loose, harvesting is easier. Therefore, brainwashing drives wherein false and unreasonable claims are being concocted. We will all have to remain alert and aware of these dangers.

Famous Bharatiya poet, Prasoon Joshi, writes in one of his poems:

"उखडे उखडे क्यों हो वृक्ष सूख जाओगे
जितनी गहरी जड़ें तुम्हारी उतने ही तुम हरियाओगे"
Gather the soil around you, oh tree,
Else you will wither.
The deeper your roots,
Greener your leaves will be

It is not a mere coincidence that the two states that are at the epicentre of the activities and that form the subject matter of this write-up have been hotspots of conversion activities. Uprooting is imperative for harvesting. If we see and analyse the forces working on this agenda and their funding sources, we can understand that creating such misconceptions for uprooting various groups from their cultural moorings is part of a larger conspiracy hatched over a period of time.t.

Endnote :

This article first appeared in *The Sunday Guardian* on May 6, 2021.

20

Article 370 Went Against the Idea of Bharat

The Bharatiya government's decision to amend Article 370 and abrogate Article 35A, combined with the bifurcation of the Jammu and Kashmir (J&K) state into two union territories has surprised, baffled and shocked many. During the debate in the parliament, the opposition parties argued that this move was unconstitutional and against the people of Jammu and Kashmir.

The Constitutional Position

Bharat, at the time of independence on 15 August 1947, comprised more than 560 princely states. They were given only two options, either to join Bharat or Pakistan. No state was permitted to remain independent by the outgoing British government. The Instrument of Accession to Bharat signed by the ruler of Jammu-Kashmir state, Maharaja Hari Singh, on 26 October 1947, was no different from all the other princely states that acceded to Bharat.

But before the Instrument of Accession was signed, the Pakistan army invaded Kashmir in the guise of Kabailis (tribals) to forcibly capture the entire Kashmir state. Though the state of Jammu & Kashmir was saved with the timely intervention of Bharatiya forces, some territory of the state remained under the illegal occupation of Pakistan, which is known as Pakistan-occupied Jammu & Kashmir, PoJK. The process of accession was complete, but as the matter was pending with the UN and some territory was under illegal occupation of Pakistan, the Bharatiya government wanted some time to normalise the situation for implementing the Bharatiya Constitution in totality to the newly accessed J&K state. For this, Article

370 was invoked till things got normal and it was mentioned that it would be temporary in nature. Defence, security, judiciary and foreign affairs were under the Central government and all other matters were to be dealt with by the J&K state assembly.

But because of Pandit Jawaharlal Nehru's bias towards Sheikh Abdullah and his communal politics, Article 35A was introduced undemocratically, surreptitiously and merely by Presidential Order in 1954 without the approval of the parliament. This was the main culprit and cause of all the trouble that gave the state powers to decide upon who the permanent resident of J&K state would be. This Article was anti Scheduled Castes (SC) and Scheduled Tribes (ST), and discriminatory to women.

The state of J&K does not comprise people living only in the Kashmir valley, but also includes people of the Jammu and Ladakh regions. The benefits or losses due to Article 370 should be reviewed in its entirety and not just be limited to the valley. Under the garb of this article, Pakistan-sponsored terrorism and separatist forces were fostered to keep the state unstable in the name of religion and politics, warring against the Bharatiya security forces that were brought here to protect the people.

This act of amending Article 370 and abrogating Article 35A to extend all the constitutional provisions to the state of J&K by the Government of Bharat is nothing but fulfilment of the promise given to the people of Bharat.

Part 2 of the Constitution of Jammu and Kashmir, 1957 mentions in Article 3, titled "Relationship of the State with the Union of Bharat" that: "The state of Jammu and Kashmir is and shall be an integral part of the Union of Bharat."

"Article 370, Temporary provision with respect to the State of J&K" Section 3 mentions that: "Notwithstanding anything in the foregoing provisions of this Article, the President may, by public notification, declare that this Article shall cease to be operative or shall be operative only with such exceptions and modifications and from such date as he may specify."

In 1964, a private bill to amend Article 370 by a member, Prakashvir Shastri got unanimous support from all the members belonging to various parties in the parliament. Those who spoke in support of this bill to delete Article 370 included socialists like Ram Manohar Lohia, Madhu Limaye, Hari Vishnu Kamath, and communists like N.C. Chatterjee, Sarjoo Pandey, MPs from Congress like Bhagvat Jha Azad, S.M. Banerjee, K. Hanumanthaiya and four MPs from Jammu & Kashmir. There was a consensus among the MPs that Article 370 was a hindrance in the development of J&K. The MPs, especially those from J&K, emphasised that it was a threat to national unity and integrity.

Gopal Datt Mengi, MP from J&K lamented that Article 370 was a "curse" for J&K. He said that "Article 370 does not give us any special status, rather it has made us second-class citizens in our own country. It is a wall between India and J&K." Another MP, Abdul Ghani Goni from J&K, who was also a close associate of Sheikh Abdullah, brought to the notice of the House the hindrances created in the overall development of the state due to the implementation of Article 370. He unhesitatingly said that "the then Prime Minister of J&K, Bakshi Ghulam Mohammad had moved for the abrogation of Article 370, but the central government did not agree. I do not know whether the central government is under the influence of the West or wants an appeasement policy towards Pakistan…they want to please their neighbours at our cost." Adding to the above points of discontent one more MP from J&K, Syed Nasir Husain Samnani, asked the House the reasons for not abrogating Article 370. He asked what the fault of the people of J&K was that Article 370 was not abrogated: "We, the people of Kashmir never demanded that we should be treated differently. We do not want Article 370. I want to end this curse in my lifetime, for my safety, for my children's safety, for the safety of our future generations." Despite such historical support, the bill was not passed because it was a private members' bill.

In 1994, the Congress-led government under the leadership of P.V. Narasimha Rao passed a historic unanimous resolution in the parliament of Bharat that J&K state is an integral part of Bharat and the only outstanding issue is to get PoJK back from Pakistan. This shows that the removal of the temporary Articles 370 and 35A was a national consensus. That is why though a major opposition party, Congress, opposed the move of the present government officially, there were rumblings and divisions in the opinion of the Congress party itself.

All these facts make the constitutional position clear that Article 370 was always temporary in nature and had to go someday. This decision will help all the residents of J&K to join the nation in its journey towards development, prosperity and democratic practices. Under the alibi of special status, which continued to be temporary even after 70 long years, benefits of reservation in education and jobs were deprived to scheduled castes and scheduled tribes. Because of the restrictions on purchasing land, no investors were ready to invest in establishing premier educational institutions, multi-speciality hospitals, and industries, depriving the people of J&K the facility of quality education, health services and job opportunities for the youth.

Taking Democracy To J & K

Article 370 was a temporary provision and our constitution-makers were clear about it. Still, under the guise of special status, only politics was played. The misuse of Article 370 led to the insertion of Article 35A through a Presidential Order, without any parliamentary approval. This provision created many constitutional anomalies and deprived J&K of the real taste of democracy and governance.

This deadly combination of Articles 370 and 35A, dynastic politics, nepotism and communalism was in play, thereby misusing the large amount of funds allocated by the central government for the development of the entire J&K state. A major chunk of the allocated funds was surreptitiously routed to benefit largely a few dynastic families and some separatist groups resorting to terrorism. In other Bharatiya states, there is a constitutional provision to appoint a Lokayukta (judicial authority to oversee the utilisation of government funds and curb corruption in the system). This special status of J&K prevented the appointment of the Lokayukta, lest all the political corruption and misuse of the allocated funds got exposed.

The RTI Act also has helped curb corruption and misuse of power in Bharat.

The recent move to amend Article 370 and abrogate Article 35A will bring RTI Act and Lokayukta to check corrupt practices by the administration, helping clean and smooth governance. This decision has put all women on par with men with regard to choosing their life partners. Under the garb of special status, injustice was done to the women in J&K. A man from J&K could marry any woman from outside the state, but if a woman married a person from outside of J&K, she would be deprived of any rights in her ancestral property.

The decision has also removed the injustice suffered by 25,000 Gorkhas living in the state.

Gorkhas settled in Jammu & Kashmir in the 19th century. A majority of them were soldiers who fought in the ranks of Maharaja Ranjit Singh of Punjab, who ruled J&K till 1846. This proves that they were staying and serving the people in Jammu & Kashmir even before 1846. Article 35A deprived these people of their rights as they were not given the Permanent Resident Certificate.

This historic decision will help 22,000 families of West Pakistan refugees to live a dignified life as free citizens of Bharat. Even after more than 70 years, these West Pakistan refugees were bearing the brunt of being refugees and could not be a part of the national mainstream.

The Valmikis, who belong to the Scheduled Castes, were brought to work as sweepers from Punjab in the year 1957. Nobody among the 15,000 Valmikis today, however educated, is entitled to do any job other than as sweepers. Now all this inhuman injustice that was shielded under the draconian Article 35A and undemocratically put into practice is undone.

This important decision has kindled hope in Kashmiri Pandits to end the life of living as refugees in their own country and opened the option and possibility of resettling in their ancestral land. The darkest day in the history of Bharat and humanity was the violent and forcible expulsion of Kashmiri Pandits who were living peacefully in the Kashmir valley and greatly contributing to the economy of the state. Only because they were Hindus nobody raised this issue of blatant violation of human rights.

The people of Ladakh, mostly Bauddha and Shia Muslims, were remotely connected with the Jammu and Kashmir region because of its special topography and extreme climate. This area was subjected to neglect and stepmotherly treatment by the incumbent governments. They had a long-standing demand for a separate union territory, which has been granted and all people cutting across political identities are happy there.

During the discussion in the parliament, some leaders termed 5 August a dark day for Kashmir. However, in reality, the surreptitious introduction of Article 35A in 1954 was a dark day for the state of J&K. Moreover, a darker day in the history of J&K was in 1989 when peaceful, wealth-creating Kashmiri Pandits, Hindus, were forcibly ousted from the Valley, after being terrorised at gunpoint. 5 August can be a dark day for only those who have indulged in dynastic politics and patronised and commercialised terrorism in the name of Islam.

The incumbent BJP government has all reasons to take this much-needed and long-awaited step to remove the constitutional anomaly as it has consistently put forth its stand regarding this temporary provision of the J&K state. The founder of Bharatiya Jan Sangh, the party which eventually became BJP, Dr. Syama Prasad Mookerjee led an agitation for the complete integration of J&K for which he was forcibly jailed. Later he died there in suspicious circumstances. The BJP has always demanded and promised the abrogation of Article 370 if voted to power. In this recent general election also the incumbent BJP had clearly mentioned that if voted to power they will take measures to abrogate this temporary provision. The people of Bharat have given the BJP a stronger mandate to fulfil the promises given in their manifesto.

In 1953, RSS passed a resolution and supported the movement led by J&K Praja Parishad for "complete integration of J&K state with Bharat". Since then RSS has passed resolutions innumerable times and occasionally conducted people awareness campaigns throughout the country about the anomaly of Article 370, a temporary provision. The last resolution passed by RSS was in 2010, where it stated: "Article 370, which was included in our constitution as a 'temporary and transient provision', instead of being abrogated, continues to be a tool in the hands of the separatist and secessionist elements."

As usual, much has been said unfoundedly about RSS and its misconstrued communal agenda. What RSS thinks about Muslims in India is very clearly elaborated in an interview of Shri Guruji, the then *sarsanghachalak* of RSS, given to senior journalist Dr. Saifuddin Jilani in 1972.

I reproduce an excerpt here for the benefit of readers.

"**Dr. Jilani**: Much has been said about 'Indianisation' and a lot of confusion has arisen over it. Could you please tell me how to remove the confusion?

"**Shri Guruji**: 'Indianisation' was of course the slogan given by Jana Sangh. Why should there be such confusion? 'Indianisation' does not mean converting all people to Hinduism.

"Let us all realise that we are all the children of this soil and we must have our allegiance to this land. We belong to the same society and share common ancestors. We also share common aspirations. Understanding this is 'Indianisation' in the true sense.

"Indianisation does not mean that one should be asked to quit his religious system. We neither said this nor are we going to say so. Rather we believe that a single religious system for the entire human society is not suitable."

During a recently held lecture series, Dr. Mohan Bhagwat said, "the Sangh works for the feeling of fraternity and the only basis for this fraternity is unity in diversity.

"The world terms this traditional thought process as '*Hindutva*'. That is why when we say our nation is a '*Hindu Rashtra*', it in no way conveys that we don't need Muslims. The day it will be said that Muslims are not required, it won't remain '*Hindutva*'." And there is no need to say separately, that this applies also to the state of J&K which inherits thousands of years of civilization like the rest of Bharat.

After two weeks of this historic decision, I had a chance to visit Jammu, Srinagar, Kargil and Leh as part of my routine travel plan. I got a chance to interact with some local people. The people of Kargil and Leh were happy about getting the UT status, which was their long-standing unanimous demand. I met one Muslim advocate from Zanskar Valley who was earlier with the People's Democratic Party (PDP) but was expelled for supporting the demand of UT for Ladakh. In Jammu and Srinagar, I was asked a common question by locals as to wouldn't it have been better if Jammu and Kashmir were made two separate UTs instead of one. I replied that that would be wrong as it was against the very idea of Bharat and an endorsement of the idea of Pakistan that Hindus and Muslims cannot live together. It is the idea of Bharat that irrespective of religious or other diversities we have a long tradition and history of living together in harmony. That is the very idea of Bharat.

Endnote :

This article first appeared in *The Sunday Guardian* on September 14, 2019.

21

Media : A Bharatiya Perspective

Trends like fake news, agenda-building, predatory mentality and media trials in the name of competitive news compilation plague the current media industry. The majority of these, it would appear, are brought on by a lack of news from a Bharatiya standpoint or by the Western influence, and getting rid of these is a challenge staring at the world of news today. I believe it is the distinction between the Bharatiya and non-Bharatiya view of life that is responsible for the differences in the representation of the news and other media. Fritjof Capra, a renowned Austrian-American particle physicist, identified the fundamental distinction between the two views of life. He stated - "The paradigm that is now receding has dominated our culture for several hundred years during which it has shaped our modern Western society and has significantly influenced the rest of the world. This paradigm consists of a number of entrenched ideas and values, among them the view of the universe as a mechanical system composed of elementary blocks, the view of the human body as a machine, the view of life in society as a competitive struggle for existence, belief in unlimited material, economic and technological growth, and last not the least- the belief that a society in which the female is everywhere subsumed under the male is one that follows a basic law of nature. These entire assumptions have been fatefully challenged by recent events. And indeed a radical revision of them is occurring."

"The new paradigm may be called a holistic worldview, seeing the world as an integrated whole rather than a dissociated collection of parts. It may also be called an ecological view, if the term ecological is used in a much broader and deeper sense than usual. Deep ecological awareness recognises the fundamental interdependence of all phenomena and the fact that as individuals and societies we are all embedded in (and ultimately depend on) the cyclic process of nature."

"Ultimately, deep ecological awareness is spiritual or religious awareness. When the concept of the human spirit is understood as the mode of consciousness in which the individual feels a sense of belonging, of connectedness, to the cosmos as a whole, it becomes clear that ecological awareness is spiritual in its deepest essence. It is therefore not surprising that the emerging new vision of reality based on deep ecological awareness is consistent with the so-called perennial philosophy of spiritual traditions."

The new paradigm that Fritjof Capra talked about resonates with the Bharatiya view of life. The Bharatiya perspective of news is fundamentally based on the Bharatiya view of life. Therefore, by acquainting oneself with the fundamental facets of the Bharatiya view of life one can easily comprehend the Bharatiya perspective of news.

The uniqueness of the Bharatiya view of life is that it is integral and holistic because it is based in spirituality. It sees the entire creation as interconnected and interdependent. Adherence to this view of life has shaped the unique persona of Bharatiya society. There are four major characteristics of this persona.

First, we believe— *'Ekam Sat Vipraha, Bahudha Vadanti'* - that is, Truth is one, scholars address it by different names. There can be various ways to know or reach the truth and they all are equal. Second, the same *chaitanya* or Supreme Being is manifested in diverse forms. Therefore, Bharat has the vision to see and experience the underlying unity in the diverse outward manifestations. The third characteristic, which relates to the current subject of discussion, is that there is potential divinity within every individual or that every soul is potentially divine. The goal of human life is to manifest the divinity within by controlling nature, internal and external. Do it either by work, worship, psychic control or meditation, either of these four or more or all and be free. This liberation (*Moksha*) or being one with the Supreme being who manifests in the entire universe, being the ultimate goal of life, all activities lead the journey of life towards it. Therefore, it has been said, *"Saa Vidya Yaa Vimuktaye"*- Knowledge is one that liberates and for art it is said, *"Saa Kala Yaa Vimuktaye"* – Art is one that liberates, and so on. Every individual is free to choose his/her own path of liberation *(Moksha)*. This signifies the fourth characteristic of the unique persona of Bharatiya society and is the precursor of Bharat's spiritual democracy.

Now there are successive steps to getting liberated. Close your "I" and open your eyes. When one does that, the circumference of 'we' gradually expands to include and experience one's own self, family, clan, neighbourhood, society, village, district, state, country, all of humanity and non-human creation as one. Despite one's existence as a distinct entity, one feels intimately connected with all. Sant Tukaram Maharaj expressed this very intimacy when he remarked, "Trees, plants and all the creatures in the forest are my close relatives" (वृक्ष वल्ली आम्हा सोयरे वनचरे). It is natural that one would then feel the need to do something for those we feel are our own. To do something for and to give back with a sense of belongingness to all, is called *dharma*. This *dharma* is different from religion. The closest term for religion is *Upasana* (worship). *Dharma* does not discriminate. It connects, unites, binds and holds all together.

Sister Nivedita, a disciple of Swami Vivekananda, once remarked "the society, whose members instead of withholding their remuneration with themselves share it with the larger society, with the accumulated remunerations (the social capital) build a wealthy and prosperous society, which in turn makes each individual of the society wealthy and prosperous. But in a society where people hoard their remuneration with themselves, instead of sharing it with the rest of the society, only a few individuals become wealthy and prosperous, while the larger society remains poor."

Dharma is best propagated by actions. Therefore it is said आचारः प्रथमो धर्मः ("*Aacharah Prathamo Dharmah*"), meaning, as per the enlightened souls, our (good) conduct is our foremost duty *(Dharma)*. *Dharma* does not discriminate. Therefore, nurturing *dharma* is equivalent to nurturing life. The reason being, "*Dharmo Rakshati Rakshitah*" – *Dharma* when protected, protects all.

Another significant feature of Bharat is that state power was never paramount in Bharat. The concept of a welfare state is not our tradition—only a few important matters of the society were addressed by the state, and for the majority of matters, the society had its own arrangements, independent of the state.

In his essay '*Swadeshi Samaj*,' Gurudev Rabindranath Thakur claims that "'*Swadeshi* society' is the one that depends the least on the state for its needs." He wrote, "welfare state is not a Bharatiya tradition. Barring defence and security, judiciary and foreign affairs the people had their autonomous systems for all other matters like education, healthcare, industry, trade & commerce, temples, fairs, art & aesthetics, music, dance, drama, pilgrimage, etc. that did not depend on the state. *Sanatan* Bharat did not rely on the state treasury to fund these activities of the society. The society had its independent arrangement which had *dharma* as its guiding principle." This '*dharma*' does not imply religion or worship. To give to the society as one would to one's own family, to give back, is considered *dharma*. Therefore upholding *dharma* enhances and enriches the social capital or capital of the whole society. And it is on the basis of this social capital that the society can run its own order, independent of the state. Most systems of the society function on the basis of the capital earned through *dharma*. In this sense, *dharma* was and still is the foundation of our society.

The coronavirus crisis has been a global concern since the start of the year 2020. Contrary to popular belief, Bharat's war with Corona is unique in comparison to that of the other nations. State power is paramount in most countries of the world. All the arrangements in society are based on state power, and hence it is called a 'welfare state.' In the face of such a calamity, the state apparatus and administration are proactive and the people also expect the government agencies to act promptly. But the scenario in Bharat is different. In the Bharatiya tradition, society has an independent existence and structure. It has its own systems. 'We' is a combination of all this together.

This 'We' alludes to the people of this society, our *rashtra* – the nation. Now in this context, it is vital to understand that our concept of *rashtra* is distinct from the 'nation-state' concept of the West. In the year 2018 when former President Dr. Pranab Mukherjee addressed Sangh *swayamsevaks* (volunteers) in Nagpur, he emphasised the same thing. He said, "The Western concept of a state-based nation and the Bharatiya concept of a nation based on the Bharatiya view of life are both different." Because of this fundamental conceptual difference, whenever a natural or man-made tragedy strikes, the entire society in Bharat becomes an active contributor in the relief and restoration efforts alongside the administration.

During the lockdown following the Corona pandemic outbreak, 5 lakh 7 thousand volunteers of Rashtriya Swayamsevak Sangh distributed ration kits to crores of families through *Sewa Bharati* at 92,656 locations throughout Bharat, from Arunachal Pradesh to Kashmir and Kanyakumari. They also distributed millions of masks, donated more than 60 thousand units of blood, assisted millions of migrant labourers, as well as nomadic tribes, members of transgender groups, those in the flesh trade, monkeys dependent on pilgrims at religious places, and fed the birds and the animals too. Their political allegiance notwithstanding, RSS *swayamsevaks* assisted the state administration wherever the administration sought help in crowd management, registering the names of the migrant workers and even testing people in infected settlements in many places.

Not only the Sangh, but many socio-religious institutions like monasteries, temples and gurudwaras also participated in this social *yajna* of the fight against corona. This is society's own system, besides the government system. It has happened only in Bharat. Outside Bharat, in many countries where social activism to support the society during the pandemic was noted, it was attributed mainly to the people of Bharatiya origin who settled there. This is the hallmark of Bharat – the Bharatiya way of life. The feeling of "*vayam rashtrangabhuta*"- (we are the constituents of the nation) makes this possible. The acute awareness of being a part of this colossal 'we' offers inspiration in extending selfless service, the life threat notwithstanding and free from expectations of making a name or fame. "People living in all states, literate, illiterate, wealthy, poor, villagers or city-dwellers, townsfolk and forest-dwellers are all my own people." Inculcating this sentiment implies awakening a nation. It is then that the consciousness expands to successively include the self, family, clan, neighbourhood, village, district, state, nation, the entire world and all creations into the scope of one's own identity. These different layers are not in conflict but are mutually complementary. In the absence of any perceptible conflicts among these layers, all components function mutually complementarily.

The incessant endeavour of the society to harmonise multiple components is the basis of the eternal, spirituality-based, integral and holistic view of life of Bharat. This view of life is what gives Bharat its unique identity since time immemorial. Our identification with these various identities of society is the very reason why 'we' have the capacity to have a feeling of affinity for these ever-expanding layers of existence. That feeling of affinity propels action in times of crisis. This strengthens the bond further and weaves the weft of society to create an organised society.

The lockdown brought all economic activities to a grinding halt. The magnitude of this unprecedented challenge induced a multitude of challenges. Arrangements and efforts to address those challenges were not free of shortcomings. It is painful that ordinary, innocent and helpless people had to bear the consequences of those shortcomings. In a democratic setup, it is natural for such issues to become the material of public discourse, media and other discussions. But a few members of society—politicians, journalists and writers—are oblivious of the fact that they too are a part of the same society. To blow matters out of proportion, generalise a condition and create the false impression of an all-pervasive gloom demoralises the entire society. It drags the well-meaning officers, workers and volunteers into a psychological courtroom, raising many question marks and in return creating general unrest. There are no two ways about it; what is wrong is wrong. But when publicly scrutinising such matters, having one's allegiance with the truth, and carefully avoiding the portrayal of an inflated, fallacious picture is our social and moral responsibility, owing to the value system rooted in the feeling *"vayam rashtrangabhuta"*.

It was not an easy task to make arrangements for infection control, keep a tab on its spread in places where there was crowding and above all to make arrangements for food, water, temporary shelter and finally the isolation of labourer families, who were in transit along with the elderly and the children. While inadequacies in arrangements were noted in a few places, at other places people lacked the practice and patience to adhere to the rules of such arrangements, which caused them immense hardships. It was heart-wrenching to see their pictures and to hear the tales of their agony. This was a much-debated topic in the media. The opposition and ruling parties got into verbal duels. Notwithstanding these arguments, the fact remains that more than 50 lakh labourers were safely ferried back to their respective villages in the states of Bihar, Uttar Pradesh, Madhya Pradesh, Jharkhand, and Orissa among other states, with the help of the resources of the government machinery and social organisations. These facts ought to be mentioned alongside other pieces of criticism in the media. How may the generalisation of a shortcoming, portrayal of an inflated, fallacious picture and deflation of the spirits of the larger, well-meaning society be justified? However, such conduct is commonplace in the aforementioned reportages and the sole reason behind such erroneous conduct is the dulling of the feeling of "*vayam rashtrangabhuta*". For those engaging in such irresponsible conduct in this society, a specific category of this society, its oddities and poverty, its illiteracy and squalor all seem like resource material in fulfilling their "agenda". This is owing to the failure to incorporate one's society in their concept of 'self', which may be because of either pursuing agenda-driven journalism to blindly favour an ideology or because of total amnesia of the *dharma* of journalism.

It frequently happens that events are reported with bias in the form of news because of a lack of understanding and sensitivity towards this sense of obligation to build a society. A leading English newspaper once claimed that the members of the Dalit community were barred from taking part in Holi celebrations in a village in Haryana. I requested the *Prant Prachar Pramukh* (Media Relations in charge of the state) of Haryana to investigate the matter, who subsequently reported that the Holi programme was attended by everyone in the said village. Only four to five young individuals who misbehaved when under the influence of alcohol were forbidden. Those young men belonged to the scheduled caste. But all the other people of that caste took part in the Holi celebrations. Those who were barred were not excluded because of their caste but rather because of their inappropriate behaviour after drinking. Thereafter, the village *Sarpanch* (Chief) offered an explanation for this. I do not claim that caste-based discrimination doesn't prevail anywhere. Unfortunately, it does happen, and it should be vehemently opposed.

However, in this case had the reporter taken the time to carefully examine the causes, inaccurate news that could potentially fuel caste animosity wouldn't have been published. Such presentations compromise the *dharma* of journalism in addition to undermining the process of building a community and weaving the social fabric.

It is unfortunate that at times persistent efforts have been made to portray Rashtriya Swayamsevak Sangh—an organisation dedicated to public welfare—as a proponent of a narrow worldview, by spinning a tale based on untrue and unfounded statements. An incident comes to mind in this context.

A communist leader's daughter once declared that the RSS would commemorate Nathuram Godse's 100th birthday in Uttar Pradesh during a Communist Party event in Vijayawada, Andhra Pradesh. This news was reported in three columns in a popular English daily in South Bharat. Now, it is common sense that a Communist leader does not have the authority to declare any Sangh program. And if she did, it is that reporter's journalistic '*dharma*' (that is if the leftists believe in '*dharma*') to verify the facts with a Sangh functionary. Nevertheless, this did not happen. Eventually, Sangh *swayamsevaks* challenged that statement in the Press Council and the publisher was compelled to publish a clarification from RSS. Despite these instances, Sangh is constantly working in the society to build a competent force that is always active and prepared to handle any crisis.

Everyone working across all fields, institutions, and organisations—not just the media—should be mindful of the fact that "I too am an integral part of this society." Although it is an inevitable aspect of life, competition is not the end goal of human existence. This society which has a heritage, its structures and its system independent of the state, the necessary coordination, cooperation and collaboration imperative for its uninterrupted flow must be kept in mind and all work plans should be centred around this thought with an acute awareness of our boundaries and limits.

While competing, it is necessary to take care that this structure, which took many years and several generations to be created, does not get uprooted because of anyone's selfishness. 'I am also an integral constituent of this nation', should be our guiding philosophy.

I recall one incident dating back to 1992. Having recently landed in the United States I soon learnt of this then-popular "GUN" tee-shirt brand that was apparently a rage amongst American teens. With his tee-shirt sales hitting the roof, the producer made huge profits. But there was another section in American society that started to point at the potential threat of those tee shirts—a spike in violent tendencies among teens. Concerned, they stirred a movement in society demanding the producer to withdraw the GUN tee-shirts from the market shelves. Unwilling, but eventually foreseeing the threat of a complete boycott of all his products, the producer relented and withdrew that particular product. In a subsequent press interview, the journalists quizzed him: "When the dangers your product posed were brought to your notice early on, why did you not withdraw it immediately?" To this, he replied: "Look, I am here in the business of making money, not morality." This implied that maybe there exist two viewpoints in business—to view one's society as a mere resource or to consider it as an extension of one's own self.

In the past few years, adherents of a particular ideology have started using the media as a tool in their arsenal. By disseminating absurdity, they "misuse" the "media" to sow the seeds of dissension in the society and foment strife against those who disagree with them or hold different opinions. All this is done in the blind pursuit of political power. Since they lack the sense of "*vayam rashtrangabhuta*" they behave like vultures looking for 'opportunities' to feed on carcasses. When the Parliament House was attacked by terrorists, one senior journalist is believed to have shamelessly admitted that his initial reaction upon hearing the news was that it would make an excellent exclusive for his channel, and he wished to be the only one reporting it before other channels could. He had no concern for the safety of the Parliament House or the nation's parliamentarians. We are also aware of how, during the 26/11 Mumbai terrorist attack, the strategic movements of the officials were broadcast live in the name of exclusive coverage without taking the safety of the security personnel into consideration, which was total malfeasance.

It is also imperative that we recall how the hijacking of an Air India flight was covered by the Bharatiya media, where the hijackers demanded the release of terrorists held by the Bharatiya government. The media utterly failed to take into account the psychological and mental stress that was mounting on the government and security personnel as they endlessly flashed photographs of the irate relatives of passengers who were trapped. This is a plain predatory mentality.

I can also recall a report that contrasts the aforementioned instances. In 2001, a massive earthquake wreaked havoc in Kutch. One photojournalist uploaded a picture of an elderly man standing next to his home turned into a heap of debris. The photo carried a caption as a way of sending a message of optimism to all his readers: "Saw your power, Nature, now you see mine." Such a caption, in my opinion, is an attempt to instil hope in such a devastating situation, thereby contributing to the process of shaping the society.

The phrase "*Vayam Rashtre Jagrayaam Purohita*" (We purohits would keep the nation awake) means that certain members of society, such as journalists and media professionals, should be more invested in the welfare of the society. Information first enters the media outlets before being disseminated widely throughout the society by means of mass communication, through the journalists. To ensure that the truth and nothing but the truth is delivered, it is expected of the media to choose, fact-check, and present the news with utmost care and responsibility. Journalistic writing should play a significant role in awakening society, persuading the heedless to change, and checking the wrongdoers. The meticulously crafted structure of the society must be protected against destruction and damage.

Unfortunately, by promoting a desperate, one-sided narrative, certain members of the society are overlooking their moral and ethical obligations to shape and see the community as a cohesive whole. Conspiracies that sow discord include misconstruing our distinctive uniqueness as divisions and turning a blind eye to the spirituality-based view of life, which is the source of unity in diversity. This agenda has been championed by the media for a while now. This attitude is the consequence of devout loyalty to the Western concept of media and unwavering faith in European liberalism. Not all journalists and editors implicated in this "conspiracy" are anti-Bharat, leftists, or jihadis. In fact, the majority of them emanate from our own education systems. They genuinely believe that our diversity essentially highlights the distinctions in our culture based on what they have read. They firmly adhere to the liberal ideology of the subculture reclaiming its identity.

However, it is noteworthy that despite the ubiquitous influence of the Western concept of popular news and European liberalism in media, traces of the Bharatiya view of life still exist in the media of our country. It is a matter of solace and an indication of hope that the media institutions that usually engage in activities that are in opposition to the Bharatiya worldview, or the "feeling of we," have also successfully defended this "feeling of we".

In the course of time, several flaws crept up in an ancient society like ours, giving rise to problems. All possible corrective measures must be taken to rid the society of these flaws and restore its former glory, but it must be done carefully, so as not to undermine the ongoing efforts to bind and weave the community as a cohesive unit. Social and economic inequities were brought about by some historically erroneous policies. They ought to be beaten back, and every effort ought to be made to build a harmonious society. As we work towards this, we must be careful to prevent the fundamentally diverse elements of our society from losing their strength or becoming weak. The phrase "Operation Successful, Patient is Dead" kind of circumstance will result if the importance of our roles in the process of weaving the society is undermined in the name of press freedom or freedom of expression. These points are important while selecting, presenting and also while considering the consequences of the news presented.

Samarth Ramdas Swami had said—

"सामर्थ्य आहे चळवळीचे, जो जे करील तयाचे। परंतु तेथे भगवंताचे, अधिष्ठान पाहिजे।।"

Meaning—"Strength is of the movement, it is of those involved in running the movement. But it's mandatory to have its foundation based on Divinity".

Therefore, bearing in mind that it is also my responsibility to be an active agent in shaping this society which is my own, while performing the duty of informing others of the wrongs, one should mindfully avoid undermining the human potential for goodness and disrupting the delicate balance of society.

The media needs to produce positive and uplifting news as well as news of events that uphold society and the country as paramount a frequent feature. Facts must be confirmed, and efforts to communicate information in a manner that awakens readers' inner divinity and raises their consciousness must be made by those who relay the news. If the wickedness and latent inhuman instincts are kept in check, the ignorant are made aware, and there is an abundance of inspiration to unleash the potential divinity of the society, then one may say that their journalistic *"dharma"* has been fulfilled.

Rigveda (1-30-5) holds *"Vibhootirastu Sunrita". Vibhooti* implies prosperity, dignity, or affluence. So it may even be said that news must contribute to the overall dignity and affluence of the society and not impoverish it by fragmenting and destabilising it. Its underlying vision must be *"Sa Vaarta ya Vibhootaye, Kadaapi na Vibhedaaya"* i.e. "news is that which enriches and never creates divisions." During the Bharatiya freedom movement, prominent veteran journalists and editors, including Lokmanya Tilak, Gandhiji, and Pandit Deendayal Upadhyay, asserted in various ways that this was the responsibility of the press and the media.

The Bharatiya view of journalism ultimately is to help the journalist and the reader to broaden their ambit of affinity and move towards liberation. News is *"Samvaad"* in Hindi and *"Vaarta"* in Sanskrit, therefore the reporter is called *'Vaartahar'* in the Marathi language. So, we may conclude – *"Sa Vaarta yaa vimuktaye"* - News is that which liberates.

Endnote :

This article first appeared in *Manthan* in the April-June, 2021 edition.

22

Denying Bharat its *Swa*

Perhaps there is not a single country in the entire world except Bharat whose people are confused over who we are, who our ancestors were and what our history is. Bharat, despite being the cradle of human settlement, the richest and the mightiest of all human civilizations suffers due to a multiplicity of narratives and opinions over these fundamental questions, but no consensus is achieved. This lack of consensus shows that we are not willing to identify and actualize our real identity, our *"swa"* (selfhood) as a unified society and one nation.

Following the devastation of World War II in 1945, Britain, Germany and Japan turned a new leaf. An unceasing struggle of hundreds of years culminated in Israel reclaiming its nationhood in 1948. Having suffered at the hands of invaders and exploiters for many centuries and over a 100-year-long freedom struggle, Bharat too attained independence in 1947. All five of these nations began anew at almost the same point in time. However, today, the socio-economic progress made by the aforementioned four countries is incomparable to that of Bharat. What might be the cause of the same?

Samuel Huntington, a social scientist, in his seminal work philosophised, "We have to know who we are before we can know what our interests are." I also believe that unless we decide who we are, as a people, we cannot decide what our priorities can be, as a nation, and this can leave us directionless. The absence of such an agreement is the underlying difference between the socio-economic progress of Bharat and the countries that marched with 'freedom' around the same time.

In his monumental essay *"Swadeshi Samaj"*, Gurudev Rabindranath Thakur opined, "First we have to be what 'we' are consciously, strongly, actively and completely." This is an amazing coincidence that the buzz of the country's 75th independence anniversary celebrations is juxtaposed with an emergent identity search, where Bharat is attempting to redefine itself with its *"swa"* as the focal point. However, why is there an aversion to this tenable search is yet another question worth pondering over.

Modern history of Bharat is replete with incidents and anecdotes of the suppression and negation of that *"swa"* of Bharat which is famed, immortal and pre-eminent. And it is now fashionable to refer to those doing so as "liberal-intellectual and progressive". It is evident that Bharat, having failed to define its developmental goals in the light of its *'swa,'* has not fully realised its potential in the progress made by the country thus far. Unfortunately, the many opportunities for the blossoming of this *"swa"* were repeatedly stubbed up early on.

It is common knowledge that "*Vande Mataram*" became the slogan of the people's movement of 1905 in opposition to the Bengal partition. "*Vande Mataram*" inspired innumerable youth and freedom fighters to take up the freedom struggle and sacrifice themselves for the cause. It was the spontaneous eruption of the *"swa"* of Bharat. All national-level sessions of Congress were witness to proud renditions of the song. Stalwarts like Pandit Omkarnath Thakur and Pandit Vishnu Digambar Paluskar lent their musical acumen to such renditions in countless meetings of the Congress. It was equally a source of inspiration to both Hindus and Muslims. Then all of a sudden, in the year 1921 it became a communal, Hindu song. But how? The mindset that fuels such thinking needs to be understood. The natural expression of patriotism that energised the freedom movement for fifteen long years since 1905 was abruptly stalled and labelled 'communal'. Investigating the 'what' and 'why' of these series of events is crucial.

In another incident of 1905 Swami Vivekananda's disciple, Sister Nivedita, put together the first-ever model of the flag for independent Bharat. The symbol of *Vajra* created with the bones of Rishi Dadhichi was inscribed on it. Thereafter she wrote, "Unfortunately we had a Chinese war flag as a model in front of us, so we made it black on red. But it doesn't appeal to Indians. So, the next one will be yellow on saffron". In the 1906 annual meeting of Congress, a saffron-coloured flag with a yellow *Vajra* symbol was displayed.

Thereon several samples of various flags were proposed. In 1921, a tricolour flag with a *Charakha* (spoked wheel) symbol was declared the representative embodiment of all the communities of Bharat. A group of Sikh representatives led by their leader, Master Tara Singh, met with Mahatma Gandhi in 1929 and opposed the idea of representation of different communities through different colours in the flag. He insisted on the need for one national flag that conveys unity among the many communities and added if they were stuck up on the idea of representation of different communities through varied colours then the yellow colour - representative of the Sikh community - must be added to the flag. A Flag Committee was constituted by the Congress Executive Committee comprising Pandit Jawaharlal Nehru, Sardar Patel, Maulana Abul Kalam Azad, Master Tara Singh, Pattabhi Sitaramaiah, Kaka Kalelkar and Dr. Hardikar. The Flag Committee in turn solicited comments (over the objections raised against the proposed flag and suggestions) from the State Congress Committees and common people. After considering all objections and suggestions the Flag Committee submitted its report that said - "it was decided that our flag should be distinct, artistic and non-communal. It was decided unanimously that it should be of one single colour. And if there is a colour that is more distinct than others, one that is more acceptable to the Indians as a whole and the one that is associated with this ancient country by long tradition, it is the *Kesari* - saffron colour." Therefore, the committee unanimously recommended a rectangular saffron-coloured flag with a device *Charakha* in blue on it. Why then was this decision reversed? What is that underlying mentality that denied Bharat its intelligible, organic "*swa*"? These factual queries are worthy of consideration.

After the independence of Bharat in 1947, the tricolour representing prosperity, peace and valour with the *dharmachakra* or the wheel of *dharma* at the centre was accepted as our national flag. It is now our national flag. It is undisputedly the rightful duty of all Bharatiya people to respect and protect it and to glorify it with our responsible actions.

On similar lines, the educational reforms that were anticipated following independence were also denied. Dr. Sarvepalli Radhakrishnan in the capacity of the Chairman of the University Education Commission wrote unambiguously about the un-Indian character of education as follows: "One of the serious complaints against the system of education which has prevailed in this country for over a century is that it neglected India's past, that it did not provide the Indian students with a knowledge of their own culture. It has produced in some cases the feeling that we are without roots, in others, what is worse, that our roots bind us to a world very different from that which surrounds us.

"The chief source of spiritual nourishment for any people must be its own past perpetually rediscovered and renewed. A society without a knowledge of the past which has made it would be lacking in depth and dignity.

"It was assumed that education should not stop with the development of intellectual powers but must provide the student, for the regulation of his personal and social life, a code of behaviour based on fundamental principles of ethics and religion. Where conscious purpose is lacking, personal integrity and consistent behaviour are not possible."

These words are evidence that spirituality is the cornerstone of Bharatiya philosophy or view of life and our education system should have evolved in the same light. However, recommendations made by education commissions appointed by the Congress-ruled governments itself were not implemented during Congress rule. When the people constituting those commissions and deliberating on these issues were their own party workers then who were the people who impeded the implementation of those recommendations? What thought process was at play then? Even to this day attempts to amend the prevalent education system are ridiculed and dubbed as saffronisation of education. What hidden motives fuel those oppositions needs serious deliberation.

It is an undisputed fact that Sanskrit is the mother of all Bharatiya languages and is comprehensible for all Bharatiya people. Malaysia is home to a largely Tamil-speaking Bharatiya diaspora. Shri Ramchandran, Hindu Swayamsevak Sangh *pracharak* in Malaysia, speaks Tamil. During his Sangh training, he attended two (20-day duration) camps in two different years in Tamil Nadu. For his third year training, he spent 25 days in Nagpur where most lectures were delivered in Hindi and were incomprehensible to him. Later when those lectures were translated into Tamil for Tamil-speaking trainees only then was he able to understand the content. He later shared with me that out of the twenty-five lectures delivered, he could fully comprehend one lecture without translation and that lecture was delivered in Sanskrit. This is glowing evidence of the fact that Sanskrit is closer to all the Bharatiya languages. Bharat Ratna Dr. Babasaheb Ambedkar and his contemporaries (ministers) were aligned on the opinion that each student in Bharat must undergo Sanskrit education. The wealth of Bharatiya knowledge is encoded in Sanskrit and all the languages spoken in the Bharatiya subcontinent have emanated from Sanskrit or have much in common with Sanskrit. The suggestion is pertinent even from the point of view of realising the Bharatiya view of unity and integrity (*ekatmata*); which is an essential part of the Bharatiya worldview. However, which ideology deemed it right to overlook an invaluable suggestion, this must be ascertained.

Most modern-day academicians are of the view that primary education must be imparted in the pupil's mother tongue. Education in one's mother tongue is crucial as it enables conceptual clarity when learning new subjects and fluent expression of one's own ideas and knowledge. If the goal is to create fluent English speakers among students, then teaching English as a subject is sufficient; there's no need to conduct all subject lessons in English. In any case, only a minuscule 9% of humans across the globe obtain education in a foreign language or a language other than their mother tongue. Bharat is a key contributor to that 9% figure. Education in the English language has been so hyped up here that the students pursuing education in their mother tongue develop a sense of inferiority in comparison to their English-educated peers. This is contrary to the "*swa*" of Bharat. Despite innumerable thinkers, including Mahatma Gandhi emphasising the need for introducing the mother tongue, especially in primary education, the outcome is contrary to the expectations. Why is that so?

With a maximum share in global business, Bharat flourished prosperously for an indefinite period of history. Ours was not an 'agrarian economy.' We were known for the trade of leather products, metals, perfumes, timber, statues, stone sculptures, textiles, spices, diamonds and precious jewels across the world. Bharatiya merchants have been trading across oceans for millennia. Therefore, it is more appropriate to call ourselves an industry-centric economy instead of an agrarian economy. Home-based cottage industries were the originators of those goods and the families running those units resided in the villages of Bharat. Villages of Bharat were opulent. But influenced by the European mindset, post-independence Bharat adopted an urban-centred economic development model. Consequently, cities became overcrowded and over-competitive, crime rose and familial ties weakened, leaving the villages neglected and backward, lacking basic amenities for living. Urban living came to be interpreted as progressive and rural dwelling was deemed regressive. The profit-maximising mentality induced by the Industrial Revolution trapped humanity in the web of greed.

The unique feature of the Bharatiya view of life is that it equally emphasises the importance of both material progress and spiritual growth and not just one at the exclusion of the other. A verse from *Isavasya Upanishad* elucidates that one who relentlessly pursues material prosperity only enters into deep darkness. In the same verse it is said that one who single-handedly pursues spiritual progress enters even greater darkness. The *Upanishad* conveys pursuing material prosperity and spiritual progress simultaneously as the true purpose of life. The village life is the ideal setting for the same. In a village, one earns less, but expenditures too are limited. Hence, one needn't hustle to afford himself a good quality of life and a decent income. The rural environment provides for both means of livelihood as well as ample time for one's spiritual meditation (*sadhana*). It is for this reason that Mahatma Gandhi also advocated for a rural-centric economic model for independent Bharat. His book *'Hind Swaraj'* revolves around the same theme. The Constituent Assembly while deliberating on the ratification of the Constitution between November 19 to 22, 1948 also expressed their hopes to embark on our journey of *'Gram Swaraj'*. However, embroiled in the socialism-capitalism duel of the West, our inclusive, eco-centric model of progress was forgotten. Former President Dr. Abdul Kalam also appealed for the remodelling of Bharatiya villages and bringing them up to speed with the urban centres. The eminent thought espoused by Bharat is that to live a prosperous, joyous, healthy and spiritually bountiful life is the essence of life. It was also the hallmark of Bharatiya life - an optimal expression of the *"swa"* of Bharat. How did we fail to adopt this approach?

Gurudev Rabindranath Thakur in his essay *"Swadeshi Samaj"* writes- "Welfare state is a Western construct; it is not Bharatiya. Traditionally Bharatiya society was never state-dependent. By the very definition *swadeshi samaj* is that society which is least state-dependent." Traditionally only judiciary, foreign relations, security and defence were under state jurisdiction. Other concerns like education, healthcare, trade and commerce, arts and culture, temples, fairs and the lore were all channelized by the societal arrangement directly.

Swami Vivekananda's disciple, Bhagini Nivedita said, "The society, whose members instead of withholding their remuneration with themselves share it with the larger society, with the accumulated remunerations (the social capital) build a wealthy and prosperous society, which in turn makes each individual of the society wealthy and prosperous. But in a society where people hoard their remuneration with themselves, instead of sharing it with the rest of the society, only a few individuals become wealthy and prosperous, while the larger society remains poor." To give to the society with a sense of belongingness and that all this belongs to the commonwealth, and to return it to the society is akin to absolute fulfilment. So, Vivekananda Kendra prayer goes like -

> जीवने यावदादानं स्यात् प्रदानं ततोऽधिकम्।
> इत्येषा प्रार्थनास्माकं भगवन् परिपूर्यताम्।
> *Jivane yavdadaanam syat pradanam tato'dhikam*
> *Ityesha prarthanasmaakam bhagawan Paripuryatam*

Meaning: "Whatever we receive in life let us give far more than that. Oh Almighty! Grant our wish."

We receive much from society. To give back is the essence of *dharma*. Religion or worship is not the same as *dharma*. Worship is a means to attain a *dharmic* attitude. But *dharma* is to conduct oneself in the spirit of giving back to the society. To offer alms is charity, but to give back to the society is *dharma*. As per Bhagini Nivedita, enriching common social wealth is *dharma*. *Dharma* is indiscriminate, it weaves the society into a whole, beholds, protects and sustains it. It is the foundation on which *Swadeshi Samaj* is built.

The essence of *dharma* captured the eye of the mind of the architects of Bharat at the time of independence which must be why *"dharmachakra pravartanaya"* (for the propagation of the timeless cycle of *dharma*) and *"satyam vad, dharmam char"* (speak the truth and act in *dharma*) are inscribed in the Lok Sabha and Rajya Sabha of Bharat respectively. The Supreme Court upholds the directive "*Yato Dharmastato Jayah*" (where there is *dharma*, there will be victory), and wheel in the center of the national flag is that very *"dharmachakra"* (wheel of *dharma*). Wheels are designed to turn. Every act of giving back to the society is an act of *dharma* and that gives a push to the wheel of *dharma* and keeps it rotating, gaining momentum.

The *dharma* that was the premise of the imagination of the Lok Sabha, Rajya Sabha, the Supreme Court and the national flag is absent in all social dialogue. In fact, discussing *dharma* is now considered 'communal.' While the term secularism, which was considered unnecessary after detailed discussions and a mutual consensus (among members of the Constituent Assembly) was in great connivance, discreetly and forcibly added to the (unamendable) Preamble of the Constitution. That non-Bharatiya (un-Indian) word is being indiscriminately hurled everywhere.

Which ideology breeds the current scenario? This question must be probed. The only way to realise the long-subdued *"swa"* (selfhood) of Bharat is to extricate ourselves out of the shackles of this non-Bharatiya (un-Indian) thinking and recalibrate our thought process in alignment with the untainted Bharatiya philosophy. And when with our efforts it proudly blossoms in all its glory Bharat will confidently march to fulfil its promise to the world.

Endnote :

This article first appeared in *The Sunday Guardian* on August 13, 2022.

23

The Invincible, Eternal 'We'

At a time when the entire world is grappling with the onslaught of the coronavirus pandemic, considering the diversity and enormity of our population we can say that Bharat is faring relatively better than other powerful nations. People here experienced the lockdown for the first time. Speculations about the merits and demerits of this measure run rife all over the world. Slowly, the lockdown is easing out. We will have to proceed further carefully. Coping with the challenges posed by this unfamiliar disease will require an extraordinary approach. The world, as we know it, will no longer be the same. Restoring normalcy in day-to-day functioning will be no cakewalk. We will have to walk into this new world together, united and with a firm resolve to be victorious.

Bharat's war against coronavirus is different from that of other nations. It is unique. State power is paramount in most of the countries of the world other than Bharat. It has a great bearing on all societal systems in those countries. For this reason, those state powers are called "welfare states".

During times of catastrophe, state systems are activated through administrative readiness and citizens await official, state-based machinery to get functional. However, the picture is different in Bharat. Traditionally, society (as people) existed independent of the state power here. We had autonomous systems that were capable of taking care of various needs of the society without the state's support. Rabindranath Thakur, in his essay, "*Swadeshi Samaj*" opined that "a welfare state is neither a Bharatiya concept nor tradition. Since time immemorial the state here was entrusted strictly with only a few critical matters. Barring defence and security, judiciary and foreign affairs, people had their autonomous systems for all other matters like education, healthcare, industry, trade & commerce, temples, fairs, art & aesthetics, music, dance, drama, pilgrimage, etc. that did not depend on the state. *Sanatan* Bharat did not rely on the state treasury to fund these activities of the society. The society had its independent arrangement which had *dharma* as its guiding principle." He stated explicitly that "a society that has minimal reliance on state power to make arrangements for itself is "*Swadeshi Samaj*".

Acharya Vinoba Bhave remarked, "State power was important to us only until we were under foreign rule. Now that we are independent, it is time to awaken the power of the people." He further added, "The society that relies heavily on the state for its needs is an indolent society; a weak society. Non-governmental work is more efficacious."

Earlier, "we" were under foreign rule. On 15 August 1947, "we" gained independence. On 26 January 1950, "we" brought our constitution into effect. This "we" under foreign rule, the "we" that became independent, and the "we" that adopted our constitution is the same timeless continuum of the people through the ages—it precisely is our existence and identity, that is our *Rashtra – the people*. Our motherland was invaded. At times, kings got defeated. Foreign rule too prevailed. But this "we" remained undefeated. "We" alludes to the people of this society, our nation. At this point, it must be understood that this "nation" is not the same as the Western "nation-state". Former President of Bharat, Dr. Pranab Mukherjee in his address to Sangh *swayamsevaks* in Nagpur highlighted this very fact, stating, "The Western concept of a nation-state and the Bharatiya concept of '*Rashtra*' seeped in our view-of-life are dissimilar." Our national identity has emerged through a long-drawn process of confluence, assimilation and co-existence. It is owing to this concept of *Rashtra – the people* that in times of natural or man-made calamity, the society seamlessly coalesces with the administration for relief and rehabilitation work, here in Bharat.

In the present situation, state employees—policemen, doctors, nurses, paramedics, cleaners and many others—are executing their duties remarkably well despite the possibility of infectious transmission and life threat. Many personnel even contracted the virus in the line of duty and a few ended up losing their lives. Therefore, it is legitimate to refer to these professionals as "corona-warriors". All sections of society, especially the army and the police have loudly applauded the care workers' efforts. They rightfully deserve this. Some might be of the opinion that "duty is an official imperative and hence they were under a compulsion to discharge it". However, the diligence, faithfulness and dedication exhibited by the members of these groups are extraordinary and worthy of honour.

Alongside these government and semi-government employees, another sizeable section of society embraced the threats to their lives to join the emergency task force from day one. Unbound by a contract with the government and a disinclination towards return gains, yet driven by a profound sense of affinity, these people convey, "in times of crisis it is my responsibility to help the members of my society" and make dedicated efforts towards this goal. This spirit of oneness with the whole society is the feeling of "*Vayam Rashtrang Bhootah*" (I am the constituent of the society and have an inextricable connection with my society). Doing relief work in times of natural calamities like floods and earthquakes is incomparable to serving in a pandemic, where a highly infectious disease amplifies the threat. The active societal contribution made by this section was consistent across the length and breadth of the country. This illuminates the power of a conscious and active nation.

From Arunachal Pradesh to Kashmir and Kanyakumari, 5,07,656 *swayamsevaks* of Rashtriya Swayamsevak Sangh, under the banner of *Sewa Bharati*, supplied dietary allowance kits to families at 92,656 different locations. 4,66,34,730 food packets were distributed to those in need of food. Approximately, 83,23,131 masks were distributed. The beneficiary groups included members of nomadic tribes, eunuchs, those in the flesh trade, monkeys, cows and other animals dependent on temple visitors for nourishment. Several students living in major metropolises and large towns also received help. A helpline to support students from the Northeast was created to facilitate communication with their family members and render all required assistance. Those who sustain themselves by gathering daily alms around temples and other religious centres also received the offerings of this "*Sewa Yajna*". *Swayamsevaks* even ventured into "*bastis*" that had infectious breakouts to help people. Regardless of any filter, unbiased help was extended to the needy in every state of the country. Crowd management, registration of workers in transit and innumerable such tasks were managed as a token of support to the local administration. Upon the administration's clarion call in the city of Pune, RSS *swayamsevaks*, flanked by volunteers of other social outfits, stepped inside densely populated, risky, red zones and screened over 1,00,000 people, handing over suspected carriers to the administration for further testing.

Besides RSS, several other social and religious organisations, congregations, *mathas*, temples and *gurudwaras* contributed to this society-led relief movement in various locations across the country. Independent of state arrangement, this is a societal system. Contemplation of the *"vayam rastrang bhootah*" (body-limb connection) sentiment gives impetus to the development and functioning of such systems. Despite the differences in dialects, caste identities and religious beliefs the realisation of this feeling connects and unifies people spread across the Bharatiya landmass to forge the "we". The eternal "we".

The acute awareness of being a part of this colossal "we" offers inspiration to extend selfless service, even in the face of life-threatening challenges, and without the expectation of gaining name or fame. "People living in all states, literate, illiterate, wealthy, poor, villagers or city-dwellers, townsfolk and forest-dwellers are all my own people"—encouraging this sentiment implies awakening a nation. It is then that the consciousness expands to successively include self, family, clan, neighbourhood, village, district, state, nation, the entire world and all creations into the scope of one's identity. These different layers are not in conflict but are mutually complementary. In the absence of any perceptible conflicts among these layers, all components function mutually complementarily. The incessant endeavour of the society to harmonise these components is the basis of the eternal, spirituality-based, integral and holistic view-of-life of Bharat. This view-of-life gives Bharat its unique identity since time immemorial. Our identification with these various identities of society is the very reason why "we" have the innate feeling of affinity for these ever-expanding layers of existence. That feeling of affinity propels action in times of crisis. This strengthens the bond further and weaves the weft of society to create an organised society.

The act of organising society is neither instantaneous nor automatic. Conscious, long-term and continuous endeavours result in an organised society. It takes generations of craftsmen to build a functional system. Rashtriya Swayamsevak Sangh is an example of such crafting agents. The goal of unifying all the people of the diverse Bharatiya society by inculcating a spirit of oneness with all was our founding purpose. The comprehensive expanse of work, influence and organised cohesion visible today for all to see has consumed the lives of five generations of Sangh *karyakartas*. Thousands of people have spent their entire lives with this very aim as their mission. Innumerable youth were consumed like camphor to fire, without leaving a single trace of ash. It is then that such results have emerged. Not only RSS, but umpteen social and religious institutions, educators, merchants, businessmen and home-maker womenfolk contribute to this task of nation-awakening each day, consistently, in their own subtle ways. However, Sangh's ability to consolidate and project nationwide efforts under one umbrella makes it perceptible.

It takes dedicated years of penance to awaken this sense of belonging to the entire society and a mindset to work as a part of a disciplined system in a given situation. One such revelatory experience came about when the Aila cyclone hit Bengal on 25 May 2009. 24 Pargana district (South) was worst affected by that devastating cyclone. On June 3, having travelled in a jeep for an hour, followed by a 40-minute boat ride and lastly a walk through knee-deep slush, I reached the distant island where relief work was undertaken. Taking cognizance of the ongoing rescue and relief operations, I enquired into the experience of the *swayamsevaks* there. I asked them to share the names of the socio-religious organisations or agencies that were also conducting relief work there. The answer was eye-opening. They said, "Other agencies have restricted their service area only to the parts having road access. Sangh alone is active in these inaccessible interiors." I wondered if those *swayamsevaks* would have ever experienced working in such dire conditions. Doubtful that they had executed such elaborate plans in remote areas before, I admired their thoughtfulness and courage to reach out to the people who needed help desperately. Such dedication can only result from cultivating the discipline to work in peculiar conditions and by identifying the self as an integral part of society.

The coronavirus pandemic has brought similar instances to the fore. Due to some rumour-mongering, thousands of waged workers gathered at Delhi's Anand Vihar bus stand. No sooner did this become known, Delhi *swayamsevaks* arranged for food and water distribution. Uttar Pradesh Sangh workers, in collaboration with the state administration organised a fleet of 5,000 buses that successfully ferried those labourers to their places of origin. Technically, the governments and administration owe those responsibilities but the *swayamsevaks* offered a glimpse into their managerial abilities and strength by undertaking such challenging tasks.

Making arrangements despite innumerable palpable challenges is no pushover. Pictures of some temporary settlements erected to accommodate travellers surfaced in the media. Some arrangements were adequate and a few were inadequate. Many people, unaware of proper conduct, became flustered and suffered in the process. Painful visuals of such incidents were heart-wrenching. This mass exodus caught many headlines and became a hot debatable topic. Pro-government and anti-government camps locked horns and engaged in mudslinging over televised debates. However, it is imperative to note that during the same period, 10 lakh waged labourers migrated back to Bihar, 30 lakh to Uttar Pradesh, 10 lakh to Madhya Pradesh and 1.15 lakh migrants successfully made it back to their villages to Jharkhand. Governmental-societal partnership made this herculean goal attainable. Such factual information also deserves its rightful place in televised debates.

The lockdown brought all economic activities to a grinding halt. The magnitude of this unprecedented challenge induced a multitude of challenges. Arrangements and efforts to address those challenges were not free of shortcomings. It is painful that ordinary, innocent and helpless people had to bear the consequences of those shortcomings. In a democratic setup, it is natural for such issues to become the material of public discourse, media and other discussions. But a few members of society—politicians, journalists, and writers—are oblivious to the fact that they too are part of the same society and often alienate themselves from it. To blow matters out of proportion and to generalise a condition, creating the false impression of an all-pervasive gloom, demoralises the entire society. It drags the well-meaning officers, workers and volunteers into a psychological courtroom, raising many question marks and, in turn, causing general unrest. There are no two ways about it; that which is wrong is wrong. But when publicly scrutinising such matters, it is our social and moral responsibility to align ourselves with the truth and to carefully avoid portraying an inflated, fallacious picture. This responsibility is deeply rooted in our value system, which is rooted in the feeling of *"vayam rashtrang bhootah"*.

I recall one incident dating back to 1992. Having recently landed in the United States I soon learnt of this then-popular "GUN" tee-shirt brand that was apparently a rage amongst American teens. With his tee-shirt sales hitting the roof, the producer made huge profits. However, another segment of American society began to raise concerns about the potential threat posed by those tee shirts—a spike in violent tendencies among teens. Concerned, they stirred a movement in society demanding the producer to withdraw the GUN tee-shirt from the market shelves. Unwilling, but eventually foreseeing the threat of a complete boycott of all his products, the producer relented and withdrew those "GUN" tee-shirts. In a subsequent press interview, the journalists quizzed him: "When the dangers your product posed were brought to your notice early on, why did you not withdraw it immediately?" To this, he replied: "Look, I am here in the business of making money, not morality." This implied that maybe there exist two viewpoints in business—to view one's society as a mere resource or to consider it as an extension of one's own self.

In the same zest, if incidents of violence, torture, exploitation, injustice or deceit plague society then people must organise their might to oppose and remedy such matters. After a thorough investigation those found guilty must be brought to trial, bearing appropriate punishment. However, is the generalisation of a shortcoming, portraying an inflated and fallacious picture, justified? Does it not deflate the spirits of the larger, well-meaning society? Unfortunately, such conduct is a truism in the present scenario, and the reason behind this erroneous behaviour is the diminishing sense of "*vayam rashtrang bhootah*". For those engaging in such irresponsible conduct, the society, its oddities and poverty, its illiteracy and squalor all seem like resource material in fulfilling their "agenda". This is owing to the failure in the incorporation of one's society in their concept of "self".

Unfortunately, in endorsing a disparate, one-sided narrative, several members of the society are overlooking their moral and social responsibility of viewing and integrating the society as a cohesive whole. Floating divisive conspiracies such as misconstruing the characteristic diversities as divisions and turning a blind eye to the spirituality-based view of life, which is the source of unity at the core of our diversity has been a norm for quite some time now. In such an ancient society, some defects emerged and became flawed which birthed many problems. Corrective measures as efforts in redeeming our ancient glory must be taken, but with care not to dampen the perpetual spirit of weaving the society together into a cohesive whole. Historically, erroneous policies have led to social and economic problems.

Efforts must be made to nullify those errors and rebuild the fabric of the society. In doing so we must be diligent and ensure that the unifying thread of our fundamentally diverse society doesn't weaken or lose strength.

Stretching from the Himalayas to the Andaman, the entire society is my own. I have to weave and create beautiful motifs in my social fabric—this should be the underlying thought behind all actions. The invincible "we" is the key to its capacity for standing tall in the face of the tribulations of the future, and emerging victorious. All of us, at all times, under every circumstance should strive to strengthen and revitalise this emotion of "we".

Endnote :

This article first appeared in *The Sunday Guardian* on June 06, 2020.

Reflections

24

Time to Get Rid of Pseudo-Secularism

The grand Shri Ram Mandir construction commencement ceremony held in Ayodhya was proudly witnessed by the people in Bharat and people of Bharatiya origin in all other parts of the world. On one hand, it was a dream come true for some, having overcome innumerable hurdles of a centuries-long battle. For the "secularists" of the nation, especially politicians, who under the garb of secularism engage in communal politics, and the "intellectuals" and journalists, who are in the business of divisive and anti-national activities, it was an unnerving moment. Fearful of dire consequences in the upcoming elections, few 'secular politicians,' cognizant of the elevated general level of national consciousness, even changed their stance on Ram Mandir! But the so-called intellectuals and journalists, who make a living by indulging in divisive activities and anarchy, cried wolf, stating, "Indian Constitution is in danger as secularism is under threat." With these cries, they tried to delude the masses into believing that the "secularism" they practise is at the heart of the Bharatiya Constitution and also that it was an integral part of the Constitution right from the beginning. This is like convincing the cart horse that he was born bridled.

For the self-professed guardians of the Constitution, this chorus claims that the Constitution has been frauded. In reality, the deceptive induction of the word 'secular' into the Constitution was the actual "fraud" committed. Our Constitution makers were not unacquainted with the concept of secularism. After an intense debate over K.T. Shah's suggestion to define Bharat as a "secular socialist republic", members of the Constituent Assembly deemed it unnecessary in the Bharatiya context and hence kept it out. Secularism is attributed to the particular socio-political context of Europe. Secularism was a reaction to the 1,000-year-long historical context of the theocratic state ruled by the Pope in Europe. To separate and free the control of non-religious matters from the Church, secularism was brought into practice. However, such a need did not arise here in the long history of Bhārat as we never had the concept of a theocratic state; considering the spirituality-based integral and holistic view of life, our Constitution makers did not visualise such a possibility at any point in the future. The all-inclusive ancient civilisation of Bharat that adheres to the holistic and integral Hindu view of life was evidence for the Constituent Assembly that even in the future no such need will arise.

The word "secularism" was inserted in the Constitution in the year 1976 when an Emergency was imposed upon the country, democratic norms were compromised, and the opposition was absent from the parliament (as opposition leaders were forcefully incarcerated, and those who escaped detention were underground). In the well-organised Bharatiya judicial system, we have a provision to challenge lower-court judgements in the higher courts. In the face of higher courts' failure to do justice one may knock at the doors of the apex court. And if the apex court judgement is inconclusive or unsatisfactory then the provision to refer the matter to a larger bench of judges is also available. Where problem-solving necessitates constitutional amendment, the parliament is empowered to proceed after a debate with the requisite type of majority. But the connivance of including the word "secular"—previously declined by the Constituent Assembly—did not undergo any such legal scrutiny. Amidst the terror of the Emergency, in the absence of any need, demand or debate, this insertion was evasively made to the (unamendable) Preamble of the Constitution and this is the real fraud dealt within the Bharatiya Constitution.

Having engulfed Bharatiya imagination over the decades, this "secularism" is causing havoc in our national and social life, but its definitive meaning still remains a matter of debate. Even the Constitution has not provided for any definition of the same. Against the backdrop of this semantical mystery, organised efforts to impose this conspiratorially added foreign concept on Bharatiya collective conscience are underway to create confusion. If assuming secularity pertains to religious neutrality on the part of the state, where followers of all religions are entitled to equal rights and opportunities, then this magnanimity has been a Hindu tradition since time immemorial. Therefore, being a country with a Hindu majority, the Bharatiya Constitution had inbuilt provisions regarding the same. Moreover, the "religious minorities" are assured of special rights under the Constitution, which the "majority" Hindus are not given. What could be the motive behind surreptitiously adding an ill-defined word, "secular," to the Constitution despite these provisions? A critical analysis of the socio-political developments that took place in the aftermath of this foul play proves that this fraud was committed to create an environment in the country that is congenial for divisive and communal politics and to nurture and protect those whose agenda is to break the nation into a fissiparous society. What is the impact of such an ill-conceived move on the society? In the name of secularism, a divisive-communal agenda is openly encouraged and promoted, while those who call out their misdeeds are labelled communal!

A "secular" prime minister openly made a blatant communal statement: "Minorities (meaning Muslims) have the first claim on resources in the country." Despite the unconstitutional nature and repudiation by the High Courts and the Supreme Court, the leaders of a few "secular" parties, time and again, propose to create reservations for religious minorities. If Bharat is secular in the true sense of the term, then the government should not provide a *Haj* subsidy. Some Islamic scholars have claimed that only a pilgrimage done using one's own means is admissible in Islam, therefore, no other Islamic country provides a *Haj* subsidy. The subsistence of this practice in post-colonial Bharat is both non-secular and anti-Islamic. Indiscriminate vote-bank politics is practised here by employing tactics like making the religious ground a criterion for giving out scholarships to students, providing cycles to Muslim school-going girls exclusively, offering financial aid for the marriage of Muslim girls alone and so on. The "secularism is under threat" brigade conveniently turns a blind eye to such aberrations. On the lines of the *Haj* subsidy, in order to acquire Christian votes, a "secular" state government announced a subsidy for a trip to Jerusalem, but we didn't hear a peep from the champions of secularism there. Overlooking the court rulings, a "secular" state government announced reservations for Muslims thrice. Did the cat get the tongues of the keepers of secularism, then?! The government must have control over the offerings made at Hindu temples, while offerings made at the places of worship of other religions may go unaudited—is this secularism? Any discrimination by the state based on religion is unacceptable as per secularism, but the defenders of secularism maintain a stoic silence over these matters.

Recently a satirical viral social media post—"religion of the mob is not known, but of the human chain protecting the temple from the mob has a religion"—about the reportage on the sponsored Bengaluru communal violence put the brand of Bharatiya "secular journalism" under the scanner. Another famous post attributed to the Canadian journalist, Tarek Fatah, making the rounds of social media reads, "India is the only major civilisational country where you are taught to hate your heritage and glorify the invaders who came to destroy it. And this (absurdity) is called 'secularism.'"

Quintessential Bharatiya secularism entails legislations and acts to annihilate *Hindutva*, Hindu beliefs and Hindu traditions. Sharing the dais with Owaisi (who openly espouses communal hatred) is "being secular" while sharing the dais with an ascetic like Yogi Adityanath is dubbed "communal"! Offering *chadar* at the dargah (Sufi shrine), government-sponsored *iftar* parties and the like are signs of secularism, whereas participating in the *prana pratishtha puja* of a temple is a grossly communal act that garners "secularism under threat" slogans. Seeped in the belief that the whole universe is inhabited by all-pervading spirituality ("ईशावास्यम इदं सर्वम यदकिंचित जगत्याम जगत") is an ancient Bharatiya praxis to commence all relevant tasks by re-establishing and re-invoking the divine forces (दैवी अधिष्ठान). This is an expression of our spirituality, not some communal act. We've inherited the knowledge that various divine manifestations perpetuate different human endeavours—*Saraswati* for scholastic pursuits, *Dhanvantri* for medicine, *Nataraja* for dance and other performing arts, *Hanuman* for wrestling, *Vishwakarma* for crafts and aesthetics and so on. To invoke the deities of one's specific vocation, regardless of one's religion, has for ages been the thumb rule in our land. In doing so we do not defy "secularism". But the insecure fundamentalists, jihadi groups and other "breaking-Bharat" forces try to relegate these pragmatic traditions here by distorting their meaning and misbranding these as "communal acts". Furthermore, political parties that made hay of the "minorities" and "communal" cards bolster these groups and in some cases act unmindful of them.

A journalist known to me engaged a Muslim contractor at her newly-constructed house for carpentry work. The work was in progress when that

Muslim contractor one day informed the journalist of his team's impending absence the following day. To satisfy my acquaintance's curiosity he said they would celebrate *Vishwakarma Jayanti*. The (Muslim) contractor then explained the significance of *Vishwakarma Jayanti* to this Hindu journalist. Where Bharatiya spirituality is second nature to a commoner like that contractor, it appears to be rocket science to the secular *jamaat* of Bharat, or maybe they are too conceited to acknowledge it. In light of this emerging brand of new secularism, it is imperative to redefine secularism as blind opposition of religion and religiosity fits just right.

The classical spirituality-based Bharatiya view of life is intrinsically holistic and integral. This philosophy or way of life came to be known as *Hindutva* among people outside Bharat. The glaring differences between the living conditions of people living under the framework of two separate constitutions of two nations that emerged from the partition of the same landmass—Bharat and Pakistan—is reason enough to believe "*Sarva Dharma Sama Bhava*" is our disposition. Pakistan has failed to display generosity towards each citizen of its country (regardless of their religion) which Bharat has exemplified. Bharatiya Constitution owes its nobility to our Hindu roots, while Pakistan's negation of granting equal opportunity to all stems from its denial of and alienation from *Hindutva*. If the essence of secularism is parity of various religious paths, then Hindus are beacons of secularism by our innate nature, our conscience is fed on the fact "एकं सत विप्रा: बहुधा वदन्ति"—"the truth is one, the wise express it in numerous ways". In 1893, during his Parliament of World Religions address in Chicago, Swami Vivekananda described Bharat as the "mother of all religions". He then illustrated how followers of several religions fleeing religious persecution and conversion in their countries of origin found asylum in Bharat at various points in time and left behind sanctuaries for their future generations to freely practice their religion and way of life here. He summarised by saying, "We go beyond tolerance and accept all ways to be true". Hindus profess, live and breathe inclusion and acceptance.

The conspiracy of labelling the benevolent *Hindutva* as communal and refashioning and serving gross unpalatable communal thoughts as secular has subdued our collective conscience and quelled our societal evolution for a few decades now. The enormity of this problem became palpable to me while reading the letter from a young woman who happens to be a Sangh *karyakarta's* sister. Gauging her interest in writing I suggested she share her thoughts over our discussion.

She wrote: "I'm an Indian, which to me until a couple of days ago meant that I belong to India. I thought this was more of a physical, geographical and maybe even a cultural reality. I'm also a Hindu. But my faith which is deeply personal to me has nothing to do with my national identity. Or so I thought. I never once thought of blending my faith and my national identity. They are not the same thing. In fact, I very strongly thought the two shouldn't mix, for we, as 'urban, modern, progressive' Indians are taught to not mix our religious and national identity. While being patriotic is great, we are taught not to wear 'being a Hindu' on our sleeve—whether it's at work or social gatherings, for it might offend other religions of India. Being Hindu and being Indian are two different things, and should be kept separate. Mixing the two is looked at as being communal and marginalising anyone who follows a different faith. India belongs to every faith equally, we are taught. India is a land of diverse cultures, we are taught."

Being anti-religion or non-religious and irreligious are not necessary conditions to enact secularism. It is impossible for any individual to be secular. If anyone claims to be one then they are either lying or are deluded. All human lives are guided by some or the other underlying philosophy or religion. A man's religion or way of life may be Hindu, Islamic, Sikh, Parsi, Jew, Jain, Buddhist, Vaishnav, Shaiva, Devi-worshipping, nature-worshipping or atheist. And every person has the right and freedom to practice his own religion. This doesn't endanger secularism. Secularism expects all religions to be treated equally but if you go beyond treating all religions as equal and accept all to be true then you are a Hindu. Acharya Vinoba Bhave made a simple distinction that sums up the matter: "Salvation through this way only—non-Hindu; Salvation through this way also—Hindu."

I believe while the state must be secular, it is neither possible nor necessary for an individual to be secular. For instance, the State Transport Corporation must be secular but demanding that for it to be secular its chairman must be secular is illogical. All passengers using the state transport service must be treated equally, but to say equal service will be available to all passengers only when the bus driver or conductor becomes irreligious is undesirable. We have all seen most Bharatiya bus drivers start the journey by paying obeisance to a deity (they believe in) and even the vehicle. How has that ever come in the way of secularism? Secularism on the part of the State Transport Corporation mandates all users have equal access to common facilities, the conductor must charge the same fare for all and no discrimination in seating arrangement must be made. Over and above, special arrangements to help the elderly, women or people with special needs are understandable. But demanding special provisions stating one's religion as the ground for privilege and calling it secularism is an oxymoron.

That young woman closed her letter by saying, "A couple of days ago, I had a conversation about this with Dr. Vaidya, of the RSS. RSS, an organisation that believes India should be a *Hindu-Rashtra*, that strongly believes in propagating the *"Hindutva"* agenda and that sees everyone in India through saffron-coloured glasses. Or so I thought, until this conversation, a couple of days ago. It was only during this conversation that I realised how far from the truth was my 'knowledge' of the subject. For the first time, I heard and absorbed what it really means to be 'Hindu' and how it isn't at all far from being 'Indian' or 'Bharatiya'. They are the same thing. *Hindutva* (Hinduism is a loose translation of the word, not quite accurate) is a way of life. It was life in this region of the world, much before religion existed. It was a way of life that continued to thrive, much after religion divided this country into two. And it will be a way of life here, despite the far-spreading business of religion today. Bharat or India is the seat of this way of life. The soul of this nation is this throbbing, thriving, celebration of diversity. Being Hindu is celebrating this diversity and recognising the underlying sameness in the glaring differences.

Bharat goes beyond the lines drawn on a map. Bharat is a concept of inclusivity and humanism that has transcended generations and generations, invasions after invasions. In the words of Ernest Renan: A nation is a spiritual principle and not a group determined by the configuration of the earth…a nation is a soul…the nation, like the individual, is the fruit of a long past spent in toil, sacrifice and devotion. It couldn't be truer for a nation like ours. Similarly, being Hindu goes beyond the God you worship. It's the celebration of the various paths that lead to the same God. In its *Hindutva* lies this nation's essence. I'm a Hindu, which makes me an Indian. I'm an Indian, which makes me a Hindu. And where I fold my hands or bow my head in worship has nothing to do with it."

The newly awakened Bharat is now ready to free itself of communal politics by rejecting the "breaking-Bharat" forces that have pitted one Bharatiya against another and bluffed them with slogans like "secularism under threat". By embracing our traditional values of plurality, diversity and unity we are strengthening the chord of integrity that binds all Bharatiya people. This process is in the national interest and also in the interest of the people following Islam or Christianity in Bharat. Getting rid of this hypocritical and artificial secularism in turn will disable the machinery that has hollowed our society and is robbing us of our priceless heritage. When these selfish and anti-social hypocrites say "secularism is in danger" they actually mean their "pseudo-secularism" and business based on the same is in danger. The nation is finally getting rid of such "secularism" to strengthen unity, integrity and fraternity.

Endnote :

This article first appeared in *The Sunday Guardian* on September 19, 2020.

25

'Liberals' Practise Modern Untouchability

A recent visit by German Ambassador Mr. Walter J. Lindner to the RSS headquarters at Nagpur has created an unnecessary controversy. He is not the first ambassador or foreign diplomat to visit RSS offices either in Nagpur or Delhi. These visits are considered routine and a welcome exchange of ideas over a cup of tea or a meal and take place often. However, he is the first ambassador to make such a visit public.

In Bharat, a clique has flourished largely with the support and patronage of the ruling dispensation during the Congress regime, known as "left-liberals". I don't know who coined this oxymoronic term. In practice, the people who adhere to this school of thought have been highly illiberal and intolerant of people with views that differ from theirs. These forces have consistently tried to condemn, defame, oppose and ostracise the RSS by spreading canards and unfounded lies about its philosophy and history. But by the grace of the Almighty and the relentless efforts of RSS workers, RSS' reach, spread and influence in Bharatiya society, pan Bharat, has only grown and continues to do so. On the other hand, this clique has been losing its grip on the narrative and the consciousness of the public and is increasingly criticised and ostracised for its elitist and discriminatory take on Bharat.

The very idea of Bharat, envisaged by the makers of Bharat and aptly represented in our constitution is that of plurality, celebrating diversity, coming together and having healthy discussions with an open mind. The "illiberal-left" absolutely opposes this. When former President Dr. Pranab Mukherjee was invited to address the RSS cadre, this very clique criticised him for accepting the invitation. Dr. Mukherjee has a long experience in public life and is a learned, veteran politician. Inviting him to address RSS workers, despite the fact that he was with the Congress party throughout his public life, demonstrated the openness of RSS, while the forces who opposed it were exposed for their illiberal, intolerant mindset. Their intolerance was also on display when they doggedly opposed the invitation of RSS functionaries to the Jaipur Literature Festival.

Recently, an article condemning the visit of the German ambassador to Nagpur came to my attention. The article was merely an aggregation of lies presented in a "scholarly" fashion, a regurgitation of other articles in the same vein that have been part of a calibrated propaganda against the RSS.

One of the lies was that RSS reveres Hitler. Nothing can be further from the truth. I have been actively involved with the RSS for four decades. Never have I heard any senior office-bearer of RSS glorifying Hitler or Nazism. On the contrary, I have, umpteen times, heard references about Israel, their heroic patriotism, national unity and commitment. During my college days, I had read and always recommended the novel *Exodus* by Leon Uris, which depicts the thrilling and inspiring story of the beginnings of the state of Israel, a dream come true after 18 centuries.

Shri N.H. Palkar, a veteran RSS *pracharak* and author of the first authentic biography of Dr. K.B. Hedgewar (the founder of RSS), has authored a book in Marathi on the victorious accomplishments of Israel—*Israel: From Torture to Strength*. When I was in RSS during my college days, the book I read on Hitler was *Nazi Bhasmasuracha Udayast*, meaning *The Rise and Fall of the Demon Nazi*.

This illiberal clique in media and intelligentsia relentlessly quotes the book, *We and Our Nationhood Defined*, authored by M.S. Golwalkar. The said book was first published in 1938 when M.S. Golwalkar was not an office-bearer of RSS. It doesn't represent RSS views. Furthermore, this book was a translation of a Marathi book by Babarao Savarkar, elder brother of V.D. Savarkar, and not authored by M.S. Golwalkar.

In an interview with the *Economic Times* (ET Sept. 8, 2016), Satyaki Savarkar, grandnephew of Nathuram Godse and Veer Savarkar said, "The relationship between Nathuram Godse and RSS *Sarsanghachalak* then, M.S. Golwalkar had soured over the latter taking credit for translating Babarao Savarkar's book *Rashtra Mimansa* in English."

M.S. Golwalkar in his detailed interview with journalist Dr. Saifuddin Jilani in 1972 elaborated on RSS' view on minorities, particularly Muslims. These so-called academicians and scholars never mention or quote this interview because this is an inconvenient truth that contradicts their propaganda, even though it is on record. I reproduce an excerpt here for the benefit of readers.

Dr. Jilani: "Much has been said about 'Indianisation' and a lot of confusion has arisen over it. Could you please tell me how to remove the confusion?"

Shri Guruji: "'Indianisation' was of course the slogan given by Jana Sangh. Why should there be such confusion? 'Indianisation' does not mean converting all people to Hinduism. Let us all realise that we are all the children of this soil and we must have our allegiance to this land. We belong to the same society and share common ancestors. We also share common aspirations. Understanding this is 'Indianisation' in the true sense.

Indianisation does not mean that one should be asked to quit his religious system. We neither said this nor are we going to say so. Rather we believe that a single religious system for the entire human society is not suitable."

During a recently held lecture series, the present *Sarsanghachalak* of RSS, Dr. Mohan Bhagwat said, "As a people, a *Rashtra*, we all have a Hindu identity. Some people take pride in referring to themselves as Hindus and there are others who do not feel that same sense of pride. Due to some material considerations or political compulsions, some may not want to say they are Hindus publicly but do so in private. And there are those who have simply forgotten. All these people are our own, they belong to Bharat. Just like in exams, we attempt easier questions first before proceeding to the difficult ones, so it is with our work. We have first chosen to approach those who consider themselves Hindus (culturally). This is because we consider no one as our enemy in the world, or in the country. There may be those who have declared us their enemies, but whilst we may defend ourselves, we have never wished to finish them. On the contrary, we aspire to take them along with us. This is the reality of *Hindutva*."

He further said: "Dr. Ambedkar had also said in the Constituent Assembly that because of our infighting, foreigners won and ruled over us. I am mentioning the spirit behind what he said, you can read his actual words. He said that in the parliament we are sitting in opposite camps but that is a compulsion of the system. In the end, all of us are one. If we don't create this feeling of fraternity, then we cannot guarantee what our future will be like. The Sangh works for the feeling of fraternity and the only basis for this fraternity is 'unity in diversity'. The world terms this traditional thought process as '*Hindutva*'. That is why when we say our nation is a '*Hindu Rashtra*', it in no way conveys that we don't need Muslims. The day it will be said that Muslims are not required, it won't remain '*Hindutva*'."

Dr. Hedgewar's biographer writes that he was an unflinching patriot and a self-made person. He had not made any person his "*guru*" or guide. He maintained excellent relationships with people from various walks of life, even those with differing and often opposing views. However, his thoughts and actions were based on "*Swa-Bodh*"—self-consciousness and self-realisation. He had great respect for Lokmanya Tilak. After the demise of Tilakji in 1920, Dr. Hedgewar accompanied Dr. Moonje to meet Yogi Aurobindo in Pondicherry, urging him to take up the leadership of the Congress. In 1921, when the Berar Prant Congress Working Committee headed by Lokanayak Ane was mulling over passing a resolution to condemn the revolutionary movement for Independence, Dr. Hedgewar intervened and persuaded them to not do it. He was equally close to revolutionary activities, and the varied groups in Congress—Tilak-supporters and Gandhi-supporters, Hindu Mahasabha leaders and even social reformers and social workers.

He had cordial relations with Dr. Moonje, V.D. Savarkar and Mahatma Gandhi. He would occasionally invite them to address *swayamsevaks* but he took every care that the decisions in RSS were taken by *swayamsevaks* only after discussion and consensus and were not influenced by these leaders. Dr. Moonje and V.D Savarkar were not a part of RSS and their opinions had no bearing on the RSS.

In a meeting in Pune addressed by Dr. Hedgewar, a person arrogantly countered him by asking, "Who is that fool who says Bharat is a *Hindu Rashtra*?" Dr. Hedgewar, without quoting any book or scholar, calmly but firmly said, "I, Dr. Hedgewar, say that Bharat is *Hindu Rashtra*." In 1937, Dr. Hedgewar arranged a tour for Veer Savarkar in Vidarbha for a month and accompanied him. Savarkarji was impressed by Sangh's work. He appreciated RSS and expressed his willingness to become a *swayamsevak* of RSS. However, Dr. Hedgewar politely suggested that his blessings were sufficient for the fledgling organisation.

It is the tradition of Bharat that there can be various interpretations of a scripture or theme. The Bhagavad Gita has been interpreted in various ways by different scholarly, learned people. The same is true for *Hindutva* also. Lokmanya Tilak gave a definition that whoever follows the Vedas is a Hindu.

> प्रामाण्यबुद्धिर्वेदेषु साधनानामनेकता ।
> उपास्यानामनियमो हिन्दुधर्मस्य लक्षणम् ।।
> *"Praamanya Buddhirvedeshu Sadhananaam Anekata.*
> *Upasyanam aniyamo Hindu Dharmasya Lakshanam"*

But this excluded Jains and Bauddha who are very much a part of Bharat.

Then Swatantryaveer V.D. Savarkar gave a broader definition saying that all the people living on this land from the Himalayas to the Indian Ocean, who treat this land as their fatherland and holy land are all Hindus.

> आसिंधु सिंधु पर्यन्ता, यस्य भारतभूमिका।
> पितृभू: पुण्यभूश्चैव स वै हिंदुरिति स्मृत: ॥
> *"Aasindhusindhuparyanta Yasya Bharatbhumika.*
> *Pitrubhu Punyabhushchaiva Sa Vai Hinduriti Smrita."*

This definition excluded Bharatiya Christians, Muslims, Parsis and Jews living in Bharat.

Shri Guruji gave a still broader definition that one who reveres Bharat as the motherland, believes in common ancestors and its age-old culture that gives a unique identity to the people living in Bharat for centuries is Hindu. In the Bharatiya context, the people are the "nation", not a "state". We were one people irrespective of different rulers or states.

In the book *Indian Ideology*, the author Perry Anderson quoted Mahatma Gandhi as saying, "India was one undivided land made by nature in which we were one nation before they came to India- ancestrally, indeed, fired with an idea of nationality unknown to other parts of the world." (Page14) The author further writes: "There was something unique about the antiquity of the subcontinent, and its tremendous impression of oneness, making its inhabitants throughout these ages distinctively Indian, with the same national heritage and the same set of moral and mental qualities. Indeed, a dream of unity has occupied the mind of India since the dawn of civilization."

This unity, a uniqueness known to the world as *Hindutva* (Hinduness) should be felt, realised and manifested in all walks of social life. This is the realisation of *Hindu Rashtra* (people). This has nothing to do with a theocratic state. Rather, a theocratic state is alien to *Hindutva* and Bharat.

Now, about *Bunch of Thoughts*. It was a compilation of M.S. Golwalkar's (Shri Guruji) thoughts expressed at various places on different occasions and under disparate circumstances from 1940 to 1965. His thoughts expressed after 1965, till 1973, are not included in it.

Present *Sarsanghachalak* Dr. Mohanji Bhagwat, during his speech recently in Delhi, discussing *Bunch of Thoughts* said, "Things are said in the context of certain circumstances and specific incidents. They are not eternally true. Guruji's eternal thoughts have been published under the title *Shri Guruji: Vision and Mission*. We have kept all those things in this which are eternally relevant while removing those which pertained to certain specific circumstances."

Often, the chapter titled "Internal challenges—Christians, Muslims and Communists" from *Bunch of Thoughts* is mentioned. In today's context, it should be interpreted as Christian evangelism, jihadi Muslim fundamentalism and Naxalism or Maoism. Their activities are a threat to the very idea of Bharat envisaged by the constitution makers. Not all Christians, but some churches and missionaries are involved in evangelical activities and wrongful conversions and they have been successful in getting the tacit support of certain members of the Christian community in the name of religion. This is why the first anti-conversion law was enacted in 1967 in Madhya Pradesh and Odisha when these states were ruled by Congress. The clause simply said that conversion by force, fraud or allurement would not be permitted, which was vehemently opposed by churches and missionaries. Similarly, not all Muslims in Bharat but some Muslim organisations are involved in propagating and spreading jihadi fundamentalism in the name of Islam and they succeed in getting support from some members of the Muslim community in the name of religion. The subversive and divisive activities of Maoists and urban Naxals are now exposed to the public. Have you ever heard of a communist organisation condemning the brutal attack and killing of Bharatiya security forces while combating Naxals and Maoists, performing their duty to protect the people and the state? The same people create a hue and cry when Bharatiya security forces are successful in nabbing or curbing the subversive activities of Naxals and Maoists. Warning Bharatiya citizens about these three anti-national activities is important and necessary.

RSS is not a banned organisation. Though the government had banned it at times, illegally, for no valid reason, the same government has had to lift the ban unconditionally. RSS is not a secret organisation. Its daily activities (*shakha*) are carried out in the open, where anybody can walk in and participate. It has a pan-Bharat presence and is consistently growing in spread, strength and influence. There is a natural curiosity and eagerness to know about its goal, methodology and philosophy.

A few years ago, a delegation of the Communist Party of China was on a visit to Bharat and they expressed their desire to meet RSS persons. I was in Delhi when this meeting was arranged. We exchanged our views on different issues over a cup of tea. They requested us not to publicise this meeting. I don't think they wanted to hide it from their masters in China, but they may have been worried about how the "left-illiberal" media and intellectuals in Bharat would react to this.

All people with open minds are welcome. The truth is that illiberal-left intelligentsia and media who vehemently oppose the RSS have never tried to meet RSS members to know and understand what the RSS is. The German ambassador did. The openness of the German Ambassador Walter J. Lindner should be welcomed.

Endnote :

This article first appeared in *The Sunday Guardian* on August 17, 2019.

26

Leftists Use Fiction to Malign Sangh

The USP of the staunch leftists, who are self-proclaimed liberal intellectuals and journalists, is their total disregard for the truth. With their agenda-driven strategies, they conclude first and then hypothesise. Weaving webs of falsehood, they have perfected the art of deception. While such fiction thrills buyers of these misrepresentations in the short run, it falls flat on its face with the test of time. The most recent example of such concoction can be seen in a Left-leaning English language magazine, wherein, efforts to malign the Sangh's *sewa* work have been made through a trumped-up fiction.

At the time of the coronavirus onslaught, when the whole country was dumbfounded, a sizeable section of society readily marched into the streets and joined the emergency task force, from day one. Assisting governmental and semi-governmental agencies, sans official accountability to the government and without expecting anything in return, these relief workers embraced life threats and tried to help out every living being in need. With death constantly looming large in one's face, serving in a pandemic is a different ball game than carrying out relief work in times of natural calamities like floods and earthquakes.

From Arunachal Pradesh to Kashmir and Kanyakumari, 5,07,656 *swayamsevaks* of the Rashtriya Swayamsevak Sangh reached out to 92,656 locations all over the country and supplied "*Sewa Bharati* ration kits" to over 73,81,802 families. 4,66,34,730 food packets were distributed to those in need of food and over 89,23,131 masks were distributed. About 19,42,179 migrants living in cities including a large number of students were helped in different ways. 60,229 units of blood were donated. 44,86,558 migrant workers on their way back home were provided with food, medicines and other emergency medical help through dedicated centres set up to cater to their needs. Members of nomadic tribes, eunuchs, those in the flesh trade, monkeys, cows and other animals dependent on temple visitors for nourishment were among the other beneficiary groups.

The *swayamsevaks* even ventured into heavily corona-infected areas to help the people there. Regardless of any filter, unbiased help was extended to those in need from every state of the country. Crowd management, registration of workers in transit and innumerable such tasks were managed as a support to the local administration. Upon the administration's clarion call in Pune city, RSS *swayamsevaks*, flanked by volunteers of other social outfits, stepped inside densely populated, risky, red zones and screened over 1,00,000 people, handing over suspected carriers to the administration for further testing.

Despite the monumental, selfless efforts of innumerable Sangh *swayamsevaks* the aforementioned magazine did not mention even an iota of these facts. Because reporting the Sangh work in a positive light is not a part of their "agenda". In fact, in the reportage of the relief work, the same old set of misinformation and falsity about Sangh is repeated to craft yet another fable that these leftists have been spinning since antiquity. In observance of journalistic ethics, these reporters did not even consider it worthwhile to approach any senior RSS functionary to confirm and discuss the allegations hurled at the Sangh. How could their conscience allow them to endorse and float such hollow stories? Oh! How did it escape my memory that leftists do not believe in concepts like conscience and "*dharma*" (ethics)?!

Another misleading claim dished out by this journalist is that RSS used government funds to aid these *sewa* activities. Even if that presumption is true, what's wrong if the government utilises funds for society through registered non-profit organisations? In reality, right from its inception, Sangh *swayamsevaks* have been carrying out their mammoth *sewa* initiatives with the funds collected from society. All initiatives are executed by different registered non-profit entities, whose accounts are periodically audited. During the Kedarnath floods, massive relief work was carried out using funds collected from the common public. At that time, we came across a letter written by a gentleman named M.D. Ramteke. It read: "I am an Ambedkarite and a staunch opponent of RSS. It is my firm belief that Dr. Ambedkar was the modern-day reincarnation of the Bhagwan Buddha. But witnessing RSS' *Sewa* work has moved me profoundly. I've observed if you donate Rs. 100/- to an RSS worker he will add Rs 10 more from his own pockets to ensure *sewa* work continues unhindered. Therefore, you can rest assured that your money will be put to the right use by RSS."

Sangh *swayamsevaks* are carrying out around 1,35,000 service projects through various registered organisations. Out of them, 90% do not take any assistance from any government, but projects are run with societal support. Invoking national consciousness and creating society-centric systems without being dependent on the State has been the fundamental belief of Sangh.

Even during corona relief work, grain distribution and food packet distribution comprised the majority of *sewa* work. A total of 95 tonnes of grain (mainly rice) was purchased at government-set prices in the states of Kerala, Assam, Nagaland, Tripura and Mumbai. One Jharkhand-based initiative (*Sarvangin Gram Vikas Samiti*, Khunti, Jharkhand) is an isolated case where a subsidy of Rs 60,000 (Rs 5 per packet) was sought over the distribution of 12,000 food packets. No governmental aid has been sought in any other state. But the agenda of tarnishing Sangh's image compels these journalists to spew hatred in the name of journalism.

That report also intends to imply that under the garb of relief activities, the Sangh is spreading its activities across the country. Misrepresentation of this sort is hardly shocking as owing to its Semitic roots, the leftist lens compels its subscribers to perceive all *sewa*-based organisations as potential missionaries, out to convert. But the Bharatiya view of life holds that *Vaishnav Jan To Tene Re Kahiye Je Peed Parai Jane Re* (call those people Vaishnav who feel the pain of others) and our society operates on the same principle. We must be specifically mindful of the fact that the communist ideology is absolutely unsympathetic to the Bharatiya view of life as it is based on spirituality, and for the leftists, spirituality is nothing but a "false consciousness".

In his address to the nation on 19 April 2020, *Sarsanghachalak* Mohan Bhagwat urged all *swayamsevaks*, "we should serve everyone selflessly with the sense of belongingness without any consideration for publicity. We must extend a helping hand with the view that I am one with the whole society. Our value system holds 'service to society is what meditation is to self'." This also is Sangh's legacy.

On the night of 12 November 1996, the news of two aeroplanes (Saudi Arabian Airlines and Kazakhstan Airlines) carrying a total of 351 migrants having had a head-on collision, crashing at Charkhi-Dadri, Haryana came in. In both the planes, a total of 351 passengers were on board out of which 300 were Muslims and 12 were Christians. Soon after, Jeetram Ji, the *sanghachalak* for the zone, along with other *swayamsevaks* and doctors of Dr. Hedgewar Hospital propelled into action, reached the site and took cognizance of the matter. They arranged for petromax and generators to illuminate the area. All the dead bodies were immediately taken to the Bhavani Government Hospital. With daybreak, the relatives of the deceased, police and administrative staff and journalists started pouring in on the site. The identified bodies were handed over to their relatives. The bodies of 76 Muslims and 3 Christians that remained unidentified were ceremoniously cremated in observance of their respective religious practice. The maulvi of a local mosque and a few people who arrived from Mumbai assisted in this process. Three days later, on 15 November, Jeetram ji was felicitated at a thanksgiving event organised at the Dadri Masjid. Most newspaper report headings reporting this event carried a title along the lines of "Khaki shorts and saffron bands are applauded at a masjid". Former Central Aviation Minister Ibrahim and another Cabinet Minister, G. Kurian, who also inspected the site, applauded the efforts of the Sangh workers by saying "We cannot appreciate your efforts enough. We are grateful for your work." Sikar's Jaffer Ali and Hakim Khan said: "These angels of God are denigrated through many demeaning suffixes but we are no longer deluded." Police superintendent Md. Shakeel thought "Sangh workers' contribution to mitigating this challenge was overwhelming. This is exactly what was expected of them."

Innumerable anecdotes like this can be stated to describe the uncanny dedication towards service by the Sangh *swayamsevaks*. It is to illustrate this point that this event has been recollected in vivid detail here. What kind of agenda these leftists must be seeing in these service activities?

Swami Vivekananda opined *"Shiva bhava se Jeeva Seva"* (serving living beings with a spirit of serving Shiva – the God). This is the message of *Hindutva*. Sangh *shakhas* echo the same sentiment and uphold service regardless of caste, creed, religion and ideology as their motto. In observance of this very value system in the past, while conducting cleanliness drives in several houses, offices and hospitals in Kerala's flood-affected areas, Sangh *swayamsevaks* even cleared water and muck from local Communist Party offices. What could be the Sangh's vested interest in this except for selfless service? Some leftist journalist should explain.

Another peculiarity of the adherents of the leftist ideology is that they don't seem to get tired of fondly referring to themselves as "liberals". When the fact is they are anything but liberal. Patient hearing of differing viewpoints is a mere overture to liberalism, the first step. Efforts to understand those follow next. Passing motions of agreement or disagreement are later steps. In case of an agreement, assimilating the decision in one's conscience, and finally, jointly working towards the actualization of previously agreed upon plans cohesively is the epitome of liberalism. It is interesting to note that the so-called liberal left lobby doesn't favour the idea of entertaining the expression of views that differ from their viewpoint. Renowned social worker and Magsaysay Award recipient Dr. Abhay Bang was once invited as the chief guest at a Sangh gathering. He graced the occasion and frankly shared his views with us. However, this did not go down well with the leftists, because they considered Dr. Bang to be "one of them". Before the event, they subjected him to negative publicity and public scrutiny through the articles published in their mouthpieces. This was done with the intent of creating psychological pressure upon him, thereby compelling him to drop the idea of addressing a Sangh gathering. To which Dr. Bang responded saying "Despite the knowledge of my political viewpoints Sangh's eagerness to hear my address is indicative of openness on their part. I will express the same views before the audience there that I have endorsed all along." But these leftists didn't relent. After his address at our event, he sent the transcript of his lecture to be published in the same mouthpiece that subjected him to blackmail. But his transcript did not feature in their magazine. This is the actual "liberal" face of the left!

Similarly, when Sangh dignitaries were invited to present their viewpoints at the Jaipur Literary Festival these "liberal" leftists made a big hue and cry against it. Ultimately, some of their top leaders boycotted the festival. Now it's worth deliberating as to why leftists evade the truth?!

The third distinguishing feature of the leftists is that they tirelessly sing unreasonable, unfounded criticisms of Sangh in a chorus and never care to check facts or quote evidence for their baseless claims. Under the smokescreen of intellectualism, they have been carrying out a covert operation against Sangh for a long time now. This involves rumour-mongering and creating illusions. The list of allegations hurled at the Sangh by these intellectuals includes myths like the Sangh was responsible for the assassination of Gandhiji because of which a ban had to be imposed upon it; that Sangh is a Manuvadi, Brahminical, patriarchal, misogynist, anti-minority, communal, Muslim-hater, anti-progressive organisation. But then again, they do not consider unearthing the truth by interacting with any Sangh functionaries and by no means do they try acquiring any first-hand experience. Simply because they are not sincere.

The Congress indeed saw the Sangh as its arch-nemesis in the days when Gandhiji was assassinated and deemed that incident as a good opportunity to annihilate the organisation by imposing a ban on its activities and making it a scapegoat. *Sarsanghachalak* Shri Guruji was arrested under Article 302 and an allegation of murder was stamped on him. However, the failure to furnish evidence to this claim compelled them to withdraw the mention of Article 302, yet, Guruji was retained in custody, citing "security issues". When the Gandhi assassination trial opened in court, it was found that Sangh's name did not even feature on the list of suspects. Nathuram Godse—who was eventually charged with Gandhiji's murder—was a member of Hindu Mahasabha, but a ban was imposed upon the RSS. Nothing explains this move other than the fact that the RSS was gaining rapidly in popularity among the countrymen. When the government could not explain the reason behind such a move, RSS launched a *satyagraha*, wherein 70,000 *swayamsevaks* from all parts of the country participated and courted arrest. Such countrywide, peaceful and disciplined *satyagraha* was one of its kind in the history of Bharat. Eventually, that same government unconditionally repealed the ban. But these leftists don't venture into the finer details.

When deliberating on the issue of repealing the ban imposed upon the Sangh, the following extract ensued in the proceedings of the Bombay Legislative Assembly of 14 October 1949, in my opinion, is noteworthy.

"Mr. Lallubhai Makanji Patel (Surat District)

Will the Hon. Minister for Home and Revenue be pleased to state—

1. Whether it is a fact that the ban on RSS has been lifted.
2. If so, what are the reasons for lifting the ban?
3. Whether lifting of the ban is conditional or unconditional.

4. If conditional, what are the conditions?
5. Whether the leader of the R.S.S has given any undertaking to the government.
6. If so, what is the undertaking?

Mr. Dinkarrao N. Desai for Mr. Morarji Desai

1. Yes.
2. The ban was lifted as it was no longer considered necessary to continue it.
3. It was unconditional.
4. Does not arise.
5. No.
6. Does not arise."

I have yet to see these facts featured in an article written by a leftist "intellectual."

I have been in contact with a Christian family for the last three years. During our first chance meeting, they bombarded me with several questions, with the question-answer round lasting well over one and a half hours. They used to be vehement Sangh opposers, then. Their last question to me was "Can a church-goer, practising Christian, who doesn't believe in idol-worship, like me, become an RSS member?" I replied with an obvious "Yes." Thereafter we happened to meet on many other occasions. On one such occasion, they quizzed me, asking "are all Sangh functionaries like you or you're an exception?" With time our association deepened and they shared with me that "the Christian community is oblivious to the facts you've shared with us". After this, they organised several meetings of Christian association leaders with me. Whenever they move into Christian gatherings, this couple makes it a point to bring up the topic of RSS. They realise the stereotypical perception of RSS among Christians is that it is opposed to Christianity. So, they ask the following questions to claimants of this claim:

1. Have you had any first-hand experience of an RSS worker opposing you (a Christian)?

2. Have you ever had an opportunity to meet an RSS functionary?

3. Have you read any RSS literature?

Most often, the answer to all three questions comes in negation. To this, they share their personal Sangh experience with the members of their community and share some Sangh literature with those interested in reading, which they regularly restock at their home.

Such receptivity or candour is not possible for the leftists. They avoid a face-off at all costs. Possibly they are insecure about their falsehood being busted.

The light of evidence can dispel the darkness of misinformation and bring about a shift in approaches if one keeps an open mind. One such anecdote is that of the North Arcot district of Tamil Nadu where the local Dravida Kazhagam leader was invited to the annual celebration of the RSS *shakha*. His acceptance of the invitation itself was a pleasant surprise to all. He arrived at the function and yet another surprise awaited the *swayamsevaks* when at the closing he went in and came back with sweets for distribution. He then explained; "In fact, a few days ago, I had come intending to stop your activities since all our DK workers were upset about your starting the *shakha* in our village. But when I saw the boys of the Savarna Brahmin locality and those from the Harijan mohallas freely mingling and playing together with joy and enthusiasm and behaving just like the children of one family, I was disarmed. I felt that our founder Periyar (E.V. Ramaswamy Naicker) too had dreamt of a similar casteless society. Whereas we of the DK have failed to achieve it, you have been silently succeeding in realising his dream. Hence I have come to convey my good wishes and brought sweets for you."

However, expecting such sincerity and honesty from leftist writers and journalists is pointless in my opinion, as they seldom write based on their experiences.

Right from its inception, RSS has been engaged in the sole objective of organising the entire Bharatiya samaj. It is owing to this goal that from our early days we made it a point to reach out to people living in as many zones, states, districts and villages of the country as possible. We have had a fair share of success in this regard. But it is not the charity or mercy of anyone that made it possible. The comprehensive breadth of work, influence and organised cohesion that is visible today for all to see took five generations of Sangh *karyakartas* to build. Thousands of people and innumerable youth were consumed like incensory (*Kapur*) to fire. It is their relentless efforts, renunciation and sacrifices that have brought such results. Despite the hurdles created by anti-Bharat forces and some political parties blinded by self-interest, Sangh's march towards the creation of a self-sufficient and self-governing Bharatiya samaj (society) remains unimpeded because of two antidotes suggested by RSS founder, Dr. Hedgewar. These antidotes are: "*Sarvesham Avirodhena*" and "*Vado Navalambyah*", which is not to oppose anyone and not to get embroiled in unnecessary debates.

Wherever Sangh *swayamsevaks* went, through their actions and behaviour, they created a favourable atmosphere. With pure compassion and a sense of responsibility towards one's society, they expanded Sangh's work. To fish out any hidden agenda in their actions is akin to putting the cart before the horse.

If one truly wants to get to the heart of the Sangh then they will need to discard the Western lens that perceives the world in binaries and adopt the Bharatiya integral and holistic view. It is the only path that will lead them to the truth of Bharat and that of the Sangh as well.

I remember a senior Sangh *karyakarta* and thinker once said: "It is very difficult to understand the Sangh using a Western or non-Bharatiya lens. It is imperative to understand the *Isha Upanishad* to understand the Sangh where the *Param Tattva* (Supreme Truth) is described in paradoxes and the paradoxes both apply equally well to the Supreme Truth." The shloka quoted by him:

> "तदेजति तन्नेजति तद्दूरे तद्वंतिके।
> तद् सर्वस्य अंतस्य तद् सर्वस्य बाह्यत: ।।"
> *Tadejati Tannejati Taddure Tadvantike*
> *Tadantarasya Sarvasya Tad Sarvasya Bahyatah*

"That moves and that moves not. That is far and the same is near; that is within all this and that is outside all this."

German theoretical physicist and philosopher, Werner Heisenberg too reckoned with the Bharatiya theory of subatomic particles when he said "It is a particle. It is a wave. It is both. What is it at a given point in time is not only difficult to decipher but impossible to find?"

To understand the Sangh one has to subscribe to the time-tested, eternal Bharatiya worldview based on spirituality which is integral and holistic in approach. But viewing the world through the prism of Bharat will mean opening the portals to the highest frontiers of human consciousness and dispelling the illusion cast by the Left. Possibly, this fear wracks their nerves and they avoid a face-off with the Sangh. Otherwise, their condition will be like that of the salt doll which jumped into the sea to test its depth and is still trying to find its way back.

Endnote :

This article first appeared in *The Sunday Guardian* on August 02, 2020.

27

Dead End on the Left

A young girl from a family known to me volunteered at the Jaipur Literature Festival this year. She noted an evident Leftist influence in the selection of topics as well as speakers – this did not surprise me. Additionally, she narrated her team leader's thoughts. This team leader, who was a self-proclaimed 'left activist,' in a matter-of-fact tone told that volunteer that the well-known lyricist, Prasoon Joshi, was not invited to JLF because "he had become a right-winger". Surprised, the girl asked- what was so wrong with being a "right-winger," isn't it just a worldview after all?! But that team leader insistently pressed, "Prasoon Joshi was acceptable when he wrote the lyrics for *Rang De Basanti*. Literature has a purpose - to invoke revolution, to take a stand against state oppression. That is what the Left stands for and hence literature is the domain of the Left. However, by writing the lyrics of *Manikarnika* he has done a disservice to the very 'idea of India' that the Left envisages. Such lyrics invoke rabid nationalism and undermine the Left philosophy."

Now, it is the prerogative of the organisers to decide who to invite and who not to. Two years ago, the organisers of the festival decided not to retract invitations sent out to Shri Dattatreya Hosabale (Joint General Secretary of RSS) and me despite severe outrage and opposition to us speaking at the JLF. This year they invited Shri Ramesh Patange, as is their prerogative. In fact, they had invited Shri Prasoon Joshi this year but he could not make it due to ill health. However, if leftists argue that Shri Prasoon Joshi should not have been called simply because writing songs for '*Manikarnika*' has made him a "right-winger," then their myopia and restrictive outlook are distinctly non-Bharatiya. It is reflective of the extreme illiberalism of the leftist ideology.

It is worth highlighting this arrogance and hypocrisy of the Left. On one hand, they are self-proclaimed warriors of free speech, considering even genuine criticism as an assault on their freedom of expression, and on the other, they do not shy away from bulldozing any viewpoint that is not to their liking. Hence, it was not at all surprising that two years ago when the organisers of the Jaipur Literature Festival invited RSS speakers for the first time ever, the Left lost its bearings. Senior communist leaders like Sitaram Yechury went ahead and boycotted the festival. Rashtriya Swayamsevak Sangh is a grassroots organisation. It exists despite serious opposition from the establishment only because it enjoys the support of the people of Bharat. Thanks to the common masses of Bharat standing solidly with Sangh, its strength and influence have multiplied manifold over time. The Left, on the other hand, is consistently losing popular support. As on today its political dominance is restricted to only one state in the South of Bharat. And this is precisely because the view of a common Bharatiya has mattered little to the Left. In the illiberal Left world, alternate thought has no space whatsoever.

Noted filmmaker and author Mr. Vivek Agnihotri shares his experiences with this illiberal Left in his book '*Urban Naxals*'. He narrates how, in 2016, he and his team were physically manhandled at Jadavpur University by "women student activists". Those activists intended to prevent him from screening his film "*Buddha in Traffic Jam*". They shouted slogans of "Go Back Bloody Fascist Brahmin". Maintaining his composure, Vivek simply suggested to the protesters that he was only screening a film and that they were free to not watch it. To which they replied, "You cannot show any movie here. There is no place for a non-communist thought in the University."

Coming back to the team leader's opposition to Prasoon Joshi's lyrics in *Manikarnika*. The song - "*Main rahoon ya na rahoon, Bharat ye rehna chahiye*" (I may or may not live, but Bharat must live on) – stuck as a sore thumb in her eye and that of her ilk and became the bone of contention. Now one cannot help but wonder what possible objection could anyone have to lyrics as benign and as moving as this. Perhaps their feelings are better conveyed through slogans like "*Bharat tere tukde honge, Insha Allah Insha Allah*" and "*Bharat ki barbadi tak jang chalegi*". No wonder "*Bharat Mata ki Jai*" holds a fascist connotation for these people.

Similar to the Semitic religions, the Left also insists on only one version of "Truth" – the only version that it subscribes to. No other narrative is allowed to exist. If one dares to differ, then their right to freedom of expression stands automatically cancelled. In fact, they even lose their right to live. Just like the Semitic thought, the Leftist-Communist ideology has been responsible for some of the most heinous political crimes in the history of the world. In Bharat too, the Left bastions (Kerala, West Bengal) have a reputation for political murders. Such intolerance is against the very spirit of Bharat and *Hindu Dharma*. Spiritual upliftment forms the cornerstone of the Bharatiya society and hence inclusiveness and freedom of thought and expression is inherently Hindu tradition. It is this nature of the *Hindu Dharma* that has allowed people of various social, religious and political strands to co-exist peacefully in Bharat since time immemorial. I am reminded of this story of Swami Vivekananda—

Having brought the rich cultural heritage of Bharat and *Hindu Dharma* to the spotlight in the West, Swami Vivekananda was getting ready to depart from London for Bharat. The year was 1897. One of his British friends asked him, "Swamiji, how do you like your motherland now after four years' experience in the luxurious, glorious, powerful West?" Swamiji's answer was poignant. He replied: "India I loved before I came away. Now the very dust of India has become holy to me, the very air is now holy to me; it is now the holy land, the place of pilgrimage, the *Tirtha*."

...and as his ship approached the shores of India, Swamiji was overcome with emotion. He stood there with hands folded and eyes moist gazing at the shoreline as if Bharat Mata had literally appeared before him. As soon as the ship pulled up in the harbour, Swami Vivekananda got off the deck and prostrated on the land of Bharat. His emotion was akin to that of a child who had finally found his way to his mother's lap and just like that he uttered, "All my worries have dissolved in the lap of my mother".

What troubles me immensely is how have we come to this point where those born on the Bharatiya land, nurtured and nourished by its food, water and air, educated by the money of its taxpayers, are somehow okay with "*Bharat tere tukde honge*", but "*Main rahoon ya na rahoon, Bharat ye rehna chahiye*" enrages them. Political parties whose existence is based in the policy of divide and rule and who nurture such '*Tukde-tukde* gangs' for their narrow, vested interests or outsource their insight-cultivation business to those Leftist think-tanks need to introspect into the fraudulence of their ideological premise. If they don't, the patriotic citizens of this country are bound to take cognizance and vanquish such groups, sooner or later.

Endnote :

This article first appeared in *The Indian Express* on March 27, 2019.

28

Sangh & Muslim Brotherhood : Comparing the Incomparable

Congress President Rahul Gandhi's feeble attempt to draw an equivalence between the Muslim Brotherhood and the RSS caused astonishment in those familiar with the RSS and people who hold a culture-based national perspective. Alternatively, those professing communist and Maoist ideology, and practitioners of opportunistic politics were predictably elated. Neither of these responses is unanticipated. However, it must not be assumed that the Congress president lacks awareness of the violence that Islamist terrorists inflict on the civilised world. Neither does this mean that he is unaware of the social work that the RSS carries out through its affiliated organisations, not to mention the growing appeal and support the Sangh receives from society. But then, why would he say such a thing?

His political advisers have succeeded in convincing him that criticising the RSS will yield political dividends, and that baseless and provocative statements will compensate for the lack of groundwork that is required to lift the grand old party out of its political misfortunes. Hence, he has been schooled to render these statements in a dramatic style without paying any attention to their veracity. When one such statement was legally challenged by a *swayamsevak*, the Congress president avoided explaining his position in court.

In reality, the Sangh is engaged in the noble work of connecting and binding Bharatiya society with the eternal thread of spirituality and the integral and holistic Bharatiya view of life. To equate this inclusive view of life with the Muslim Brotherhood is an affront to our great civilisational heritage and history. If one was to view the Islamist ideology in practise, the word "brotherhood" itself is inappropriate. In fact, the Muslim Brotherhood, which he chose to cite as an example, views not only the non-Muslims as outsiders, but even Muslims outside the Salafi Sunni fold as outside their ideological commune, and not Muslim.

11 September 2018 will be the 125th anniversary of Swami Vivekananda's Chicago address in the Parliament of the World's Religions. In that historic address, he presented to a world audience the inclusive worldview of Hindu culture. This was not merely an exercise in intellectualism, but one where the strings of the heart were playing a unique tune for an audience unfamiliar with the Hindu view of life but responsive to the music in those sincere words. Swami Vivekananda began his address with "My American Brothers and Sisters…", an endearment that was received with a standing ovation that lasted a few minutes.

In that speech, Swami Vivekananda said, "I am proud to belong to a religion which has taught the world both tolerance and universal acceptance. We believe not only in universal toleration, but we accept all religions as true. I am proud to belong to a nation that has sheltered the persecuted and the refugees of all religions and all nations of the earth. I am proud to tell you that we have gathered in our bosom the purest remnant of the Israelites, who came to southern India and took refuge with us in the very year in which their holy temple was shattered to pieces by Roman tyranny. I am proud to belong to the religion which has sheltered and is still fostering the remnant of the grand Zoroastrian nation."

"Sectarianism, bigotry, and its horrible descendant, fanaticism, have long possessed this beautiful earth. They have filled the earth with violence, drenched it often and often with human blood, destroyed civilisation and sent whole nations to despair. Had it not been for these horrible demons, human society would be far more advanced than it is now."

Dr. Ambedkar has also written about the Islamic view of the world. In his book '*Thoughts on Pakistan,*' he says, "Islam is a close corporation and the distinction that it makes between Muslims and non-Muslims is a very real, very positive and very alienating distinction. The brotherhood of Islam is not the universal brotherhood of man. It is the brotherhood of Muslims for Muslims only. There is a fraternity but its benefit is confined to those within that corporation. For those who are outside the corporation, there is nothing but contempt and enmity."

Muslim Brotherhood wants to bring the Shariat state everywhere, whereas the Sangh stands for a *Hindu Rashtra* that is based on the ideal of spreading universal acceptance, as propagated by Swami Vivekananda.

How can the fundamentalist Islamist ideology of the Muslim Brotherhood be equated with the universal brotherhood of Swami Vivekananda? Furthermore, why does Rahul Gandhi feel compelled to speak ill of an organisation that follows the precepts of universal brotherhood and is focused on organising the entire society?

A senior columnist once said to me a few years ago, that the Congress has been reduced to a party desperately trying to come to power by any means and is outsourcing its intellectual activity to the communists. Ever since the Congress has carried out this outsourcing to the communists, it has allied itself with intolerance and has opposed the national perspective and activities.

Before independence, the Congress was an open platform, amongst its members were Hindu Mahasabhaites, supporters of revolutionaries, those with a radical approach (*garam dal*) and also those having a moderate approach (*naram dal*). There was space for everyone. However, when this platform started taking the shape of a political party, it went from being a large tent of ideas to an organisation alienating and excluding those having different views. It was, however, a gradual progression. Even after independence, there was space for diverse viewpoints; if Pandit Jawaharlal Nehru was a staunch critic of the RSS, Sardar Patel invited *swayamsevaks* to join the Congress party. In 1962, during the Indo-China war, Nehru, once a critic of the RSS, was so impressed by the selfless service of the Sangh that he invited the RSS to participate in the Republic Day parade of 1963. And even though the invitation came at very short notice, as many as 3,000 *swayamsevaks* participated with pride in the parade.

During the 1965 Pakistan invasion, Lal Bahadur Shastri called for a meeting with prominent leaders, including the second RSS *Sarsanghachalak* Guruji Gowalkar, going so far as to arrange his immediate transport to the national capital. During this meeting, a Communist party leader repeatedly asked Shastri, "What was your army doing when India was invaded?" Agitated by this stance, especially at such a critical time, Guruji Gowalkar intervened and asked the gentleman why he couldn't say, "our army"? He asked him if he belonged to some other country.

Setting politics aside, this tradition of dialogue (*samvaad*) continued till the 1970s. Subsequently, the influence of the communist ideology started gaining traction in the Congress and the intolerance and "otherness" so closely linked with Stalinist ideals began rearing its ugly head. Confrontational language and an "us vs. them" discourse started dominating.

Apart from the BJP, most political parties reflect communist influence in their intellectual cell to varying degrees. Hence, we find that for short-sighted political gains, there is a tendency to side with attempts (inspired by Leftist ideology) of breaking or weakening the unity of the people of the country, and at the same time opposing national ideas and forces. This enervating influence over the past few decades has left the Congress in a strange condition, almost as if its body is but a shell that is now occupied by a Maoist soul. This is not merely an observation but is borne out by the display of support the Congress routinely expresses for Maoist protests. It is obvious that the authors who wrote articles in support of the above-mentioned statement of the Congress president seem to have links with the Left ideology.

Is it not alarming that Congress leaders stand in solidarity with those who raised slogans of "*Bharat tere tukde honge, Inshallah, Inshallah*", "*Bharat ki barbadi tak jung rahegi*" or "*Afzal Guru hum sharminda hai, tere qatil zinda hai*". Afzal Guru was the mastermind behind the terrorist attack on the Parliament, the temple of democracy; a person who was sentenced to death by the Supreme Court during the UPA regime. When the Congress leaders support those who instigate caste violence, undermining and violating the Constitution, one is compelled to feel that the Maoist soul guides their action, using the Congress' identity as a cover. The infiltration of disruptive urban Maoists into mainstream life and their influence has only recently come to light. When a mainstream party like the Congress, which has held power for so many years, supports their destructive designs, it is not an occasion to be surprised but to be saddened. Despite ideological differences, it is important to concede that the Congress of the past never spoke in the terms used by their current leaders or aligned with disruptive forces that undermined the country and national interest.

It is deeply worrying to see the oldest political party in the country, the one that was supported by people across the country, stand with such anti-national elements. As a result, the Congress' support base is being eroded.

Swami Vivekananda had crossed the oceans to plant the flag of Bharatiya civilisational and cultural values on foreign land. Today, a politician from the same country travels abroad and equates the Bharatiya cultural ethos with the Muslim Brotherhood. This is an insult to Bharatiya civilisational values and culture.

In a democracy, it is expected that there will be differences in opinion and ideologies. However, it is imperative to rise above these differences for the good of the nation. It is only when this unity supersedes politics will the country find solutions to the problems that ail us and move towards realising the Bharat that Swami Vivekananda presented to the world all those years ago.

Endnote :

This article first appeared in *First Post* on September 13, 2018.

29

Bharat Won't Become a Hindu Pakistan

It is indeed a sad commentary that some Congress leaders, under the influence of the Church as well as the Communist ideology, have resorted to making anti-national comments with the narrow intent of reaping political dividends, thereby dealing a blow to our national identity and self-esteem. Since these leaders are the so-called eminent scholars whose curriculum vitae can put many to shame, I am reminded of the comments made by former President of Bharat Dr. S. Radhakrishnan in his *'Report on Higher Education in free India'* published in 1948.

In the report, he talks about "The Un-Indian Character of Education", where he laments how the modern education system is not at all in sync with the Indian philosophical heritage and ethos. "One of the major complaints against the system of education which has prevailed in this country for over a century is that it obliterated India's glorious past and that it deprived the Indian students of knowledge about their own culture and traditions. Unfortunately, this has produced in some cases a feeling that we as a civilization are without roots; and, what is worse, that our roots limit us to a world which is completely shorn of the present reality of the modern world outside."

Recently, a senior Congress leader stated that if BJP returns to power in 2019, Bharat will become a "Hindu Pakistan". In fact, it is the pursuit of foreign philosophies like communism that has not only impacted the *Bharatiyata* of our people but also their language and terminology. In reality, the very terminology "Hindu Pakistan" is an oxymoron. The usage of words like 'Hindu Pakistan', 'Hindu Taliban' and 'Hindu Terror' is an attempt to change the Bharatiya narrative and a prime example of the expression of the 'un-Indian' thought process of such pseudo-intellectuals.

Before we move on to the irrelevance of this misconstrued narrative, it is important to understand what defines Bharat and *Hindutva*.

I may recall here that recently, during his speech at the RSS program in Nagpur, former President Dr. Pranab Mukherjee said, "The concept of a 'nation-state' as in the West is completely different from our concept of a nation. India was a state long before the concept of the European nation-state gained ground. This model of a defined territory, a single language, shared religion and a common enemy is the model which led to the formation of various nation-states in Europe. On the other hand, Indian nationalism emanated from "universalism", the philosophy of *Vasudhaiva Kutumbakam* and *Sarve Bhavantu Sukhinah, Sarve Santu Niramayah.* We see the whole world as one family and pray for the happiness and good health of all. Our national identity has emerged through a long-drawn process of confluence, assimilation, and co-existence. The multiplicity of culture, faith and language is what makes India special. We derive strength from tolerance. We accept and respect our pluralism. We celebrate our diversity. These have been a part of our collective consciousnesses for centuries. Any attempt at defining our nationalism in terms of dogmas and identities of religion, region, hatred and intolerance will only lead to dilution of our national identity."

It is this fundamental philosophy of generosity, acceptance, inclusiveness and universal care that forms the bedrock of our country's spirituality-based identity and an all-encompassing view of life. This is well known to the whole world. This has been described as the 'Hindu view of life' by Dr. Radhakrishnan. He says: "The Hindu method of reform enables every group to retain its past associations and preserve its individuality and interest. For as students are proud of their colleges, so are groups of their gods. We need not move students from one college to another, but should do our best to raise the tone of each college, improve its standards and refine its ideals, with the result that each college enables us to attain the same goal."

"We see that the Hindu recognises one Supreme spirit though different names are given to it. In the social economy, there are many castes but one society. In the population, there are many races and tribes but all are bound together by one common spirit."

In his book, *Swadeshi Samaj*, Gurudev Rabindranath Thakur underlines this very fact. Therein he says, "To feel unity in diversity and to establish unity amongst variety - this is the underlying *dharma* of Bharat. Bharat does not regard difference as hostility, she does not regard other as enemy. That is why without sacrifice or destruction she wants to accommodate everybody within one great system. That is why she accepts all ways and sees the greatness of each in his own sphere." Further, he says, "Because of this virtue in Bharat we shall not be frightened considering any society as our opponent. Each fresh conflict will enable us to expand ourselves. The Hindus, the Bauddha, the Muslims and the Christians will not fight each other and die in Bharat. Here they will find a meeting point. That meeting point will not be non-Hindu, but very specifically Hindu. However foreign maybe her body parts, her life and spirit will be of Bharat."

Congress leaders seem to forget that it was a contradiction of this very generosity, inclusiveness, integral and all-encompassing spirituality that gave birth to Pakistan. The entire event was a consequence of an education system that encouraged philosophies such as Communism that negated "*Bharatiyata*" on the hollow presumption that to do so was a necessity in order to "move with the times". Basic lessons of history that Pakistan was born as an antithesis to "*Bharatiyata*" were forgotten.

The identity of Bharat is its territorial integrity, its self-reliance, its spiritual reservoir of wisdom that passed down thousands of years, its cultural ethos and the deep resonance of its philosophy. Is it therefore not surprising that these 'ultra-modern' and 'well-educated' Congress leaders are destroying this unparalleled legacy of Bharat just for electoral benefits? What they are doing is in fact threatening the very existence of Bharat, negating its present and recreating the same scenario which had led to the Partition of Bharat!

Our more than 5000-year-old civilizational values of inclusiveness, the celebration of diversity and cultural ethos which were described by Dr. Pranab Mukherjee, Dr. S. Radhakrishnan and Gurudev Rabindranath Thakur as the "*Hindu Way of Life*" are all equal legacy of Pakistan as well. However, I consider it pitiable that Pakistan chose to forego this rich legacy. Pakistan could well have claimed this ancient legacy while simultaneously choosing to practice its own religion. It would still have remained Hindu! The two identities were not in conflict with each other. The Hindu view of life would have assisted it in finding a place of respect in the world. Mr. M.C. Chagla, Dr. APJ Abdul Kalam and Pakistan-born Canadian citizen Mr. Tarek Fateh were among the many Muslims who continue to claim their

Hindu civilizational identity. Hence, if Pakistan had remained a Muslim nation but continued to follow its ancient legacy of tolerance, we could have today labelled it as "Hindu Pakistan". In this respect, look at the example of Nepal which despite being a separate nation has enjoined itself to this legacy and heritage. It has been a neighbour as well and there has been no conflict. Moreover, both countries have set forth exemplary peaceful co-existence.

It is due to its deep cultural roots that Bharat has developed a unique identity in the world. This unique identity was made distinct by the "Hindu Identity" or "Hindu view of life" as described by Gurudev Thakur and Dr. Radhakrishnan. If people are averse to the term "Hindu" it may be referred to as Indic or Bharatiya as well. However, its content, cultural imperatives and resonance do not change. In either case, the Hindu faith believes that the truth is unequivocal, and it may be called by different names. However, the main question is how does one remain rooted in Hindu philosophy and tradition? An example of this may be found in an anecdote about Acharya Mahapragya, a monk and the spiritual head of the Terapanth sect emanated from Shwetambara Jain. He once said, "I am a Terapanthi because I am a Sthanakvasi. I am a Sthanakvasi because I am a Shwetamabara Jain. I am a Shwetambara Jain because I am a Jain. And I am a Jain because I am a Hindu". This is a beautiful example of Bharatiya thought that one can hold many identities simultaneously, embody diversity and yet see no contradiction in this existence.

This has been Bharat's traditional thinking forever, a celebration of diversity. However, over a period of time, this connection to one's roots got weakened and the narrative changed. The new paradigm became – I am a Hindu, but I am a Jain. I am a Jain, but I am a Shwetambar. I am a Shwetambar, but I am a Sthanakvasi Jain or I am a Terapanthi Jain.

It is this disconnect with our roots that creates a situation where we delve into petty and narrow-minded politics and try to change the very basis of our identity and existence. This is exactly what is happening now where some Congress leaders have chosen to make irresponsible statements and chant slogans like 'Hindu Pakistan', 'Hindu Taliban', 'Hindu Terror', etc. The nadir is reached when in utter disregard of our own identity, we bring down the esteem of an entire nation through anti-national slogans like *'Bharat tere tukde honge..', 'Bharat ki barbadi tak jung chalegi, jung chalegi…'*

It is a pity that such terminology and slogans are the brainchild of the so-called elite, educated and progressive people, considered "enlightened". I reiterate that it is not the poor and backward who chant these anti-national slogans. These are chanted by students studying in most modern and progressive government-funded institutions. Where universities must remain the organs of civilization, these students are aided and abetted in this anti-national exercise by none other than some of their own professors who have been educated in our country but have fallen prey to shallow foreign ideologies. It is not the poor who speak in these tones but the privileged and the entitled. There is no better example of 'non-Bharatiya' behaviour than them.

It is for this reason that Dr. Pranab Mukherjee reminded us of the 5000-year-old heritage of our country. One thing which is for sure is that only if we choose to retain the connection with our roots and our civilizational heritage, can we stay true to our identity.

The famous poet Prasoon Joshi has written :

> उखड़े उखड़े क्यों हो वृक्ष, सूख जाओगे।
> जितनी गहरीं जड़ें तुम्हारी, उतने ही तुम हरियाओगे।
>
> "If you lose touch with your roots, you will fail in all your endeavours.
> As you embark in a new direction or in pursuit of your dreams, never forget your roots.
> The deeper your roots, the more you will prosper and rise.
> Understanding your heritage and ancestry will ensure a secure and bright future."

Endnote :

This article first appeared in *Hindustan Times* on August 8, 2018.

30

Akhand Bharat : A Geo-Cultural Concept

Some time back in the city of Mumbai, a Shiv Sainik threatened the shop owner of one "Karachi Sweet Mart", demanding a change in the title of his shop. Pakistan instigates terrorist activities against Bharat, therefore the name must go, he reasoned. To safeguard his commercial interests and defuse tension the shop owner promptly complied and shrouded the word "Karachi" under a sheet of paper, thus averting a conflict. It has also been reported that Shiv Sena has officially distanced itself from this incident. This pitiable exchange is an indicator of the lowly mindset, a lack of historical insight and political power-fuelled arrogance on that Shiv Sainik's part. Had he developed a little sense of the history of Bharat he would've shown sensitivity towards the agony of the tumultuous times which compelled that shop owner's ancestors to wind up businesses and flee from Karachi overnight to arrive in Bharat. It is possible that in their heydays in Karachi ten servants like that tormentor were at the beck and call of the members of that business house. Either due to weaknesses or the helpless attitude of the then Hindu society and the political leadership of Bharat, such families were forced into exile and took refuge in their own country. Slowly, bit by bit, without indulging in any malpractices they pieced together their business here again; generating wealth and employment for the country. Numerous migrants from Sindh and Punjab regions have made their fair share of contribution in enriching the country's wealth reserves since their arrival. They also established many educational and vocational institutions that continue to serve and aid all sections of society till date. Firmly holding the memory of one's roots in the mind is a moral responsibility for each successive generation of migrants so that someday when the conditions are conducive, they can lead their kin back into their homeland.

"Akhand Bharat Smriti Divas", a day that commemorates and celebrates pre-partition integrated Bharat is celebrated on 14 August among the youth of Bharat in a big way. The heart-wrenching tale of the partition catastrophe is reminded and the resolve to reunite the separated parts of Bharat is reaffirmed. This Shiv Sainik may be oblivious of this fact. At the time of partition, Yogi Arvind remarked, "It is an unnatural partition and unnatural things are impermanent. Sooner or later Bharat will be reintegrated." That our roots lie in Karachi or we were under compulsion to leave our homeland and that one day we will return where we belong—such volition should not offend anyone. And for future generations to behold the memory of their roots in their hearts, retaining the name "Karachi" is important.

Forced out of their homeland the people of Israel were in exile for over 1,800 years. For those 1,800 years, each New Year's Day they renewed their vow by chanting "Next year in Jerusalem," and today Israel is a prosperous and powerful nation.

Supporters of Pakistani terrorist activities and jihadi militants and anti-national elements disguised as legitimate organisations operate within Bharat and are active in Mumbai too. A review of their audacious activities can send shivers down the spine of any regular patriot. Stills of Mumbai's Raza Academy followers kicking and desecrating the *Shaheed Smarak* (martyrs' memorial) testifies to one such incident. However, any Shiv Sainik's vehement opposition to it is yet to be heard.

The mention of integrated Bharat causes many to raise their eyebrows. It is imperative that this concept be differentiated from typical geopolitical expansionism. No one king ever was the sole ruler of the entire landmass of Bharat before the one-regime umbrella rule of the British government, yet Bharatiya life was intricately interwoven across kingdoms. Bharat is a geo-cultural phenomenon, deeply rooted in the conscience of its land. This eternal truth of our lives deserves to be embraced. A spirituality based holistic and integral view of life that we have been adherents of is what gives Bharat its distinct identity and character. This is how the world has known us for ages now. It is this identity that has come to be popularised as "*Hindutva*" or Hinduness in lands outside of Bharat. "*Hindutva*" as a mere clarion call of some political sub-group is one thing. But identification with *Hindutva* as the cultural essence of this landmass will force one to stop and think. In his seminal research work titled "World History of Economics", the famous British economist Angus Maddison claimed that between the 1st Century AD and 17th century AD, Bharatiya contribution to global trade was up to 33%, which was the highest in the whole world. Members of various ethnic groups and followers of different belief systems sought asylum in varied parts of Bharat at different points in time—Jews in the 2nd century AD, Parsis in the 6th century AD and Syrian Christians in the 8th century AD. Despite having received asylum in varied geographies, ruled by different kings, and the people speaking various languages and worshipping different deities, aliens to the land from a denominational, linguistic and dynastic viewpoint, those victims of homelessness and persecution were welcomed, accepted, nurtured and integrated within existing cultures because Bharat was geo-culturally uniform. Therefore, there's a prevalence of the places of worship of Bharatiya people across this landmass. Hinglaj Devi temple, Nankana Sahib gurudwara in present-day Pakistan, Dhakeshwari Devi temple in modern-day Bangladesh, Pashupatinath temple and Goddess Sita's birthplace in Nepal, Ramayan-era sites in Sri Lanka. Holy sites for Buddhists residing in Brahmadesh (present-day Myanmar), Sri Lanka, Tibet, Bhutan and several other countries are located in Bharat. Bharatiya people have venerated and circumambulated the Kailash Mansarovar for time immemorial. Undertaking pilgrimages to these holy places has been a way of life for the people of integrated Bharat. One can witness a consolidation of the collective conscience of our land in a newborn's "*naamkaran sanskaar*" (naming rite) at times. A family that hailed from Karnataka was residing in Gujarat. They named their daughters Sindhu and Saryu. Saryu river does not flow through Karnataka and Sindhu river flows through present-day Pakistan. Given the current scenario, it is possible that this family might be threatened that they need to change their daughter's name as Pakistan instigates terrorist activities against Bharat. One ISRO scientist based in Karnavati, who hailed from Faizabad, Uttar Pradesh named his daughter Kaveri. The daughter of a family in Gujarat's Bhavnagar is named Jhelum and a girl who was born in a family in Vidarbha has been named Raavi. This conscience that has flowed seamlessly and been a source of great cultural splendour is backed by the spirit of geo-cultural oneness.

If we pan our view towards our neighbouring countries, it is evident that not a single country that distanced itself from the cultural spirit of our land and severed ties with Bharat is contented or happy. The essence of wholeness through security, prosperity, peace and happiness for all those countries lies in seamless integration with Bharat because those countries are not just neighbours of Bharat, they are in fact integral units of a larger geo-cultural consciousness and were always so. However, to realise this in a concrete form, Bharat has a considerable role to play. Its initiatives since 2014 in that direction are notable and consoling. Attendance of the leaders of all the neighbouring countries at the Prime Minister's oath-taking ceremony in 2014 and Bharat's promise of unconditional support to strengthen their economic condition is well-known to the rest of the world. While retaining the governance structures of all these countries, if efforts are made to strengthen the emotional bonds around the geo-cultural component then together we will be able to reclaim our economic glory. History of the modern world holds that the economic prosperity of the so-called developed nations of Western liberal democracies is based in torture, plunder and inhuman trade of slaves. But these were never the basis of the economic prosperity of the Bharatiya geo-cultural unit. Merchants, traders and businessmen from this landmass travelled great distances to carry out trade with people from distant lands, but they never enslaved the native people, plundered their wealth, colonised their land, forcibly convert them or tortured them in any way. In fact, the Bharatiya people enriched the lands where they engaged in trade in terms of both economic and cultural prosperity. The sweet memory of this unique exchange is still fresh in many minds. Chinese ambassador to America, Hu Shih, for this reason, said: "India conquered and dominated China culturally for over 20 centuries without ever having to send a single soldier across her border."

People of Bharatiya origin were enslaved and forced into labour in the Caribbean islands by the Englishmen 150 years ago. Countries like Trinidad, Barbados, Jamaica, Suriname, and Guyana have retained a common identity that is based in the shared geo-cultural past of these countries. Their history as independent nation-states is recent but the memory of a long-shared common past is intact and guides the policies around inter-state travel, trade and culture despite the separate governments of each country. A general sentiment of overall mutual cooperation and support prevails between these countries, making the exchange of goods, knowledge and ideas easier to flow.

The geo-cultural history of the integrated Bharatiya landmass predates at least 10,000 years. The heights of economic prosperity and cultural prowess achieved by human civilization here served as lighthouses guiding the path for many newer civilisations that sought her knowledge and wisdom. If the larger, integrated Bharat were to achieve similar economic and cultural heights then the memory of the shared values and shared past of this geo-cultural entity must be remembered. Lowly mindset, the lack of historical insight and political power-fuelled arrogance deserve to be frankly and openly criticised and forbidden. Every effort must be undertaken to retain the memory of the past glory of the civilisation our ancestors erected and strive to achieve similar or even greater civilisational heights by routinely repeating the resolve to ourselves. We must not forget that the 1,800-year-long struggle did not prevent Israel from realising the goal of reclaiming the lost land.

Endnote :

This article first appeared in *The Sunday Guardian* on January 9, 2021.

Inspiration Continues

31

Dr. Hedgewar : A Leader Par Excellence

RSS founder, Dr. Hedgewar bore the humble appearance of just another Bharatiya. His extraordinary thoughts made his character exceptional. He was a visionary. The ability of his mind to see the future set him apart. When he was a grade three student, sweets were being distributed at his school at an event held in honour of Queen Victoria. A born patriot, at mere eight or nine years of age, when children desire multiple servings of sweets, he threw away the sweet that was given to him. This event is unusual because up until that point neither the ripples of the independence movement had touched Nagpur nor was the environment at his home charged with revolutionary thoughts of national significance. It would only be later, in 1905, that the freedom movement knocked there yet Doctor ji had been averse to slavery and had an inborn affinity towards freedom. This was not a reaction to an external situation, but his natural instinct.

Organiser Extraordinaire & Unyielding:

Similarly, in 1907, when the public chanting of *Vande Mataram* was banned, under his guidance, all the students of both sections of his matriculation class welcomed the school inspector with the slogan "*Vande Mataram*". This spells Keshav's (first name of Dr. Hedgewar) organising deftness. The protest that he spearheaded was so well-knit that the consequent principal's inquiry saw not one pupil disclose who the leader of their demonstration was. The school remained shut for some days thereafter. Later guardians convened on the idea that all the students should go to the principal's office individually and when quizzed whether they would commit such an act again, they should shake their heads in denial. This will mean re-entry into the school and continuation of school operations. But Keshav rejected this idea. He reasoned that he had the right to worship and praise his motherland, which led to his expulsion from the school. Later upon completing his matriculation from Poona, he went to Calcutta to study Medicine because that was the hub of all revolutionary activity.

Incessant Activity:

After graduating in Medicine in 1916, he returned to Nagpur. One can extrapolate when a member of an ordinary family returned home after becoming a doctor in those days, what his family and the society might have expected of him. Most of the senior Congress leaders of the time were married then. Some worked as teachers, doctors, farmers, and advocates, while others ran businesses to sustain their families. Even as family men these people were actively involved in the independence movement. Doctor ji could have very well emulated his contemporaries, however, his desire for independence was so intense that he often said- "I don't have time to think about myself until the country is free from enslavement". Therefore, he channelized all his energy towards the freedom movement. He participated actively in both armed revolutions as well as the non-violent movement led by the Congress. Upon Gandhiji's call for the Non-Cooperation Movement and Civil Disobedience Movement, he participated in those and faced imprisonment as a consequence.

Visionary & Global Thinker:

He was the managing coordinator for logistics at the Congress session that was to be held in Nagpur in 1920. He trained to engaged 1200 volunteers for that event. The resolution that he suggested to the all-India plenary committee where he proposed that the motto of the Congress should be to help Bharat achieve complete and total independence and to free the whole world from the shackles of capitalism is noteworthy. However, the resolution for complete and total independence was accepted by the Congress in December 1929 in a meeting in Lahore. For this reason, on January 26, 1930, all the *shakhas* were instructed to laude the Congress. Doctor ji's proposal of complete and total independence was validated by the Congress after ten full years is a shining example of his foresight.

Lokasangraha (Mobilisation of the masses):

The people of Nagpur, Vidarbha were divided into several groups then. Tilak followers and Gandhi followers in Congress, Congress and the Revolutionary Movement, Congress and Hindu Mahasabha would not get along. Doctor ji on the other hand shared an equally good rapport with all the different groups. Despite not having an exclusive allegiance to any single group, instead of being equally distant from all he shared similar proximity with all. This was his unusual and unique achievement. Therefore, in the 1921 Wardha meeting, when Congress was planning to pass a motion to condemn the then-ongoing revolutionary activities, Doctor ji met with Loknayak Ane who was the then president of the forum. He said, "We understand that you do not agree with their ways but their spirit of patriotism should not be doubted. We, instead of fighting against the foreign rulers, are fighting amongst ourselves. This is not desirable." Eventually, the Congress did not pass the motion against the revolutionaries.

People's Leader:

He participated in the Non-Cooperation Movement of 1921. To get imprisoned epitomises patriotism was a widely held belief at the time, therefore pleading defence in court was deemed cowardice. Doctor ji did not subscribe to such notions. So he also participated in the *satyagraha*, defended his own case in court thereby defending one's right to defend oneself and finally embraced imprisonment despite getting bail. Even though he didn't agree with Gandhiji's decision to support the Khilafat movement, he did not hesitate to work with Gandhiji. He would say, differences of opinion should not become a bane in the movement against British oppressive rule. He spent one year in confinement in a prison. Heavy rainfall couldn't prevent crowds consisting of thousands of people from turning up to receive him outside the jail the day he was freed. There they sang his praises to which he responded by saying, "Going to the prison has not elevated my merit in any way, but if this is your opinion, then the British government should be thanked." An event was organised in the Venkatesh Hall in Nagpur to welcome him back where prominent Congress leaders like Vitthalbhai Patel, Pandit Motilal Nehru, Rajagopalachari and Dr. Ansari were present. There also he echoed the same thought. He opined that going to jail being the sole indicator of patriotism is a flawed notion. Bringing about social awakening while living in the thick of the society is an equally important task.

Curing the root cause of the disease and not just the symptoms:

Shri Triloknath Chakraborty who was Dr. Hedgewar's fellow member in *Anushilan Samiti* came to Nagpur in 1989 to participate in the Dr. Hedgewar Birth centenary celebrations (1989). He shared at that event that while in Calcutta Dr. Hedgewar would say, "I want to unify Hindus." That vision precisely manifested into Sangh's vision when he started Rashtriya Swayamsevak Sangh (RSS) in 1925. Hence it is clear that his actions were preempted and not a reaction to any specific incident.

"Sangh" Method – Teamwork:

Sangh was founded on the auspicious occasion of Vijayadashami in October 1925, however, its name was decided after six months. 22 *swayamsevaks* deliberated and convened on its name in April 1926. Dr. Hedgewar was way senior to all the *swayamsevaks* present in terms of age, intellectual capacity, experience and vision still he participated in the brainstorming session to finalise the name of the organisation and solicited suggestions from each one of them. Had Dr. Hedgewar announced that Sangh would be named so and so it would have been irrefutably accepted, still he chose a team-oriented approach towards the goal. He chose this approach because the goal was not merely to select a name but also to demonstrate the desired style of working. With this demonstration, he proclaimed Sangh implies teamwork and that we must join hands and make cohesive, informed decisions.

Unique, self-dependent working style:

The practice of obtaining charity from wealthy people of the society for social work was a trend that prevailed in those days and is still prevalent. A similar funding model aided Sangh's work for the first two years. However, Doctor ji had envisioned a self-dependent organisation, whatever it takes to continue Sangh's work – time, effort, sacrifice, wealth – should be contributed by the *swayamsevak*. The virtue of serving Sangh as serving one's own work is the essence of the work style espoused by Sangh. The practice of *guru dakshina* is not new to Bharat. However, in those years it was prevalent only in the religious field. He innovated the unique idea to utilise this ancient practice in the larger social context. Most Sangh *swayamsevaks* then were students and the concept of pocket money was non-existent. These students would accept any opportunity to lend their services and contribute the remuneration earned as *guru dakshina*. To look up to one's *guru* with reverence has been the norm of our culture. Therefore, seeing Doctor ji as that figure and paying obeisance to him was a natural resort. But Doctor ji was of the opinion that Sangh is not an organisation within the society but is the organisation of the entire society. So a symbol that is as archaic as our society deserves to be glorified as the '*Guru*' in Sangh. Such thinking was truly magnanimous and ahead of its time. What could that symbol be? Without a doubt the saffron flag. Saffron is the indicator of knowledge, renunciation and the dawn. Hence he chose the natural choice of the Bharatiya society, the saffron flag.

Old foundation, new structure:

Dr. Hedgewar did not hesitate in employing modern technology to generate the necessary qualities among the members of the Hindu *samaj* in those days. Uniform *(Ganavesh)* was a novel concept for the Hindu *samaj* back then. While we stood for unity in diversity, the task of bringing about unity and discipline rendered uniforms necessary. Sangh adopted a modern uniform then. Traditions of parading and drills were not usual for the Hindu *samaj* but with the understanding that drill is essential for inculcating discipline, it was carried out using the commands followed in the British army during the initial years which have later come to be communicated in Sanskrit.

Marching on the drum beats of the military band was also alien to the Hindu *samaj*, still, it was thought indispensable in igniting a martial feeling and discipline. So the band was incorporated too. Marches of British army bands like "scout," "be prepared," "forward," etc. were in parlance for many years in the beginning at Sangh.

Sangh is not an institution or an organisation within the society but the organisation of the entire society:

Following the incorporation of Sangh, Dr. Hedgewar participated in the Civil Disobedience Movement in his personal capacity in 1930. This *satyagraha* called *'Jungle Satyagraha'* in Vidarbha did not garner public participation despite two attempts. Innumerable people participated in the movement under the leadership of Doctor ji. He went to Pusad to do *jungle satyagraha* to disobey British rule. A formal farewell function was organised in a meeting hall in Nagpur to see him off before he left for Pusad. During this event, he declared that he was not participating in the *satyagraha* as a Sangh office-bearer but in his individual capacity, and encouraged other *swayamsevaks* to do the same. Other *swayamsevaks* also participated in their individual capacity. To ensure that Sangh's work could continue uninterrupted, he handed over the charge of *sarsanghachalak* to his trusted colleague Dr. L. V. Paranjpe. Shri Babasaheb Aapte and Bapurao Bhedi were entrusted with the responsibility of travelling to ensure unhindered Sangh work.

Self-sacrificing personality:

In the meeting of all *sanghachalaks* in 1929, the members decided that Doctor ji should be conferred upon with the title of '*sarsanghachalak*' (head of all *sanghachalaks*). They offered him *sarsanghachalak* salutations to which he responded by saying, "I cannot accept the *pranaam* of honourable stalwarts like you all." To this Appaji Joshi remarked, "it may not be acceptable to you but as we have all collectively arrived at this decision, you must accept this responsibility." While addressing a meeting of all *sanghachalaks* in 1931, Doctor ji said, "Not me alone but we all are the founders of Sangh, this much is clear to me. I am accepting this responsibility at your behest. While discharging the responsibilities of my role I will not be self-indulgent in any way. Well until the point I am useful for this task, I will serve it earnestly. When another better-suited candidate comes to be known you must all freely confer this role upon him. I am eager to happily hand over the charge to such a person and will continue to serve in the capacity of a *swayamsevak* thereafter." Such was the exemplary detachment of a founder of an organisation that is unheard of and is truly rare. In 1934, the Shankaracharya of Kurtkoti of Nasik announced the conferment of the title of "*Rashtra Senapati*" upon Dr. Hedgewar. This news made it to the newspapers and congratulatory letters made their way to Doctor ji. He alerted all the *shakhas* that such a title is not at all relevant for our work. Sangh must avoid the usage of such titles. He shared a great rapport with many political and social leaders of the day and oftentimes they were provided with a platform to present their thoughts before the *swayamsevaks*. However, he did not let his personal relationship with those politicians sway the decision-making process within Sangh. The Sangh independently took all decisions pertaining to Sangh.

Sangh work relevant till date:

In 1940, against the doctor's advice and despite failing health he came to a Sangh training camp. The first few words that made their way out of his mouth were: "Kindly forgive me for my inability to serve you all. I have come here just to be amid your graceful presence." Thereafter he categorically said that Sangh's work should not be confined to the *shakha* only but it must be carried out in the society. This is how he set a strong foundation for creating a self-sufficient organisation. The unerring and successful working style for *karyakarta* development is the result of his acumen. This methodology is the basis on which fifty-five thousand *shakhas* encompassing the length and breadth of the country, from Ladakh to Andamans and from Manipur-Tripura to Kutch respectively, have functioned and sustained six successive generations within the organisation despite several oppositions and impediments. This methodological framework has been emulated in 35 countries internationally to organise Hindu *samaj* under Hindu Swayamsevak Sangh (HSS) and has yielded positive results.

Up until Dr. Hedgewar birth centenary year, many people were not even familiar with his name, yet they were aware of his work. Sangh, which is the brainchild of a self-sacrificing founding father like Dr. Hedgewar, is becoming exceedingly more relevant to our national life today. It is essential for the country. The society has immense faith in Sangh, it has become more supportive of Sangh's activities and more and more people are coming forward to contribute to the society through its several initiatives. These are the effects of the strong foundation for Sangh's work laid by Dr. Hedgewar. A visionary, simple-looking yet an achiever par excellence, such was Dr. Hedgewar. Sincere obeisance to his jubilant memory on his birth centenary.

Endnote :

This article first appeared in *VSK Bharat* on September 17, 2019.

32

Dattopant Thengadi ji : A Yogi who Nationalised the Labour Movement

At the time when the late Dattopant Thengadi ji set the foundation stone of *Bharatiya Mazdoor Sangh*, communism was at its pinnacle across the world. Starting a grassroots national labour movement rooted in the pure Bharatiya Darshan and building it brick by brick amidst odds was a lofty task then. It called for conviction, devotion, and persistence on his part. When I try to grasp the frame of mind he would've had then, I am reminded of this allegory:

> The spring breeze was still a distant memory. Mango flowers had yet to appear on the trees.
>
> Just then, a tiny creature stepped out from his warm earthly dwelling.
>
> Indifferent to the rouge winter winds shaking his little frame, he began his walk.
>
> "Stay put," his well-wishers tried convincing him, they warned him of the impending dangers.
>
> He, however, didn't heed a single piece of advice.
>
> At long last, after an arduous march, he reached the mango tree.
>
> Taking a brief glance at the tall tree trunk he proceeded onto a steep upward climb.
>
> Perched on one of the tree branches, a parakeet was intently watching his moves.

Bending his neck, he finally asked, "oh petty creature, what brings you here, in this cold weather?"

"Mango nectar," pat came a reply.

Laughing hysterically, the parakeet thought to himself, "he sure is the king of fools." "My bird's-eye view has inspected every nook and cranny. There isn't a hint of Mango here, Silly," he smirked.

Steadying his wobbly steps the little creature retorted "You might be seeing what you see, but when I get there the Mango will surely appear."

The response of that creature is like that of a yogi. One who does not wallow in self-pity; who doesn't fear unfavourable circumstances. Without a trace of even a band of colour on the horizon, he believes in the promise of the inevitable dawn. He doesn't doubt that each step of his walk is consequential and will bear fruits.

No matter how much the clever and the wise try to beat sense into him, he remains true to the music of the drummer deep within. His heart resounds with the verse— हरि से लागी रहो मेरे भाई, तेरी बनत बनत बन जाई "absorb yourself in *'Hari'*, and you will find *Hari* in everything that absorbs you."

It is for all to see, as of today *Bharatiya Mazdoor Sangh* is the largest labour organisation in Bharat.

No matter how accomplished one is, an able organiser is open to his co-worker's thoughts and suggestions and promptly accepts the appropriate ones in the interest of the organisation. Thengadi ji was such a gifted organiser. When the decision to take up some organisational activity among workers (trade unions) was made, the nomenclature contemplated was—"*Bharatiya Shramik Sangh*". Yet the discussion that ensued among the *karyakartas* illuminated the fact that the group of the society that this organisation will work with will find the word '*Shramik*' too difficult to comprehend. People of some states might not be able to even pronounce it. Therefore in place of '*shramik*', the colloquial '*mazdoor*' should be used. This suggestion was duly accepted and the organisation came to be known as '*Bharatiya Mazdoor Sangh*.'

Working in an organisation entails the journey from 'me' to 'we'. This transition is not easy for any extraordinarily adept person. Usually, such a person is a shadow of his ego. This ego crops up from time to time. Sages, the realised souls, have illustrated the irony of the ego when they said, "it is that evil which spares the ignorant and throttles the knowledgeable" (नवल अहंकाराचे गोठी, न लागे अज्ञानीयाच्या पाठी, ज्ञानीयाच्या कंठी झोंबीतसे). However, safeguarding oneself from such ego is necessary for those who work within, for or with an organisation. Thengadi ji had mastered this art. Even in casual dialogue, while expressing an opinion, offering an insight or a solution he used 'we' and not an 'I'. Elevating one's sense of self so thin so as to integrate all the people that one is associated with is requisite for an organiser and Thengadi ji was a prolific organiser in this sense.

Another noteworthy quality of Thengadi ji was that he was warm and friendly to all co-workers, their designation and qualification notwithstanding. Placing his hand on their shoulders, he would promenade with even an ordinary worker, making the worker indistinguishable from him. These gestures put the workers seeking his counsel at great ease. Forgetting that they were speaking to a national leader or a renowned thinker of international stature, they came to see him as their own family elder or a wise community member. While doing so, no artificial efforts were required for Thengadi ji, it used to be effortless and natural.

He was also very well-read with an in-depth understanding. Oftentimes while in a conversation, he would refer to texts from many books and mention anecdotes of several political leaders. But one trait of his that shines bright in my memory is when a novice *karyakarta* like me would narrate an anecdote or say a joke that was originally told to us by him, he would listen to it sincerely. Such patience is extraordinary. Many senior *karyakartas* are sometimes tempted to dismiss a conversation by saying "I know that." But Thengadi ji listened to each and every word intently, as if hearing it for the first time. Not only that, he would go a step further and mindfully reflect upon that remark and unmistakably add a new anecdote or joke thereon. A deep connection with ground-level co-workers is indeed a sign of a great leader.

Despite the temptation, intention and efforts to broaden the work undertaken, avoiding needless hurry is also the quality of an excellent organiser. Parampujaniya Shri Guruji would often say *"Dheere-Dheere Jaldi Karo"* (hasten slowly). One must not be in haste. A friend of mine was a senior leader in Shri Sharad Joshi's '*Shetkari Sanghatana*'- a farmers' movement in the Vidarbha region. Eventually, he got disillusioned with the movement and came in contact with my younger brother who was also an agriculturist at the time. Given *Bharatiya Kisan Sangh's* recent commencement, my brother deemed connecting this farmers' leader to the appropriate organisation. He shared this thought with me. Thengadi ji was overseeing the operations of the *Bharatiya Kisan Sangh* in those days, therefore I approached him with this proposition at Nagpur. Thengadi ji was familiar with this person. I was optimistic that the association of an established leader would aid the momentum of Kisan Sangh's work and Thengadi ji would welcome him into the organisation. However, no sooner had I finished drawing the backdrop and pinning my suggestion on top, he declined it. I was baffled. Later Thengadi ji explained to me that he rejected this leader because Kisan Sangh was a small organisation then. He was afraid the organisation would not be able to absorb a leader of that man's stature and he, in turn, would engulf the organisation, diluting our efforts. He didn't want that to happen. To which I said, "If *Kisan Sangh* doesn't absorb him then BJP will assimilate him in their party and give him a ticket to contest the elections." Unphased, Thengdi ji calmly responded, "BJP might be in a hurry, we are not." His lucid and confident response was enlightening and it was then that Shri Guru ji's words, "hasten slowly" had a new-found meaning for me.

Besides being a great organiser, Thengadi ji was also a philosopher. The depths of Bharatiya philosophy would subtly unravel in one's dialogues with him. The domination of communist thought on the labour movement was such that their thought process and terminology managed to percolate among almost all labour organisations of that era, becoming apparent in their slogans. At that time he replaced communism-oriented slogans with slogans that were pertinent reflections of Bharatiya Darshan. "*Udyogon Ka Rashtriyakaran*—Nationalisation of industries" was replaced with "*Rashtra Ka Audyogikaran— Udyogon Ka Shramikikaran aur Shramikon ka Rashtriyakaran*," meaning "Industrialisation of the nation— Nationalisation of labours—Labourisation of industries (worker-centric culture in industries)" Inconsiderate and unreasonable slogans that intensified the strife among workers and employers like, "*Hamari Mange Puri Ho—Chahe Jo Majboori Ho* (fulfil our demands, no matter whatever be the constraints)" were replaced with "*Desh ke Liye Karenge Kaam—Kaam ke Lenge Poore*

Daam (we will work for the nation and will also take the due compensation for the same)"

In the form of these subtle but paramount changes, he awakened the spirit of patriotism.

Besides *Bharatiya Mazdoor Sangh* and *Bharatiya Kisan Sangh*, Thengadi ji was instrumental as a key participant in setting a foundation for many other organisations. *Akhil Bharatiya Vidyarthi Parishad, Swadeshi Jagran Manch, Prajna Pravah, Vigyan Bharati* are a few among those. His essay on *Bharatiya Kala Drishti* (Indic perspective on performing arts) became the intellectual foundation of *Sanskar Bharati.*

Walking in the midst of a stalwart thinker, organiser and visionary like Thengadi ji, witnessing the seemingly mundane yet exceptional activities like the manner of his speaking, his style of conducting himself and being blessed with his guidance are moments of bliss and great honour for me. My humble tribute on the auspicious occasion of his birth centenary.

Endnote :

This article first appeared in *Organiser* on September 26, 2020.

33

Pranab Da : A Star Flies Into Sky

A bright star has disappeared from the political landscape of Bharat. The demise of former President Dr. Pranab Mukherjee is a huge loss for Bharatiya politics. Openly mingling with all, even with people having contrarian ideologies, while remaining true to one's own ideology is a nearly extinct practice now. Discussing, debating and deliberating diverse thought processes was the norm in Bharatiya society. Indian National Congress of the pre-Independence era was a palette of varied political hues that amalgamated to renew the vigour of the Independence Movement of our country. Communism-bred political intolerance and ideological untouchability is the new norm, which has become palpable in the recent past. Let alone freedom of expression, the deadly combination of communist philosophy and terror deny even the right to exist to those who differ with their views, all over the world.

When the late Pranab Da consented to grace an RSS event he faced a huge backlash. Many forces schemed to prevent him from addressing a Sangh gathering. The petty politics of pitting his own daughter against her father through public opposition was orchestrated. Pranab Da was a sincere and seasoned statesman. At that stage of his political career, he had not set out to join the RSS by addressing its members. In fact, he was there to share his well-thought-out political philosophy with the *swayamsevaks* and other countrymen. His close allies and his well-wishers should have known better and trusted him, as he was there to represent their ideology (read, core Congress ideology) to a brand new audience. Sadly, that didn't happen!

Sangh's third *Sarsanghachalak*, Shri Rajju Bhaiya, who hailed from Prayagraj (UP), shared a long-standing, intimate bond with Shri Lal Bahadur Shastri. Once during Shastriji's active years in Uttar Pradesh politics, a tea gathering was organised for a few dignitaries in the presence of the then *Sarsanghachalak*, Shri Guruji. Rajju Bhaiya had also invited Shastri ji to that event, who, however, declined citing the fear of garnering bizarre speculation from party members if spotted there. Dismayed by this response Rajju Bhaiya asked, "Shastri ji, who will ever doubt a leader of your stature?" Shastri ji answered, "Oh, you don't understand politics." Rajju Bhaiya told him, "That is not the case with RSS. If one *swayamsevak* sees me talking to you (a Congress leader) he will assume Rajju Bhaiya is explaining Sangh to Shastri ji."

This is natural. Leaders of an organisation deserve trust. In order to create a social atmosphere conducive for democracy, sincere efforts to comprehend the thoughts and perspectives of others while staying committed to one's own belief system are essential.

The political arena of Bharat is progressively bulging with new politicians each day, but the number of politicians who engage in the sincere politics of nation-building is limited. Politics that deemed national interest paramount has been pushed to the back and instead, politics based on parties, one community or caste, region and language, even one family have got the centre stage. The gospel of a single family possessing a rare leadership potion that mystically qualifies all its members, generation after generation, as national leaders has eluded me for a long time. These members on the other hand have all along carefully branded themselves as the "guardians of democracy". But what is even more shocking is to see members of the oldest political party of the country having conviction in an inexperienced person's leadership skills to lead their organisation.

Pranab Da was an icon of the league of politicians who prioritised the country's welfare, and this league is fast dwindling. This makes his demise at this turn in time doubly painful. I am told that during his tenure as the finance minister, he sought the counsel of adherents of diverse political ideologies with an intent to expand his knowledge about the neighbouring countries. This attitude is the prerequisite of a healthy democracy and a strong polity. Therefore, Pranab Da's consent to attend a Sangh event, -i.e. an organisation which is in existence since the pre-Independence era, has embodied the values of nation-building through service, ever-growing and multi-faceted in nature—exemplified his allegiance to the cause of national stewardship. It takes a certain degree of open-mindedness and strength of character to be able to grasp such intentions, which in my opinion is beyond many people's capacity.

K.M. Munshi, a cabinet minister in the Nehru-led government, painted a portrait of Sangh which is unimaginable for those who now do business in the name of politics. Such insights can be developed only by someone who is in the service of this nation and engages in the politics of nation-building. His ability to pierce reasons behind Sangh's aversion to mainstream politics and its interference in matters of social welfare, despite being in the midst of his active political career indicates the character and ability of the individual. He penned those interpretations in the book, *Pilgrimage to Freedom*: "I attended a rally of the Rashtriya Swayamsevak Sangh which we, Congressmen, had looked upon as an 'unseeable' pariah. I was struck by the discipline, determination and the spirit of selflessness which characterises its members. It had no financial backing behind it and no leaders of all-India fame to give it a status, and yet it functioned efficiently on an emotional bond."

"I met M.S. Golwalkar, the Guruji (second *Sarsanghachalak*) of the RSS. Whatever our differences in political aims and methods, I could not help admiring the dedicated life he lived, his great power of organisation and his skill in building up the RSS, at the same time resisting the temptation to throw it into the vortex of politics." (*Pilgrimage to Freedom*, P.86 by K.M. Munshi.)

A Marathi article commemorating Dr. Mukherjee claimed Pranab Da distanced himself from the Congress party at the time when it needed him the most and shook hands with the RSS. The writer was hinting at his address to the Sangh. I feel pity for that writer who fails to see that Pranab Da is inseparable from Congress and vice-versa. It was foul play on the party's part to reprimand a noble statesman like him by cornering him for a tiny difference of opinion. It is this immature politics of Congress that has weakened it and if continued, will lead to its decline.

Pranab Da's unrelenting critics have misread his actions and misinterpreted his choices because the ideological heritage they have inherited has never seen the practice of decent, frank discussions with one's opponents. Hunting elephants is commonplace for a lion's pride, but the fox clan cannot even imagine doing that. This may well be understood through this fable: Once upon a time unable to find prey, a lion brings home a fox kit one day. Overcome by her maternal instincts the lioness refuses to eat the kit. Both parents decide to raise him alongside their newborn cubs. Later, one day, the cubs and the kit while playing in the forest, run into an elephant. Following their natural instinct, the cubs plan to leap up to disarm the elephant. However, the kit, intimidated by the size of the elephant, stops the cubs from doing so. While narrating this incident to their mother, the lioness, the cubs poke fun at the kit. Taking the hint the lioness reveals his true identity to the fox kit and advises him to leave the place, for she fears once grown up the cubs would prove to be a threat to his life. She consoles him using the following words-

शूरोसि कृतविद्योसि दर्शनीयोसि पुत्रक।
यस्मिन् कुले त्वमुत्पन्नो गजस्तत्र न हन्यते॥
Shoorosi kritavidyosi darshaneeyosi putraka
Yasmin kule twamutpannah gajastatra na hanyate

Meaning: You are brave, intelligent, and handsome, my child! Just that the family you're born into, doesn't have the tradition of killing an elephant.

No matter how many changes one goes through, there comes a time when their natural strengths and weaknesses come out! The time when the Congress must seriously rethink its values has come—whether to embrace the inclusiveness championed by Pranab Da and Munshi ji or to remain shrouded in the communist dogma that promotes political untouchability.

The brand of political ethics practised by Dr. Rajendra Prasad, K.M. Munshi, Dr. Radhakrishnan, Purushottam Das Tandon and Pranab Da was integrative. The correct interpretation of their actions takes extraordinary curiosity and moral courage, which is beyond the reach of those who engage in self-interest-driven petty party politics, communal politics, caste-based politics and dynastic politics. Instilling and emulating the values that Pranab Da embodied among a new generation of politicians will be the real tribute to his unmatched legacy. Pranab Da is no more. Long live Pranab Da. May the tribe grow and flourish.

Endnote :

This article first appeared in *The Sunday Guardian* on October 3, 2020.

34

M.G. Vaidya : Tribute to a Swayamsevak, Father & Thinker

When I received a phone call suggesting I write an article about my late beloved father, my mind scattered in all directions. Scores of episodes and incidents flitted across my mind's eye. Thereafter, I decided to write about the incidents that have shaped my life; that moulded me into the person I am. I am often asked who inspired me to become a *pracharak* (full-time worker of RSS) and my unflinching answer is that my inspiration to take up my way of life came from my father, M.G. Vaidya.

My father M.G. Vaidya, better known as Baburao Vaidya, whom we address as Baba, became one with the Supreme Divinity on December 19, 2020. He led an active, meaningful and inspiring life of 97 years. His life was affectionate towards the family, committed to his goal and dedicated to the Sangh. In 1931, having moved to Nagpur from a village called Taroda to pursue his education, my father became a *swayamsevak* of the Rashtriya Swayamsevak Sangh (RSS) at the tender age of eight. Accepting to shoulder the responsibilities of Sangh in 1938, he regularly attended the daily *shakha* from the age of 15 until the age of 95. First as an office-bearer of the Sangh (RSS), then while at Jana Sangh, thereafter as a journalist, then a member of Maharashtra Legislative Council (MLC), again as the *Akhil Bharatiya Bauddhik Pramukh* of RSS, then *Akhil Bharatiya Prachar Pramukh*, thereon the spokesperson of Sangh, and finally in the capacity of an ordinary *swayamsevak*, his insistence on attending the daily *shakha* persisted. The way he planned his life, his time, his finances, his economic acuity, his insistence on the ethical use of resources, and the manner in which he planned even his death, was nothing short of remarkable.

Vision For Life

Succeeding in simply the material sense—securing a high-profile position or job, cannot be and should not be the goal of life. This is because securing a livelihood is not the sole purpose of life. Our father lived by this principle and led a meaningful and successful life. It is this mindset that inspired him to espouse a society-centric and meaningful approach to life, over a position-centric careerist approach, which was instilled in all of us siblings as well. Out of the various incidents that shaped our distinct approach to life, the first one dates back to when I was in the 10th grade. At school, we were asked to write an essay on the topic "The Aim of my Life". This was around 1969-70. Most of my classmates had written about wanting to become a doctor, engineer, or government officer. I, on the other hand, decided to discuss the topic with Baba. He asked me to begin my essay with the line, "The aim of my life is to be a social revolutionary," and the sentence that followed was, "To earn my livelihood, I may be an engineer, doctor, IAS officer, or a military officer." With these two simple sentences, he brought home the fact that earning a livelihood is not the end goal of life and from then on this idea was subconsciously imprinted in my mind.

I secured good marks in 10th grade examinations and chemistry happened to be my favourite subject. Anyone in my place would aspire to get into a medical college, especially given that one of my sisters was already pursuing medicine. However, when I broached this topic with Baba, he remarked, "Our country does not need only doctors." A year after that, we discussed the option of getting admission to an engineering college. This time again, Baba said, "Our country does not need just engineers." Through such precise, simple statements, he got all of us brothers and sisters into the habit of exploring what could be the needs of our country.

Baba was an avid reader. He read a wide range of subjects– from English fiction to serious philosophical treatises. While pursuing my M.Sc., I noticed his reading time would normally exceed my study time. His collection of books was rich, diversified, and well-organised, he could easily pick out any title from his vast collection.

Keep Reading

In 1983 after submitting my PhD thesis to the university, I became an RSS *pracharak*. I was asked to go to Gujarat but was not aware which part of the state would be assigned to me. None of our relatives or close friends lived in Gujarat then. It being a new region with a different language, promised to be a novel experience for me. On the day I was to leave for Gujarat by a late-night train, I attended the evening *shakha* and returned home to have dinner with my family. Baba, instead of advising me to travel carefully, look after my health, write regularly etc., proceeded to instruct me about something of great importance to him—reading. He said, "A *pracharak* should always be reading something new. Whichever region you are assigned duties in, you will find a library there. You will be able to get good books to read by availing a membership there. Suppose you are assigned to work in a small hamlet where there is no library, there will definitely be homes that house a good collection of books; scout them. If you acquaint yourself with the people living there, you will be able to find books worth reading even there." Thus, he advised me on how to procure books and emphasised that I should be constantly reading something new.

A Family Man

Our father was a quintessential family man. During our school days, there were hardly any means of entertainment, but he would keep us occupied by playing cards with us during Diwali and summer vacations and teaching us new card games such as bridge and heart. Our circle of relatives has always been huge, but he always found time to keep in touch with all of them, participating actively in family events and celebrations.

He was also an industrious farmer who initiated several agricultural experiments in our ancestral village. He had a great eye for bulls. Bulls were inevitable for agriculture. He would travel all the way to Telangana, to the well-known Nirmal and Mhaisa bull markets to procure the best pair of bulls—not just for our family but even for others in the village. I had accompanied him to bull markets several times. Even after we sold off our farmland, he always remained in close contact with the village—making it a point to visit during the famed village celebration *Yatra of Sant Kejaji Maharaj*, as well as during *Pola*, one of the most important festivals of farmers. During *Pola* celebrations, he would also award the most beautifully decorated bulls, and encourage people to take good care of them.

On completing 50 years of age, he decided to devote more time at home. During the *Chaaturmaas*—the four months from the *Ekadashi* of the month of *Ashadh* to the month of *Kartik*, all family members would gather between 9 and 10 at night and recite a *stotra* together, an *adhyaya* of the Bhagavad Gita, and collectively read a book on Gita. It was a rule for everyone to return home before 9 pm. He would also decline participation in any public event post 9 pm, during those four months. This continued for many years, incessantly.

Self-Discipline

At the age of 60, Baba retired as the editor of *Tarun Bharat*, despite the board of directors insisting on him to continue for a few more years. Thereafter, he was offered the position of managing director of the *Narkesari Prakashan* that managed *Tarun Bharat*, and later he was asked to come on board as the chairman of the same organisation. He accepted but was determined to not carry on in these positions beyond the age of 70. This spirit of renunciation extended to the national-level responsibilities of Sangh—despite enjoying great health, he stepped down at the age of 75. Thereafter, he remained active only in the capacity of an ordinary *swayamsevak*. In the year 2000, it was decided for the first time that a spokesperson be appointed for Sangh. After much coaxing, he relented and accepted the responsibility, but only upon categorically stating that he would shoulder it for three years only. A man of his words that he was, at the end of his three-year tenure, he continued his participation in public life as a *swayamsevak*.

Strict Time Management

His planning of hours was as precise as his planning of years. His time for *shakha*, for his family, for reading, for listening to the news on the radio, and later, after the advent of television, for watching the news, was always predetermined. His insistence on punctuality was extraordinary. When I was serving as the *Akhil Bharatiya Prachar Pramukh*, I met several journalists who told me that they had been turned down by my father for reaching five minutes late. When one such journalist, who was forced to return empty-handed on reaching five minutes late, was assigned an appointment for 4 pm the next time, he reached our home at 3:30 pm to avoid getting late again. At that time, Baba was reading a book. Finding Baba sitting there all by himself, the journalist attempted to initiate a conversation, but Baba chided him. He pointed out that the clock was yet to strike 4 and went back to his book. Sharp at 4 pm he closed his book and started the discussion with the journalist.

Financial Planning

At the behest of Sangh *adhikaris*, he decided to leave his 17-year-old stable and secure job – that of a professor of Sanskrit – and ventured into the field of journalism—an impractical decision, to say the least, given that his family was growing and journalism paid lesser than his previous job. But to him, his larger goals mattered most and he took this decision with the consent and cooperation of *Aai*—our mother. When Baba was asked how they would make ends meet with such a paltry income, his answer was simple – that he knew many such families who were able to survive within the same means. And thus, by minimising financial requirements, maintaining his self-respect by not seeking anybody's support and with the cooperation of *Aai*, he managed the financial needs of the family well.

Taking into account the sources of income, his financial planning would be thorough. When my younger brother, Dr. Ram Vaidya, who is currently a *pracharak* based in the UK, was in the final year of his graduation, the Maharashtra government had a scheme to waive the fees of students coming from economically weaker sections. Given that Baba had retired, Ram applied for the waiver on the advice of the university officials and it was sanctioned. Four months later when Baba came to know about it, he told Ram that he had made enough financial arrangements for his education, and promptly proceeded to write to the university saying that the waiver granted to his son was a mistake and that he shall not only pay the fees for the past four months but also the penalty for late payment.

Ethical Use Of Resources

When Baba was an editor at *Tarun Bharat*, my elder brother, Dhananjay, used to run a small business alongside his bank job. He was required to make calls outside Nagpur for his business. The phone, however, belonged to *Tarun Bharat*, so Baba insisted on paying the charges for the STD calls made by Dhananjay.

Similarly, as the chairman of the *Narkesari Prakashan*, he had a car and a driver at his disposal. The day he resigned from that position, he returned home from the office in a cycle rickshaw instead of the car despite repeated entreaties of the new chairman. The managing director also suggested to my elder brother, Dhananjay, to purchase the same car for a mere eleven thousand rupees, so it could be of use to our father. But Baba did not agree to that either. Later, when the same car was sold for fifty-five thousand rupees, Baba reiterated the appropriateness of his decision. Such was his monetary discipline and insistence on the ethical use of resources.

Unattached To Positions

When Sharad Pawar formed the government and became the chief minister of Maharashtra in coalition with the Janata Party, the governor was apparently mulling the appointment of Baba in the legislative council as MLC. When Sharad Pawar and Baba met each other during an event in *Tarun Bharat*, Pune, Sharad Pawar mentioned to Baba that his name was being considered for appointment as the governor's nominee in the Legislative Council. But he added, "Only your people are recommending your name at the moment. If you make some effort to get other people to recommend you as well, then the task would become easier." To which Baba replied, "You should forget that I'll ever make efforts to get my name recommended. Rather, you should drop my name altogether. I will send you the names of two to three deserving persons from Vidarbha."

Even after this incident, Baba's name got selected as the nominated member of the legislative council. A senior member of the Janata Party, Sumatitai Sukalikar, came home to convey this decision to Baba. When I reached home after winding up the evening *shakha*, I saw Sumatitai stepping out of the house and Baba standing outside to see her off. I could overhear Sumatitai saying, "Baburao, please don't refuse." To this, Baba replied, "Tai, without asking or informing those who have entrusted me with the responsibility of *Tarun Bharat*, how can I say yes?" The kind of efforts people including *karyakartas* put to bag such a position is common knowledge. But to Baba, propriety was more important.

The then *Sarsanghachalak*, Balasaheb Deoras was touring at that time. When he returned to Nagpur after three days, Baba met him and sought his permission, and only then did he accept the nomination. During those three days, congratulatory calls for Baba kept pouring in, but, at our home, the appointment was celebrated only after three days.

I recall one more episode in this context. Everyone in the daily *shakha* was naturally ecstatic that one of their own was now an MLC. A few days later, Baba's lecture had been scheduled on the occasion of *Kojagiri*, the full moon day, at the *Gorakshan shakha*. The *swayamsevaks* of that *shakha* decided to felicitate Baba for becoming an MLC. I too was present at the event and distinctly recall how, after being felicitated when Baba stood up to speak, he began his address by reprimanding the *swayamsevaks*. He said, "What difference has getting appointed in a political position brought about in me? I am still the same, a *swayamsevak*. Since when did the custom of celebrating a political appointment kickstart amongst *swayamsevaks*? If others considered such a thing to be an achievement, it is a different matter; but it is inappropriate for a *swayamsevak* of the Sangh to look at it in this way. If a *swayamsevak* resolves to begin a new life as a *pracharak*, that surely would be a reason to congratulate him."

Man Of His Word

He felt an exceptional obligation to always keep his word. In 1947, while on one hand, talks about his marriage were underway, the then *Karyawaha* of Nagpur—Balasaheb Deoras checked with him if he would be willing to go as the chief instructor to the *Sangh Shiksha Varg* commencing from 9 May in Madras. Baba said yes to him. He was required to leave Nagpur on 7 May itself. As the duration of the *Varg* was 30 days, he was to return to Nagpur after 9 June. After much discussion over the marriage, the date was finally getting fixed for 15 May. However, Baba made it clear that he was not available from 7 May to 11 June, as he had to be in Madras for the *Varg*. The bride's party met Balasaheb Deoras and discussed the matter, and Balasaheb said, "ask him to meet me. We will send him for the next *Varg* taking place in a different state". However, when Baba was informed of this, he asserted, "I have already said yes to Balasaheb once, I shall not go to meet him again, and you can fix a suitable date after the Varg ends". The bridal party was naturally infuriated upon hearing this. They said, "Then do not depend on us!" And lo! On hearing these words, our grandfather also got angry and said, "Alright! So the next time you come to us, we will begin again by asking the boy to rethink the match with the girl."

Later, the same people approached our family after Diwali, and our grandfather broached the subject of bringing the girl to Nagpur again to be reconsidered as a match by the family. The opposite party also agreed. When grandfather asked Baba to come along to meet the girl, he said, "I have already met her before and given my assent, so I won't come again. I have agreed to the match. If in the past ten months, the girl has been paralysed, handicapped, or even had a major illness, it will not affect my decision." In this way, the wedding that was to take place in May 1947, took place in March 1948. So firm was he on his word.

I have recounted the event of him being selected as the governor's nominee in the Maharashtra Legislative Council above. The swearing-in ceremony had to be organised in a hurry because the speaker of the Vidhan Parishad, Mr. R.S. Gavai was to leave for a two-month tour abroad. However, on the designated day Baba had accepted the invitation to an event at the Vinayakrao Deshmukh Vidyalaya in Nagpur. When Baba was urged to come to the swearing-in ceremony instead and was also informed of the unavailability of the speaker for the next two months, he said that he would prefer being sworn in after two months instead of turning down the invitation of the Vidyalaya.

Exceptional Dedication To Sangh

The important quality of being able to "devote oneself to the cause of Sangh" can only be developed by attending the *shakha* regularly. For the past several years, the *Akhil Bharatiya Pratinidhi Sabha* (All-India Representatives Body meeting) of Sangh is held in Nagpur once in three years. One such meeting was underway in Nagpur in March 2018. Baba was present at such meetings for the past several years. But owing to his advanced age, he was no longer obligated to attend it. The respected *Sarkaryawah* Bhaiyyaji Joshi invited Baba to remain present at the meeting for a short while, with a view of getting to meet the *karyakartas* from across the country. Baba reached the meeting venue on March 11, 2018. Bhaiyyaji Joshi learnt that March 11 was Baba's birthday as per the Gregorian calendar. As a result, Baba was felicitated at the meeting for completing 95 years of age at the hands of the present *Sarsanghachalak* of RSS, Dr. Mohan Bhagwat. Baba was wheelchair-bound. Hence, the *sarsanghachalak* got down from the dais and felicitated Baba with a customary shawl and coconut. Baba (aged 95 years) attempted to bow down to the *sarsanghachalak* (aged 68 years) when the latter held Baba's hands to prevent him from doing so. Everyone witnessed this. It was an extremely touching moment. After that, Baba was to share his thoughts for about five minutes. Baba commenced his address by saying, "The revered *sarsanghachalak* did not allow me to touch his feet. Hence, I mentally bow down to him." Listening to these words, the entire gathering was moved. Baba's speech that went on for the next three minutes was deep and poignant. He said, "It is not easy to understand Sangh. In order to understand Sangh, it is important to understand the *Ishavaasyopnishad*. In one of the shlokas of this *Upanishad*, the *'Aatmatattva'* (loosely translated as the 'Self') has been described using paradoxical elements. The shloka goes like this:

तदेजति तन्नैजति तद्दूरे तद्वन्तिके।
तदन्तरस्य सर्वस्य तदु सर्वस्यास्य बाह्यत: ॥

Meaning- it (*Aatmatattva*) moves but also does not move. It is far and it is near. It is inside all, and also outside all. The same description also applies to the Sangh. Sangh is political but is also apolitical. Sangh is a religious organisation but is also not one. Sangh is a social organisation but is also not so. Because; Sangh wants to organise the entire society. Sangh is one with the society. Sangh is the entire society itself."

He imparted such a fundamental understanding in a span of merely a few minutes. I reached home after the meeting concluded. While discussing the events of the evening with Baba, when I told him, "everyone really liked your speech", he said, "I am extremely embarrassed and upset about the fact that, due to my physical infirmity, I was unable to go to the dais and the *sarsanghachalak* had to get down from the dais for my sake." This episode has remained etched in my memory.

Planning Death

He had even pre-planned his own death. 'अनायासेन मरणं विना दैन्येन जीवनम्।' — "A life not dependent on anyone, easy arrival of death" was a line he would often recite. He had vowed to live for 100 years. On 11 March 2021, that is, merely three months later, he was going to complete 98 years and enter the 99th year of life. He would also often speak about welcoming death like an old friend. In the year 2017, he had written down that his last rites should be performed at the same place where he breathed his last. On bringing the dead body home, it should not be kept for more than 12 hours. Further that he should be cremated in an electric or diesel incinerator, and that no speeches be made at his funeral. If required, different organisations may organise independent events to pay tribute to him.

Such small incidents, episodes, and instances have consciously or unconsciously moulded, shaped and supported our lives. Baba's physical body is not with us anymore, yet we feel that he continues to be with us through the guiding light of his thoughts and ideals. Our prayers go out to him, and the Almighty, to grant us the strength to walk on this path illuminated by him.

Endnote :

This article first appeared in *The Sunday Guardian* on January 30, 2021.